EDWARDIAN PROMENADE

Marie Tempest. Painting by Jacques Emile Blanche, 1908. By courtesy of the Garrick Club.

EDWARDIAN
Promenade

by

James Laver

HOUGHTON MIFFLIN COMPANY

Boston, The Riverside Press, Cambridge

FIRST PUBLISHED IN 1958 BY
E. HULTON AND COMPANY LIMITED
HULTON HOUSE · FLEET STREET
LONDON, E.C.4
PRINTED IN GREAT BRITAIN BY
BALDING AND MANSELL
LONDON AND WISBECH

©
JAMES LAVER
1958

INTRODUCTION

THE PRESENT WORK is conceived as a sequel (which is logical enough) to *Victorian Vista*, and is constructed very much on the same plan; that is to say, it devotes its attention to the surface-pattern of an epoch, in the hope and belief that such a pattern will suggest the depths.

> For not in the historian's crowded page
> Hides the true secret of the course of Man;
> Seek rather for the Spirit of the Age
> In flounce, or frill, or fragment of a fan . . .

Perhaps there is no period more susceptible to this treatment than the reign of Edward VII and the few years that followed it before the First World War. It had not only a surface-pattern, but a surface-glitter which still dazzles our eyes a little. Although still comparatively recent it seems to us incredibly remote.

In retrospect it has already detached itself from history and become one of those little islands in Time on which (and in which) the imagination loves to dwell. There are several such islands floating about in the collective unconscious and they have this in common: they are the scene of a perpetual fête. There is a party going on, although we, alas! are born too late to have our share in it.

Such a party was the Edwardian period, before people had begun to read *The Economist* instead of *The Pink 'Un*, when bridge and bicycles were still fascinating novelties, when income tax was a flea-bite and the British pound was received with respect in the remotest corners of the globe; a party presided over by the portly and cheerful

3

figure of the Monarch himself, who was so very clearly enjoying himself and expecting his subjects to do the same.

Of course it was not all sunshine in the Edwardian epoch. There were subterranean tremors, and, every now and then, the rumblings on the distant horizon of the coming storm; but at least the surface was gay enough. It was an age when people were not afraid to enjoy themselves, before envy had darkened the world.

The Edwardian age was probably the last period in history when the fortunate thought they could give pleasure to others by displaying their good fortune before them. All most reprehensible, no doubt, in our egalitarian eyes, and yet the doubt sometimes obtrudes itself whether the general level of happiness was not higher, even among the 'down-trodden masses', than it is today. For in *our* world there are no countries of escape, no Fortunate Islands, no Eldorado, no Earthly Paradise, no kingdom east of the sun and west of the morn. It is all such a short time ago — less than the life of a man — and yet all we can do, at the present moment, is to compose as best we can our *Ode on a Distant Prospect of the Edwardian Epoch*:

> Ye distant times, ye vanished hours
> Thrice happy first decade,
> Above whose ghostly people towers
> Great Edward's genial shade;
> We who have lost the generous way
> You used to frolic while 'twas May,
> And in a meaner epoch set,
> Look backward from our vale of tears
> And see across the gulf of years
> Your glory gleaming yet.
>
> Say, Father Time, for thou has seen
> Full many a year since then,
> May not the splendour that has been
> Come back to us again?
> Where are they now, who, long ago,
> Galloped triumphant in the Row,
> Or drove to Epsom, four-in-hand?
> Or when the Danube still was blue,
> Cut ice at Prince's two by two,
> To a Hungarian band?

4

They rated loveliness so high,
They stood on chairs to view
The Jersey Lily driving by,
And Lady Dudley too;
And she, by some esteemed the best
Whom mortals called Cornwallis-West:
Their fame was borne by every breeze,
And gentlemen who dined alone
Would drain a bumper on their own
To one, or all, of these!

Once more, methought, I saw them stand
('Twas but a dream, I know),
That elegant and noble band
Of fifty years ago,
The men, frock-coated, tall and proud,
The women in a silken cloud,
While in the midst of them appeared
(A vision that I still retain)
The Monarch sipping pink champagne,
And smiling through his beard.

Ah, pleasant and primeval ways!
Ah, times beloved in vain!
Ah, good King Edward's golden days!
They'll never come again.
See, see how all around us wait
The ministers of human fate!
Ah! if there is a man alive
Who fifty years ago foreknew
What all the world was coming to,
'Twas folly to survive!

                                        J.L.

ACKNOWLEDGEMENTS

THE PUBLISHERS and Editor gratefully acknowledge permission given by the following for the quotations used:

Messrs W. H. Allen and Mr W. MacQueen-Pope (*Gaiety, Theatre of Enchantment* and *The Melodies Linger On*); Messrs B. T. Batsford (*A History of Flying* by C. H. Gibbs-Smith); Messrs G. Bell (*The Cause* by Ray Strachey); Mr John Brown, Mr W. MacQueen-Pope, Mr Cecil Beaton, Miss Daphne Fielding, Sir Osbert Sitwell, Mr James Bone (contributions to *The Age of Extravagance*); Messrs Chatto & Windus and Mrs Montague (*Disenchantment* by C. E. Montague); Messrs William Collins (*The Day Before Yesterday* by Noel Streatfeild); Messrs Constable ('I Have a Rendezvous with Death' by Alan Seeger); Dr C. Willett Cunnington and Messrs Faber & Faber (*English Women's Clothing in the Present Century*); Messrs Hamish Hamilton (*Edward VII and His Circle* by Virginia Cowles); Messrs George G. Harrap (*Taste and Fashion* by James Laver and *They Were Singing* by Christopher Pulling); Messrs George G. Harrap and Messrs Alfred A. Knopf (*The Shelbourne* by Elizabeth Bowen — American title, *The Shelbourne Hotel*); Messrs Hutchinson and Miss Joyce Weiner (*Elinor Glyn* by Anthony Glyn); Messrs Herbert Jenkins (*Woman and Tomorrow* by W. L. George); Messrs John Lane The Bodley Head (*Russian Ballet in Western Europe* by W. A. Propert); Messrs John Lane The Bodley Head and Mrs Cecilic Straker (*Life's Enchanted Cup* by Mrs C. S. Peel); Messrs MacGibbon & Kee (*Memories* by Desmond MacCarthy); Mrs Masterman and Messrs Hodder & Stoughton (*England After War* by Charles F. G. Masterman); Messrs Methuen (*Aviation* by Algernon E. Berriman); Captain Francis Newbolt, C.M.G. and Messrs John Murray ('The Vigil' by Sir Henry Newbolt — from *Poems New and Old*); *Punch* ('In Flanders Fields' by John McCrae, 'A Sketch at the Grafton Galleries' and 'Bargains for Suffragettes'); Miss V. Sackville-West (*The Edwardians*); Lady Salmond ('Into Battle' by Julian Grenfell); Messrs Sidgwick & Jackson and the representatives of Rupert Brooke ('Peace' and 'The Dead I' by Rupert Brooke) — from *Collected Poems*; Mr Siegfried Sassoon and Messrs Faber & Faber (*Siegfried's Journey*); Mr André Simon and Messrs Michael Joseph (*The Art of Good Living*); Messrs Skeffington (*The Lamp of Memory* by Desmond Chapman-Huston); Major C. C. Turner (*The Old Flying Days*); the Executors of the Estate of the late H. G. Wells (*Tono-Bungay*); the Executors of the Estate of the late H. G. Wells and Messrs J. M. Dent (*Ann Veronica*); Messrs T. Werner Laurie (*Master and Man, Pink 'Un Yesterdays* by J. B. Booth); Messrs Allan Wingate (*Sacred Cowes* by Anthony Heckstall-Smith); Messrs Weidenfeld & Nicolson (*The Glass of Fashion* by Cecil Beaton).

The source of the quotations from S. F. Edge, Charles Jarrott, Sir Francis Jeune, Hercules Langrishe, the Hon. John Scott-Montagu and J. St. Loe Strachey on pages 128, 129 and 133 is *Motors and Motor Driving*, 1902.

CONTENTS

LIST OF ILLUSTRATIONS

9

96. Patrons of the British Drama. Drawing by Will Owen. From *The Tatler,* August 10th, 1904.

97. 'Old Studio' sideboard, designed by Liberty's, 1903.

112. 'A Green-eyed Woman.' Painting by Henri Matisse.

113. 'Tahitian Women with Mango Blossoms.' Painting by Paul Gauguin, 1899. *New York, Metropolitan Museum of Art.*

116. 'Blackfriars.' Painting by André Derain, 1910. *Glasgow, City Art Gallery.*

117. A donkey painting a picture for the Salon des Independents, and, *below,* the result as exhibited. From *L'Illustration,* 1910.

124. *Above:* King Edward, when Prince of Wales, in Lord Montagu's 12 h.p. Daimler, 1900.
Below: King Edward with Wilbur Wright.

125. A lady in Hyde Park, 1906.

128. *Above:* Irish A.C. Trials, 1908.
Below: Tourist Trophy, Isle of Man, 1905. Drawing a car to the starting point.

129. *Above:* A typical landaulette of 1906.
Below: Miss Ridge Jones at Brooklands, 1908.

132. Motor fashions in Paris, 1903.

133. *Above:* M. Guillon prepares to make an attempt with the Guillon and Clonzy aeroplane on Epsom Downs, April 11th, 1907.
Below: The Hon. C. S. Rolls in his machine on the Aero Club's ground at Eastchurch, 1910.

140. 'The Sport of the Century.' Mr Wilbur Wright in flight, with the Comtesse de Lambert. From *The Sketch.*

141. August Bank Holiday at Brooklands, 1910.

144. Hanriot's aeroplane crashes in the River Wey after a flight from Brooklands on August Bank Holiday, 1910.

145. *Above:* Adolphe Pégoud with Blériot after 'looping the loop', September 25th, 1913.
Below: Gustav Hamel (facing the camera) with his machine at Brooklands, 1911.

coffin of Miss Davison who threw herself under the horses at the Derby, 1913.
Below: Suffragette sandwichwomen, 1914.

208. *Above:* Taking the oath at the Recruiting Station at the White City, December 1915.
Below: Recruits assembling at Southwark Town Hall in response to Lord Derby's campaign, December 1915.

209. Picture postcards of the war years, French and English.

224. Photograph by F. J. Mortimer.

225. Cartoons by Bruce Bairnsfather from *The Bystander.*

228. 'Tommy Atkins.' Photograph by F. J. Mortimer.

229. *Above:* Women war workers, October 1916.
Below: The first of the clippies, September 1917.

236. 'We are making a new World.' Painting by Paul Nash. *London, Imperial War Museum.*

13

CHAPTER I

THE NEW REIGN

QUEEN VICTORIA died at Osborne on Tuesday, January 22nd, 1901. At 6.45 p.m. the Prince of Wales telegraphed to the Lord Mayor of London: 'My beloved mother, the Queen, has just passed away surrounded by her children and grandchildren.' 'For two hours', says the *Illustrated London News*, 'the great bell of St. Paul's tolled the news to the grief-stricken citizens of London; and the wires carried it to the farthest ends of the earth.'

The whole world recognized the death of the Queen as the end of an epoch. She had reigned for so long that it was almost impossible to imagine the Nation and Empire without her.

'Under this great name has been begotten all that we citizens of the British Empire know of civilization in the range of our daily lives. The passing of that name from the symbols of our allegiance, from the forms of worship, from the current speech, is a shock to the imagination of which we have no parallel. Think what it means that we can never again sing the National Anthem in its present wording. The point is rather delicate, but I cannot help asking whether public sentiment can sanction the restoration of the anthem to Henry Carey's original composition? Its associations are so solemnly woven with the great personality that has been taken from us that propriety may, to many minds, seem to demand a new anthem. . . The very depth of the affection inspired by the Queen makes the simple change to title nothing less than a domestic revolution. Popular as the Prince of Wales most justly is, "Our King" is a phrase so strange upon our lips that it almost makes a stranger of him. Within the last few days I have heard men murmuring "The King", as if they were groping in their memories for some ancient and unfamiliar charm.'

'Illustrated London News', Jan 26, 1901

15

¶ But if the great Queen was universally mourned, there was already a hint that her wishes were already beginning to be disregarded.

'Illustrated London News', Jan. 26, 1901

'Our English sentiment will weave its tendrils again around "The King", but it would be well to give the title an English tradition. On this account I venture to hope that our new Sovereign will be styled Edward VII and not Albert I. Personal reasons, which must be deeply respected, made the name of Albert very dear to the Queen; but in the roll of British monarchs it would have a foreign ring.'

¶ The Government of the day was of the same opinion, and when Rouge Dragon, Pursuivant of Arms was halted at Temple Bar with the challenge "Who goes there?" he replied: "The Officer of Arms, who demands entrance into the City to proclaim his Royal Majesty, Edward the Seventh." The Edwardian Epoch has begun.

The word "King", might still seem strange on the lips of Englishmen but there was nothing strange to them in the man who had for so long been the Prince of Wales.

'The Queen', Feb. 2, 1901

'King Edward VII ascends the throne under conditions more favourable to the lasting benefit of his subjects than any other monarch in English history, inasmuch as he has been throughout his fifty-nine years of life in closest touch with people of every class, and his character, disposition, acquirements, and natural abilities are well known to all. . . A well-known physiognomist has formulated the axiom that full, blue eyes are generally associated with a cheerful and happy disposition; that they evidence a candid and generous nature, and belong to those who make the best of unpleasant circumstances; that they indicate a talent for, or a great appreciation of, music, painting or acting, also a preference for rich colours and highly decorative surroundings; and that they hint at strong feelings, love of children, and a general fondness for pleasure. . . Those who know His Majesty best could also bear ample witness to his less generally known powers of endurance, his capacity for business and his great tact. None of us are without faults, and, of course, the King has his imperfections and peculiarities; but to these we are bound, in loyalty and respect, to be "a little blind". . . Most charming and genial is the King's smile, but the expression of his face in repose is somewhat grave, at times even stern, and does not always relax when speaking in public. . . His Majesty's voice is quite unmistakable, his pronuncia-

Reception of the Kaiser by the King and the Prince of Wales at Charing Cross Station, January 20th, 1901, on his arrival for Queen Victoria's funeral. Drawing by R. Caton Woodville.

tion I should be inclined to describe as syllabic, as for instance, the word "interest" would be pronounced "in-ter-est".'

¶ This was a tactful way of saying that he spoke with a pronounced German accent. But the public prejudice against all things German was still in the future. The King was cosmopolitan.

'Edward VII excited more interest than any other figure of the decade. The Kaiser was spectacular, and the Czar was all-powerful, but the King of England was the leader of high society. The glittering world of wealth and privilege, from one end of Europe to the other, took its cue from London and accepted without question the dicta of the British Sovereign.

Virginia Cowles. 'Edward VII and His Circle', 1956.

'Edward was the picture of opulence. With his heavy-lidded protruding eyes, his sensual mouth, his air of geniality, his enormous cigars, and his huge, over-fed body, always superbly attired, he was the symbol of the good life. He had never made any pretence of deriving pleasure from intellectual pursuits. His pleasures were the pleasures of the senses—food, women, magnificence, and above all else, comfort. He had indulged his tastes for forty years, but his appetite was still unsatisfied. As a result the Edwardian era sprang into being.

'Edwardian society modelled itself to suit the King's personal demands. Everything was larger than life-size. There was an avalanche of balls and dinners and country house parties. More money was spent on clothes, more food was consumed, more horses were raced, more infidelities were committed, more birds were shot, more yachts were commissioned, more late hours were kept, than ever before. It was, in short, the most ostentatious and extravagant decade that England had known.

'The Edwardian era had other distinguishing features about it. It was vibrant and adventurous. The fact that the King liked City millionaires and Jewish jokes and American heiresses and pretty women (regardless of their origin) meant that the doors were open to anyone who succeeded in titillating the monarch's fancy. . . The three men closest to the King were the Duke of Devonshire, the Marquis de Soveral and Mr. Ernest Cassel. They perfectly represented the new social order. The aristocracy with its immense estates was still predominant; but foreign diplomats and modern Jewish Croesuses also had their place. Oddly enough, Edward VII was immensely popular with the working classes.'

B

King Edward and Queen Alexandra in their Coronation robes.

17

Virginia Cowles.
'Edward VII and His
Circle', 1956.
'Royalty, the world over, was at the height of its glory and splendour as the new century progressed. Thrones sparkled thickly in Europe and stretched across the Middle East and Asia to the far reaches of Japan. As preparations for the Coronation of Edward VII rolled forward, scheduled for June 26, 1902, people declared that the event would be unparalleled in history for its brilliance. Although Edward had declared flatly that "crowned heads should not come, only representatives, owing to the extreme difficulty of precedence," the reigning houses had agreed to send their sons and heirs, Crown princes galore were due to arrive; from Russia, Italy, Denmark, Rumania, Portugal, Saxony, Greece, Sweden and Norway, Siam, Montenegro and Belgium. Austria was to be represented by the ill-fated Archduke Franz Ferdinand; Spain by the Prince of the Asturias; China by Prince Tsai Chen; Japan by Prince Akihito Komatsu. . . Only the Kaiser threw a spanner into the works. He refused to allow his son, the Crown Prince, to attend the ceremony because, he said, he disapproved of the unseemly frivolity into which the young man had been drawn during his last visit to England. . . He was the only heir to a throne in all Europe not present.'

¶ Then, suddenly, the King was taken ill. On the very next day, the country learned that he had undergone an operation for appendicitis and that the Coronation was indefinitely postponed.

Virginia Cowles.
'Edward VII and His
Circle', 1956
'The Coronation took place in August, seven weeks after the date originally set. The foreign princes, with the exception of those related to the British Royal Family, did not return to England. Only the members of the Abyssinian Special Mission were present, for the simple reason that they had never dared to go home. They would lose face, they explained, if they returned to Abyssinia without having seen the crowning of the great white potentate.'

'It might be said that the Edwardian era officially began when the King and Queen moved into Buckingham Palace. The first season of the new occupancy was that of 1903, and it was suitably spectacular. The tedious "Drawing Rooms" of Queen Victoria's day were abolished, and instead King Edward gave a series of splendid Court Balls. He entertained profusely, and on many evenings of the summer months carriages rolled into the Palace yard with the handsome men and women who had been bidden to dine with their Sovereign.'

18

'The first State Ball given by the King since he ascended the throne... *'The Queen',*
July 18, 1903
was certainly one of the most memorable occasions of State festivity
we have had for years. The dresses worn were specially magnificent.
The Countess of Wicklow had long sprays of pink roses on her tulle
gown, covered with rose petals. Dove-coloured crêpe de Chine
embroidered in opals and paste was worn by the Countess of Leven
and Melville; and the Marchioness of Lansdowne was in cream satin,
trimmed with chiffon and old lace, with very wonderful diamonds; she
wore the Orders of Victoria and Albert, the Crown of India and the
Jubilee and Coronation Medals, as did also any other fortunate lady
who was entitled to that high honour; the bodices were not so much
pouched as they have been... Very soft and becoming was the Countess
of Dalkeith's mousseline de soie, embroidered in blue and hand-
painted with forget-me-nots. . . The Countess of Dundonald wore a
handsome jet embroidered black satin. The Countess of Powis looked
singularly beautiful in a pale blue satin, embroidered with diamonds.
The Countess of Bandon's white tulle was veiled with black and worked
with black sequins. The Countess of Cromartie's grey iridescent and
mother-of-pearl embroidery mingled with white tulle and grey pearls,
trimmed with grey and white hyacinths [&c., &c., &c.,]. . . The
gowns were well seen in the ballroom, notwithstanding over 2000
guests had been invited, but possibly when they began to disperse for
supper they were more *en evidence*. . . The supper room, where
Royalty supped, was not kept exclusively for them, as is often the case;
there was a table there for the Ambassadors and other special guests.
Most of the young ladies came in late to the supper, Lady Marjorie
Greville among them in a pretty white tulle gown, and Miss Barbara
Lister, also in white. Lady Hillingdon wore one of the few Princess
gowns, all soft tulle and chiffon. Lady Ashburton was in pale blue
chiffon and cloth of silver, embroidered with stripes of brilliants, the
swathed bodice fastened with diamonds. . . Lady Ermyntrude Mallet's
was really a superb gown of tulle and mousseline de soie, but with such
wonderful embroideries of crystals, topazs (*sic*) and chains of the same;
Viscountess Duncannon's maize dress was worked in jet and silver
with point d'esprit, her all round diamond tiara collar and chain of
diamonds were much admired [&c., &c., &c.,]'

¶ It was, however, possible to 'go to Court' a little less gorgeously
clad:

Mrs C. S. Peel,
O.B.E.
'Life's Enchanted
Cup', 1933
'After the accession of King Edward, Drawing-Rooms became Courts, and took place in the evening. A luxurious buffet-supper, accompanied by particularly good champagne, was served from tables set out with the Royal gold plate.

'I attended a Court after the accession of King Edward, wearing a home-made train of white brocade lines with pale pink satin and garlanded with La France roses which I bought at Stagg and Mantle's in Leicester Square where artificial flowers were both good and cheap.'

¶ Society was quick to realize that a new era had indeed dawned. It was not that the King did not take his duties seriously.

A Foreign Resident.
'Society in the New
Reign', 1904
'At home King Edward used the protracted series of ministerial crises, occurring in the autumn of 1903, to assert himself in a strictly constitutional way as head of the State. Mr. Balfour had expected to find in his Sovereign the figurehead of the bureaucracy with which it was the minister's idea to replace both Parliament and Cabinet. Instead, his royal master gave him from the beginning to understand that the new bureaucracy, if a bureaucracy there was to be, would be rigorously presided over by a crowned chairman, who had no notion of being an ornamental supernumerary. Abroad, the wearer of the crown had already impressed his personality on his brother Sovereigns and their statesmen. If hunting be the traditional pastime of kings, diplomacy has ever ranked in a special degree as their more serious employment. All the circumstances of the time have therefore conspired to increase the interest and importance of the diplomatic circle, whose centre is St. James's Court.'

¶ The King was, however, an adept at combining duty with pleasure:

A Foreign Resident.
'Society in the New
Reign', 1904
'Le roi s'amuse is as applicable to English monarchy now as it ever was. The single change seems to be that His Majesty's pastimes have lost a certain aimlessness they may once have had and generally subordinate themselves to one pervading idea. The King grants interviews to his ministers at the palace in London. He receives them as family guests when he plays the squire at Sandringham. He converses with them not a little when they are "in attendance" at Windsor or Balmoral. Each of these statesmen leaves the presence-chamber with the sense of having been drained dry by his royal master on any subject that may have turned up. In the same way the father of his people cruises with Sir Thomas Lipton in his yacht, visits a former Irish

20

'Les conseils d'un oncle.' King Edward, in the uniform of a Colonel of Dragoons in the Prussian Guard, with the Kaiser in the uniform of a British Field-Marshal. Drawing by L. Sabattier, from 'L'Illustration', February 13th, 1909.

Ena and Betty, daughters of Asher and Mrs Wertheimer. Painting by John S. Sargent, R.A., c. 1901. London, Tate Gallery.

Viceroy, Lord Cadogan, at Culford Hall, drops in quietly to tea with the chief of the Cathcart clan in the Highlands, is entertained by the head of the Rothschild dynasty at Tring or in Piccadilly, more frequently, at Palace House, Newmarket, dines with his special favourites of this family, the Leopold Rothschilds. Whatever the little rite may be, while adding to his subjects' happiness, the illustrious visitor has made just the addition he wanted to his own store of information.

While Queen Victoria's successor was only mounting the throne a notion went abroad that the great Jews were not to enjoy the same favour with the new Sovereign as they had found with the heir-apparent. The very notion of such a break being possible was of course absurd. The single fact underlying the fiction was that, on a flying visit to Brighton soon after his coronation, the King had not been able to look in upon any of the Sassoons. As for dropping the Semites, one might as well talk of His Majesty's giving the cut direct to his ministers in Downing Street.'

¶ Of course, there were old-fashioned people who did not at all approve of this mingling of races and classes, although it is a little surprising to find the future socialist Lady Warwick instructing Elinor Glyn in the exclusiveness which should still be maintained:

'Lady Warwick was . . . successful in instructing her in her social duties, for though Elinor [Glyn] had often been to the great houses of England. . . being a hostess was a new experience for her. Army or naval officers, diplomats or clergymen, it was explained, might be invited to lunch or dinner. The vicar might be invited regularly to Sunday lunch or supper, if he was a gentleman. Doctors and solicitors might be invited to garden parties, though never, of course, to lunch or dinner. Anyone engaged in the arts, the stage, trade or commerce, no matter how well-connected, could not be asked to the house at all.' *Anthony Glyn. 'Elinor Glyn', 1955*

¶ Some people had a horror of the Jews who were now beginning to make their way into Society.

'When, in extreme youth, I first knew England, there were whole families of the most respectable and intelligent sort who could scarcely sleep because of the Jesuit scare. The Romanists had got the press into their hands; they had undermined the foundations of sound Protestant training in the schools and colleges of the country. It was *A Foreign Resident. 'Society in the New Reign', 1904* only a question of time when the Pope and his English prelates *in partibus* would claim an equal share in Westminster Abbey with the dean and chapter. A little later came the Puseyite horror. The penny newspaper was then becoming an institution. In proof of the subtle encroachment of papal influence, bishops and deans pointed out that instead of execrating him as a bloody-minded traitor, the leading articles only spoke of Guy Fawkes as "that greatly misguided gentleman". Since then countless bogeys of foreign or domestic origin have periodically agitated the body-politic. The possible demoralisation of a high-minded and virtuous aristocracy by the new mammon-worship, dating from the era of Australian gold discovery and of "railway kingship", had no sooner somewhat receded than one heard about the Judaising of the West End and the degrading materialism of its spiritually minded denizens which was sure to follow. What has really happened? Such humanising influences as leaven fashionable London to-day largely come from the Jewish element. Apart from the fostering Hebrew, English art and music could scarcely live in the English capital. The encampments of the Israelitish army, from their City headquarters near Swithin's Lane, extend due West first, then by way of Piccadilly, in a north-westerly direction, into the heart of Beds. and Bucks. Other investing armies bring havoc in their van and leave desolation in their rear. The invader's line of march is marked by bounties distributed at every point. The nobility could to-day as ill dispense with the Jews as could the Monarchy itself.'

¶ It was not only the old established English Jewish families for which the King showed a liking:

A Foreign Resident. 'Society in the New Reign', 1904 'No one expected or wished Edward VII to pose as the regenerator of Society. His Court is highly respectable, with as much tendency to what passes for cosmopolitan as aristocratic and smart prejudices allow. To international relations, when acting as his own ambassador, the King has applied a social cement, the secret of which is known to Royalties alone. The rich men from the East are to-day only where he found them on his accession. With the tact which keeps Jew and Gentile alike in high good-humour, he has contrived to make them pay in philanthropy for what they have received in honours. A final word about the Rothschild *personnel:* Baron Alphonse of Paris can still perhaps boast the best brains on the French Bourse. The head of the English branch is of course an able man, whose manners do him less

22

than justice. All the partners everywhere must belong to the family. The Frankfort house was recently closed. Unless New Court develops some fresh genius, within fifty years, it may probably cease to exist. Eclipse has already overtaken the Sterns, who have so declined as scarcely to be a power in the City. The South African gold-mines have brought to the front a host of German Jews — Beits, Neumanns, Cassels, &c. — but the Rothschilds and the old British Hebrews reluctantly recognise them, hold aloof from them in business as much as possible, and entirely avoid them in Society. The Montefiores represent, though not in the smart Society, which they seldom enter, but to the popular eye generally, Israelitism in its intellectual aspect. The old Sir Joseph's successor, Sir Sebag, is a worthy, but obscure, figure. Since Leonard Montefiore's death, the family has a good deal gone out of social evidence. The Muriettas, wrongly classed as Jews, being Roman Catholics, have for the present disappeared. Of the Goldsmids only one has been in the way of receiving titular dignities. In the same birthday honours list that included Sir Nathaniel Nathan, Sir Harry Samuel, and Mr. Arthur Sassoon, 'Colonel Goldsmid" was found. At the Coronation itself the City reply to the Royal Proclamation had a Rothschild's among its chief signatures. That was followed by the promotion of the head of this house to the Privy Council. Among the other decorations of that auspicious event were the knighting of a second Nathan and the baroneting of the Ely Place solicitor, Sir George Lewis, that professional vindicator of affluent innocence and unveiler of impecunious guilt.

'To talk of Jew influence materialising Society in London is silly *blague*. The Israelite might rather claim to be considered a spiritualising force. Not only from Houndsditch to Hyde Park Corner does he supply a whetstone for the wits of his adopted countrymen, but he gives the self-sufficient islanders the few opportunities they enjoy of meeting men distinguished in art and letters, who, but for their Jew *proxeni* in Piccadilly, would never entrust their existences to the British climate.'

¶ It was not only the men of finance but the great tradesmen who basked in the Royal favour:

'The interval separating the social life of retail traders from that of the professional classes has been largely bridged over by the rural hospitalities of others who, during business hours, stand behind their

A Foreign Resident. 'Society in the New Reign', 1904

Bond Street counters. The strawberry feasts, at which the head of a hair-cutting dynasty entertains his customers, almost next-door to the Rothschilds at Gunnersbury, are still smartly patronised. The riverside hospitalities of the Chappell family were at first frequented only by the lights of the musical stage. Gradually they expanded into reunions of any or of all who might consider themselves interested in music, letters, and art. Latter-day Liberalism has found a notable supporter in Mr. J. Barker, head of a mammoth drapery firm in Kensington. After long and lavish expenditure on party objects, he is now in Parliament, and, if with good reason expectant of a baronetcy, is not likely to let a title shame him out of his trade. Mr. C. D. Harrod is visited by academics and parliamentarians at his hunting-box in the Exmoor region. Mr. Whiteley, of Westbourne Grove, from among his young ladies, provides wives for Indian staff-officers.'

¶ Old fashioned gentility, however, still showed a certain reluctance in following the King's lead:

A Foreign Resident. *'Society in the New Reign', 1904* 'Marylebone is one of the London districts whose shopocracy already rivals that Society into which, so far, no retail trader has been admitted. The late Sir Blundell Maple was doing the honours of his Tottenham Court Road establishment to a stately dowager shopping there in her son's company. "I think," naïvely observed the dealer, "I had the pleasure of seeing your Ladyship at the Opera last night." Turning round to her companion, the lady of quality indignantly asked, in an intentionally audible aside, "What does this man mean?" "That he will lend you his box whenever you want it, and if I were you I should borrow it like a shot," came the son's reply. Any fulfilment the words might have had in fact would merely have marked another stage in that process of social fusion which nobody supposes to be finished yet. The Western quarter of the town possesses many other tradesmen of as much social consequence in their way as was the first upholsterer, converted by Royal favour into a baronet.'

¶ Even doctors, whom Lady Warwick in her advice to Elinor Glyn, had so pointedly excluded from the luncheon and dinner tables of the great, were now, if sufficiently eminent, making their way into Society:

A Foreign Resident. *'Society in the New Reign', 1904* 'The chief son of Galen, beneath whose roof the sons and daughters of fashion occasionally dine to-day, is Mr. Alfred Cooper, of the silken manner and the discerning eye. As the wearer of the Victorian decoration and brother-in-law of a real princess — the Duchess of Fife — he may claim to be in a manner related, not only to the greatest nobles in the land, but to royalty itself. No other professional Englishman holds such a position; but Mr. Alfred Cooper's distinctions may remind one of the fact that the social fusion, beginning in the last half of the Victorian Age, has now become so complete as to have deprived the old professional Society of its former independent being, and, in all its sections and departments, to have blended it inseparably with the richly veneered ornaments of both sexes, whose business it is to do nothing but loaf through life and lounge daintily along a path strewn with roses and bank-notes.'

¶ As if even this were not enough Society was invaded by a swarm of rich Colonials:

'The succession of King Edward to the throne of his ancestors completed the social sovereignty of wealth over every class in his realm. The prosperous Australian about the middle of the nineteenth century, having found his nugget, or sheared a thousand flocks, settled down for the residue of his days in Westbourne Terrace. The lucky man's successor finds Tyburnia insufficiently smart; he acquires a palace in Curzon Street or Piccadilly. He had been prepared for glitter and profusion; he had not dreamed of the aggregation of pecuniary interests which dominate the fashionable world in the Old Country. He had heard of plutocracy; he finds it reigning supreme over all other social forces, such as rank, beauty, and wit. At the Turf Club our returned Colonial meets Mr. Henry Chaplin as well as Sir Ernest Cassel. Both have the same social plating, belong to the same clubs, and generally move in the same society. The wealthy Australian has heard, on the other side of the world, of "Harry Chaplin" as a genuine type of Tory squire, living the free, generous life proper to a typical territorial magnate. He is therefore a little perplexed and even disappointed when, on becoming personally acquainted with him, he finds the ideal Tory squire to differ only in appearance from the Prussian Croesus.'

A Foreign Resident. 'Society in the New Reign', 1904

¶ The American invasion was even more significant:

'No Fair Trader is known to have asked Mr. Chamberlain to put a tax on the Chicago and New York heiresses who have become the

A Foreign Resident. 'Society in the New Reign', 1904

25

most considerable exports from the New World to the Old. Besides, if there is to be a tariff against the American conqueresses of the British peerage, ought there not to be like retaliatory measures in the case of Jewesses from Germany? Failing the dowries of Israel and the plums of the United States the British peerage would go to pieces tomorrow. The two principals in this system of matrimonial barter *á la mode*, each bring an article of the same marketable value to the transaction. The reciprocity of the arrangement is complete. It is based on common advantage and cemented by mutual interest; there can be no sense of mutual obligation. The bride contributes the fortune, the bridegroom's wedding gift consists of the position and the title. No business of the sort could be more frank and straightforward, or more thoroughly in harmony with the temper of the time, and here it will be useful to recall, with the help of figures supplied by the *New York World*, some of these hymeneal contracts, more or less recent, and the pecuniary influx into Europe which they represent. The latest is that of their Roxburghe Graces, involving the transfer of a little less than £2,000,000 from the New World to the Old. The wealthiest American bride of all, Miss Roberts with her £2,400,000 had already gone to a commoner (Vivian).

To return to the peerage, Miss Yznaga brought the eighth Duke of Manchester £200,000. With Miss Zimmerman, the ninth Duke of Manchester received twice that sum. The ninth Duchess of Marlborough had a dowry of £2,000,000. On a lower grade of titles, Lady Halkett's fortune equalled that of the mistress of Blenheim. Among the smaller dowries were those of Lady Donoughmore and Mrs Douglas Campbell (£100,000 each). Yet the English record has been beaten across the Dover Straits by Miss Gould who brought her husband, the Count Castellane, not far short of £3,000,000 in cash. In round numbers, then, New World heiresses have enriched Old World husbands to the sum of £40,000,000.

¶ Even when they were not great heiresses, the American girls had a way with them. Let us take the case of Miss Georgiana Robinson who had actually been on the stage:

Desmond Chapman-Huston. 'The Lamp of Memory', 1949 'Harry, when I arrived in London an unknown provincial, opened his own and many other doors to me, including that of Stafford House, where his lovely and gracious sister, the Duchess of Sutherland (Millicent), gave regularly small evening parties at which one met the

26

cleverest, most amusing, and most distinguished people in London. With Harry's auburn, wavy hair, a tall, lovely figure, perfect taste in dress, the Duchess's splendid historic background apparently suited her to perfection. In addition to Stafford House, which, if I remember correctly, was built as a royal residence by that Duke of York who has the statue and the Steps, she became, upon marriage, mistress of Lillieshall, Trentham, Branksome Tower, Cliveden, lordly Dunrobin in wild Sutherlandshire overlooking the North Sea, and a young palace on the French Riviera!

'Like all the St. Clair Erskines, the Duchess has brains, charm, and a very considerable literary ability, inherited from her father, the fourth Earl, who was a remarkable man. Her mother, Blanche, Lady Rosslyn, born a Fitzroy, was also a most unusual personage and survived until fairly recently. Through Harry I also came to know his half-sister Frances, the beautiful Lady Warwick, who entertained royally and who also possessed the family itch to write. Harry's younger sister, Lady Westmorland, I only met a few times as she was little in London, but her exquisite features and delicate beauty are unforgettable.

'Harry had met at Monte Carlo Miss Georgiana Robinson, a rich American who, mainly because of her great beauty, had made something of a success in fashionable light comedies in New York and London. Easily inflammable, Harry fell madly in love and, without either of them knowing the other, they hastily got married. They had a small house in Norfolk Street, Park Lane, and Anna had it furnished by the most popular interior decorator of the moment, the male of that odd species becoming about then all the rage. Harry gave his bride a present of a smart electric brougham painted in his livery colours and with a large cypher made of two large R's crossed and surmounted by an outsized coronet.

'In many ways very simple, one of Harry's little weaknesses was an undue liking for the insignia of his rank and an exaggerated idea of the historic importance of his family. That autumn he took Thurso Castle from his grand old kinsman, Sir Archibald Sinclair, father of the present baronet. He organised large house parties, chartered a yacht which spent most of its time lying in the bay. I joined the party at the end of August or early in September with the second and third-rate shots — and thoroughly enjoyed myself. Anna was very fascinating and, like most Americans, a good hostess.

'I have an unforgettable vision of her in the floppy, lacy gowns of the period, her eyes protected from the sun by a picture hat and a lingerie parasol, while servants dispensed drinks and tea on the deck of the safely anchored yacht. Anna disliked rough tweed suits, country-clothes, tramps over sodden, windswept Caithness where, as she rightly felt, she was at a disadvantage. She found the wild splendour of Thurso almost frightening. Once or twice we drove miles and miles to Dunrobin and the Duchess, whatever her private thoughts, was charming to her sister-in-law. Rumour had it that her verdict was: "she is certainly a lady. Harry might have done worse." '

John Brown in 'The Age of Extravagance', 1956 'Then there were the Professional Beauties, Ladies who, when they went driving in the park, would have people leaping up on chairs and benches, in order that they might catch a better glimpse of them as they passed. If you were one of those, you would be offered a large sum of money, either by Bassano, or Foulsham and Banfield, or Ellis and Wallery, to go to their studio where, for a whole day, you would be arranged in a variety of different poses, in front of such a diversity of different backgrounds, all the pictures showing an extravagance of sentimentality. There would be twenty to thirty pictures, all made to be sold to the Picture Post Card Trade. To begin with you might be shown as a simple country maid, peeping out from bales of straw. Then you would be made more worldly, smiling a little more wantonly from under the brim of an enormous hat that was just a little bigger, and a little more showy, than any that a real lady would care to wear. Following that you would be put into flowing Greek draperies; and you would be seen wafting about in a clump of silver birches that had been planted in sockets in the studio floor, which had artificial roses growing up the trunks tied on with string; and you would never be able to resist pointing out one naughty foot to meet its reflection in a little looking-glass pool that lay in front of you. Finally, you would be seen swinging in a hammock up in the tree-tops, even in the lap of the crescent moon itself. It was all such fun to see oneself, covered with tinsel and imitation snow, sparkling away in the little shop windows, back in the high-street at home.'

¶ The period has been rightly named the Age of Extravagance. The more sedate landed gentry found themselves unable to compete with the New Rich. The King himself set the example:

A Foreign Resident. 'Society in the New Reign', 1904 'The shooting parties of the new reign, as high functions, are not less important than State entertainments in London. Here Royalty has

28

The Countess of Craven (Cornelia, daughter of Mr Bradley Martin of New York).

The Countess of Tankerville (Leonora, daughter of Mr Van Marter of New York).

The Duchess of Marlborough (Consuelo, daughter of Mr William K. Vanderbilt of New York).

The Marchioness of Dufferin and Ava (Florence, daughter of Mr John H. Davis of New York).

AMERICA AND THE PEERAGE

VINS

..MENU..

—o—

Coronation Sherry,
1837

Consommé Printanier à l'Impériale.
Consommé froid à l'Indienne.

———

Madeira, 1853

Blanchailles au Naturel et à la Diable.
Filets de Truites à la Russe.

———

Rudesheim, 1893

Côtelettes de Cailles à la Clamart.
Poulardes à la Norvégienne.

———

Moet,
"Dry Imperial"
1892

Selles de Présalé à la Niçoise.
Jambon d'Espagne à la Basque.

———

Château Langoa
1874

Ortolans rôtis sur Canapés.
Salade des quatre Saisons.

———

Asperges froides à la Vinaigrette.

———

Gâteau Punch granit au Champagne.
Gradins de Pâtisseries.

———

Royal Tawny Port

Port, 1863

Canapés d'Anchois à la Provençale.

———

Sherry, George IV.

Petits Soufflés Glacés Princesse.

Brandy, 1800

Gaufrettes.

BUCKINGHAM PALACE,
23 Juin, 1902.

set the inexorable fashion. The luncheons at Sandringham and at the appointed *rendezvous* in the other royal preserves were always banqucts. To-day, to entertain the King or any of his family at a specially reserved shoot is a much more expensive affair than a country ball used to be.'

¶ Even the King's appetite for food was on a gargantuan scale:

'Although King Edward ate a Continental breakfast when he was abroad, he always liked "an English Breakfast" consisting of haddock, poached eggs, bacon, chicken and woodcock, before setting out on a day's shooting or racing. Luncheon and dinner, of course, were meals that stretched from ten to fourteen courses, and tea was an elaborate affair with every sort of scone and crumpet, tart and roll and cake. Besides this, snacks consisting of lobster salad and cold chicken were often served at eleven in the morning to appease the King's hunger, and even after dinner a plate of sandwiches, and sometimes a quail or a cutlet, was sent to the Royal apartments.'

Virginia Cowles. 'Edward VII and His Circle', 1956

¶ A similar state of affairs existed in all the great houses:

'Those meals! Those endless, extravagant meals, in which they all indulged all the year round! Sebastian wondered how their constitutions and their figures could stand it; then he remembered that in the summer they went as a matter of course to Homburg or Marienbad, to get rid of the accumulated excess, and then returned to start on another year's course of rich living. Really there was very little difference, essentially, between Marienbad and the vomitorium of the Romans. How strange that eating should play so important a part in social life! They were eating quails and cracking jokes. That particular dish of the Chevron chef was famous: an ortolan within the quail, a truffle within the ortolan, and pate de foie gras within the truffle; by the time all the disembowelling had taken place, there was not much left of any of the constituents. From his place at the head of the table, Sebastian watched the jaws going up and down, and wished that he did not always see people as though they were caricatures. There was Sir Harry Tremaine, the perfect courtier, with his waved white hair, turning his head rigidly above his high collar, rather like a bird; there was Mrs. Levison, with her raucous voice and her hair like a frizzed yellow sponge. They were all people whose names were familiar to

V. Sackville-West. 'The Edwardians', 1930

every reader of the society titbits in the papers. Sebastian saw them suddenly as a ventriloquist's box of puppets.'

¶ By modern standards, of course, food was cheap — that is for those who looked after their own affairs and had some notion of economy. But for the others—

Mrs C. S. Peel,
O.B.E.
'Life's Enchanted
Cup', 1933

'In the rich years of the late Victorian and Edwardian periods, the extravagance in many large houses was appalling. The owners of these establishments had neither the time nor the desire to look into the details of their household expenditure. Other people were employed to attend to that, and it was not surprising that those to whom even smalls sums of money mattered very much should use their opportunities to provide for their later years. The perquisite system was carried to great lengths; indeed in numerous cases the term perquisite was a polite synonym for what was neither more nor less than theft.

'In allowing such a state of affairs the careless rich created social plague spots. Every boy and girl who took service in their houses was contaminated by the atmosphere, and it was not only the servants whose standard of moral values was harmed, but the inhabitants of the neighbouring villages.

'In one case, it was found that in a household numbering thirty persons, not including guests and their servants or the cost of parties, the expenditure for food and cleaning materials worked out at £4 per head per week, and this although mutton, game, rabbits, garden produce, milk, cream, butter and eggs were obtained free from the estate. At prices such as ruled during the first ten years of the twentieth century it was impossible that any person could eat even £4 worth of food each week and remain long alive. In this case effort was made to put matters on a different footing, but in the end, though greatly against the desire of the owners of the property who were distressed at the amount of unemployment which would be the result of such a step, this house was shut up.

'I think it is Frances, Countess of Warwick who, in one of her books, refers to the extravagance of a ducal establishment, where for a week-end party three turtles costing £20 each would be sent down from London and perhaps only partly used. The rotting corpse of one of these reptiles was commented upon by a disapproving farmer who remarked that "it did cost as much as a cow".

'In another case where economies had to be made dissection of the

30

house accounts showed that the number of eggs used was unreasonable. The *chef* never troubled to teach his underlings to examine each egg as it was broken. For a dish for which perhaps thirty or forty eggs might be needed, one after another they were broken into a large bowl. If one tainted egg went in, then the whole bowlful would be thrown away.

'Commission on all goods ordered was regarded as the perquisite of the upper servant who gave the order. It was putting too much faith in human nature to suppose that the average person would refuse to avail himself of the opportunity of making easy money, though in justice to the servant one must bear in mind that he saw nothing wrong in the perquisite system, but many did draw the line at deliberately ordering goods to be given to their friends or thrown away.

'Generally speaking, even when luxurious living was required in the dining-room, which meant it was also enjoyed by the upper servants, an average sum of £2 per head per week throughout the household throughout the year should have been sufficient to buy every article of food required. In lesser houses where the management was good, 25/- a head for the dining-room, £1 for the nurseries, schoolroom, and the housekeeper's room, and 15/- a head for the servants' hall, allowed for as good living as most people require. The same estimate is applicable to-day.'

¶ Our leading historian of the theatre, who himself lived through the epoch he describes, has given us a vivid picture of Edwardian feeding habits:

'Only the really improper Edwardians had breakfast in their rooms. The others met, on that Sunday morning, in the dining-room. The smell of last night's port had given place to the smell of this morning's spirits of wine. Rows of little spirit lamps warmed rows of large silver dishes. On a table to the right between the windows were grouped Hams, Tongues, Galantines, Cold Grouse, ditto Pheasant, ditto Partridge, ditto Ptarmigan. No Edwardian meal was complete without Ptarmigan. Hot or cold. Just Ptarmigan. There would also be a little delicate rectangle of pressed beef from the shop of M. Benoist. On a further table, to the left between the doors, stood fruits of different calibre, and jugs of cold water, and jugs of lemonade. A fourth table contained porridge utensils. A fifth coffee, and pots of Indian and China tea. The latter were differentiated from each other by little

W. MacQueen-Pope
in
'The Age of
Extravagance', 1956

ribbons of yellow (indicating China) and of red (indicating, without *arrière pensée,* our Indian Empire). The centre table, which was prepared for twenty-three people, would be bright with Malmaisons and toast-racks. No newspapers were, at that stage, allowed.

'The atmosphere of the Edwardian dining-room at nine-thirty was essentially daring. A pleasant scene of confederacy and sin hung above the smell of the spirit-lamps. For had they not all been brought up to attend family prayers? And had they not all eluded that obligation? It was true, of course, that the host and hostess, with their niece, had at nine proceeded to the family chapel and heard the butler reading a short collect for the day. But the guests had for their part evaded these Victorian obligations. This corporate evasion gave to the proceedings an atmosphere of dash.

'Edwardian breakfasts were in no sense a hurried proceeding. The porridge was disposed of negligently, people walking about and watching the rain descend upon the Italian garden. Then would come whiting and omelette and devilled kidneys and little fishy messes in shells. And then tongue and ham and a slice of Ptarmigan. And then scones and honey and marmalade. And then a little melon, and a nectarine or two, and just one or two of those delicious raspberries. The men at that stage would drift (I employ the accepted term) to the smoking room. The women would idle in the saloon watching the rain descend upon the Italian garden. It was then 10.30.'

¶ What a party it was! But it didn't, after all, last very long:

Cecil Beaton. 'The Glass of Fashion', 1954 'Whereas Queen Victoria's reign lasted for more than sixty stolid years, the Edwardian age of opulence proved to be a short-lived wedding party, confined to one brief decade. Someone has said that each age is an age that is dying, or one that is coming to birth; but the nostalgic eye always seems to choose to regard change as a form of dying. Meanwhile, though it would have been difficult to forsee the war that was to come four years later, King Edward's prestige was such that his death in 1910 brought a first suggestion of the profound organic break-up which many of the component parts of Western European society and culture were to undergo in the next three or four decades. The most significant aspect of England's mourning period for King Edward was the social event that came to be known as 'Black Ascot'. At the first Ascot racing season after the popular monarch's death, society appeared dressed from head to foot in black.

Ascot Races, 1907. Outside the refreshment tent of the Bachelors' Club.

Above: the Enclosure at Goodwood Races, 1907.

Below: the 'Black Ascot', in mourning for King Edward, 1910.

The men wore black silk top hats with morning or frock coats, black trousers, black waistcoats, black ties, while in their black-gloved hands they carried tightly rolled black umbrellas. Their funeral ladies must have seemed like strange giant crows or morbid birds of paradise strutting at some Gothic entertainment. As far as the eye could see there were black dresses trimmed with long black fringes, black lace parasols and huge black hats, wider than they had ever been before. Fashions tend to extremes before being dropped, and the elaborate headgear had now become like the last spurt of a Catherine wheel. These vast picture hats, perhaps set on one side of the head and piled high with black ostrich feathers mixed with osprey or black paradise feathers combined with black tulle, were worn not only in mourning for a king but for a glory that had gone forever.'

¶ That admirable social commentator Mrs Peel may, perhaps, be allowed to sum up the whole matter:

'What a rushing, glittering time it was, that of King Edward's reign. *Mrs C. S. Peel,* *O.B.E.* The Court set an example of splendour, and American, South African, *'Life's Enchanted* and Jewish magnates were made welcome. Social conventions became *Cup', 1933* less strict and, where rank, or position gained by outstanding mental capacity backed by wealth had been passports into exclusive society, now money, unbacked by other qualifications, began to talk, though not invariably to just those people to whom it desired to talk.

'There was a vast amount of entertaining of a lavish order, with red carpets and awnings, rows of men-servants and champagne suppers. As the motor car came into more general use, the week-end habit grew, and well-to-do folk ceased to use the Park and went further afield for their Saturday to Monday pleasuring. Even people of no account like ourselves were affected. We went to quantities of all kinds of parties and when we could get away took a holiday abroad or rented a house in the country, sufficiently near London for Charles to travel up and down to his office and for me to keep in touch with my newspapers.

'Then came the illness and death of King Edward. Everyone, I think, felt sorry that he should have lived so short a time to enjoy the Kingship which for so long had been denied him, but his death did not mark the end of a period, as that of his Royal Mother had done, and neither was it mourned by members of the general public as a personal loss.'

¶ On the contrary, there was a feeling of personal loss which was shared by the meanest of the King's subjects:

Broadsheet sold in the London Streets at King Edward's funeral.

' "*On the Death of King Edward VII*

"Greatest sorrow England ever had
When death took away our dear Dad;
A king was he from head to sole,
Loved by his people one and all.

"His mighty work for the Nation,
Making peace and strengthening Union —
Always at it since on the throne:
Saved the country more than one billion." '

¶ Many a King has had a worse epitaph.

CHAPTER II

THE SOCIAL ROUND

EDWARDIAN SOCIAL LIFE revolved round 'The Season' and the great country houses. It is hard for anyone today to realize how rigid and regimented the life of pleasure was. The taboos were absolute. Bernard Shaw once remarked that 'acquired notions of propriety are stronger than natural instincts. It is easier to recruit for monasteries and convents than to induce an Arab woman to uncover her mouth in public or a British officer to walk through Bond Street in a golfing cap on an afternoon in May.' Impossible perhaps at any time of the year, but doubly impossible (if the phrase may be permitted) in May for that was 'the height of the Season'.

A young man of 'good family', with a modest unearned income of £500 could have a very good time on one condition: that he kept rigidly to the time-schedule. He could have a flat in Jermyn Street and be a member of several clubs in the neighbourhood. He probably had more invitations than he was able to accept and was hardly ever in the regrettable position of having to pay for his own dinner. If he did find himself 'on his own' in the evening, he would dine at his club. 'Never dine alone in public restaurants', was the advice of the redoubtable Jimmy Glover. 'People will think you have no friends.'

Of course, having dined at someone's house, it was necessary, on the following day, to call and leave a card:

'After receiving any particular hospitality, such as a dinner or ball, it is necessary to call or merely to leave cards at the door within the few following days. The hours for calling are between three and six o'clock pm. No call should be paid before luncheon, unless on a very familiar friend.'

Lady Colin Campbell
'Etiquette of
Good Society', 1911

35

¶ Leaving cards, indeed, was almost an occupation in itself:

Cecil Beaton in 'The Age of Extravagance', 1956 'These ladies of the upper middle classes rolled along in hansom carriages as they paid afternoon calls. Their white kid gloves were of an immaculate quality. Over one wrist they carried a small, square gold mesh bag containing a gold pencil, a handerchief, and a flat gold wallet which held their calling cards. If the lady of the house was "not at home", the visitor handed the servant two of her cards with the corner turned down to indicate that she had "left cards" in person. The shining wheels of her carriage revolved on the freshly gravelled surface of the road to the next place of call, their sound muted if they were passing a door where the sick or dying lay, for it was customary to spread a thick carpet of straw in the streets before houses of invalids.'

¶ If anyone under the age of seventy could return to this Edwardian epoch he would find its formality stifling. However, *some* things had changed since Queen Victoria's day.

'The Queen', 1905 'It is significant of the position taken up by the unmarried women of to-day that, as hostesses, they occupy a prominent place in society amongst dinner givers. In the sixties "To dine with an old maid, oh, dear no!" would be said if an invitation to dinner was received. "Much too dull." There was little opportunity, it must be admitted, for refusing to join a spinster's dinner party, as unmarried ladies at that epoch did not enter the lists as dinner givers, neither were they habitual diners out; for while their married sisters, the mothers of the present generation, were both giving entertainments and going to them throughout the London seasons, the unmarried ladies, their contemporaries, were, with but few exceptional exceptions, left out of most that society had to offer, notably dining out and giving dinners.'

¶ Being a spinster-hostess, however, had its own pitfalls:

'The Queen', 1905 'An unmarried lady, when acting as hostess, is often at a loss as to whether, in her unattached condition, she should give the lead or follow it. Should she go in to dinner first or last — act as a host or a hostess? A widow lady frequently experiences a like hesitation. Actually, whether she is a widow or a maiden lady she should follow last, as would a married lady, and send her guests in before her. A male relative, the son of the widowed hostess, or the brother of the

36

The Earl and Countess of Normanton driving in Hyde Park, July 1911.

The Misses Acheson. Painting by John S. Sargent, R.A.

unmarried lady, is, when possible, asked to act as host; failing these, a more distant relative can with advantage take the place; but oftener than not, neither can fall back upon such aid and act independently of it, in which case the man second in rank takes the lady first in rank, and the other couples follow, according to their precedency, the hostess going last with the man of highest rank or importance. The hostess herself tells each man the name of the lady he is to take in to dinner, and, if necessary, introduces him to her soon after arrival.

'Seating the guests is arranged by means of name cards, and, failing a host, a lady often occupies the seat that would otherwise be his, and faces the hostess. If more ladies than men are present, the hostess sends the married ladies in to dinner with the men present, allowing the young ladies to go in together and precede her; or she walks in with one of the ladies following last of all, and allows the man of highest rank who should have gone in with her to take the lady highest in rank and lead the way with her. Should they, however, be husband and wife, the lady second in rank must be chosen instead, and follow as second couple. The first plan is best, when possible, but, if unavoidable, it is always preferable to ask a man to take a second place than a lady. It involves a good deal of explanation on the part of a hostess to make these changes, therefore it is wiser to ask two ladies to go in together and seat each beside a man, or one beside the hostess if the numbers do not admit of placing than as aforesaid.

'The man who takes in the hostess is asked by her to take her place when she and the other ladies leave the table, and to pass the wine and cigarettes to the men as a host would do, to ring for more wine if required, and for coffee. Also he makes the move for adjournment to the drawing room, as being the man of highest rank, which is his privilege to do when a host is present; being deputy host, he is still entitled to do this. He leads the way to the drawing-room, followed by the other men, and does not act as does a host and enter after the men, but before them. When a relative is deputed to act as host, he follows the same lines as does a husband when his wife is hostess; he does not propose adjourning to the drawing-room, but leaves it to the man who has taken the hostess down to dinner to make the move.'

¶ Formality still ruled even when away from home:

'When unmarried ladies entertain at hotels, it is usual for the couples to walk to the dining-room side by side, not arm in arm, from

'The Queen', 1905

the lounge or sitting-room where they have assembled; and although they precede the hostess to the dining hall, yet they await her coming, and she then leads the way to the table set apart from her and her party. The man of highest rank sits at her left hand. She gives the signal for leaving the table by rising from her seat, and the ladies leave walking together in twos and threes. Here, again, the man of highest rank is deputed by her to act as host to the men of the party when she and the ladies have left the dinner table. When more ladies than men are present, they, with their hostess, go first together, followed by the men, as at luncheon.'

¶ It was a little simpler if the spinster were not entirely on her own but kept house for her brother:

'The Queen', 1910 'When a sister is at the head of her brother's house she always takes the position of a married woman in the estimation of her friends; the mantle of his presence in the household completely envelopes her in its folds of conventionality. The two are invited together to dinners, to dances, to At homes, to everything.

'But as a set off against this advantage a sister who keeps her brother's house is regarded with so much respect by her brother's friends that she is seldom asked to relinquish that position, and as years roll on she is still her brother's housekeeper, until quite unexpectedly he takes unto himself a wife, and she is then left to roam the world, or to settle down in some quiet spot, a maiden lady, with her youth behind her.'

¶ Married ladies had their own problems, but life, although lacking in 'modern amenities', was still pretty comfortable for anyone with any pretensions to belong to the upper classes:

Mrs C. S. Peel, O.B.E. 'Life's Enchanted Cup', 1933 'When we went to Brompton Square it had not so long before been a favourite haunt, together with St. Michael's Grove, now Egerton Terrace, of ladies of the half-world. Earlier still its reputation had been exceedingly black, rumours suggesting that many a man had been lured to what was then a rural neighbourhood, robbed and murdered.

'I think my husband's uncle, Sir Baldwin Wake Walker, was one of the first respectable persons to install his family in a house in this Square. His example was soon followed, until in the early nineteen-hundreds it was considered quite a good situation.

'Our home was one of the two last lodging houses. We proceeded to modernise it, adding a kitchen, larder, boxroom and storeroom, a large drawing-room, small sitting-room and bathroom, a service lift, electric light and a telephone, not as usual a piece of domestic equipment as it now is.

'Neither architect nor builder suggested central heating, a second bathroom, or indeed any labour-saving arrangements.

'This house when rebuilt contained a large basement, three sitting-rooms, what house agents now call a lounge-hall, and seven bedrooms. All the rooms were warmed by coal fires. There were nursery meals to be carried up and down, hot water to be taken to the bedrooms, and we entertained a good deal in a small way. Yet we found little difficulty in running the house with a staff consisting of a Norland nurse, a parlourmaid, a housemaid, and a cook. Later we kept a manservant who had been head footman of three, and asked £70 a year. The cook, and a very fair cook too, earned £28. If my memory serves me rightly, the Norland nurse's salary was £40. Norland nurses, who were women of the educated classes trained at the Norland Institute, wore a special uniform and were a novelty. Later, while our second child was in the nursery meal stage, we had a between maid.

'Old account books show that we spent about 12/- a head each week on food and cleaning materials, and this sum included the cost of come-and-go guests, but not of parties. We bought coal at 15/- a ton taking six tons at a time, laundry charges were no more than half what they are now, and the cost of the upkeep of a house much less because labour was cheaper, and the rent and upkeep of shops and business premises very much less. There was penny postage, no insurance to pay for domestic servants, stamps on cheques cost 1d. each and, most important of all, Income Tax was but 1/- in the £. An income of £1,500 a year was, I think, equivalent to one of £2,500 to-day.'

¶ It is interesting to find the sensible — and not very wealthy — Mrs Peel falling a victim to the universal passion for bridge:

'Now that our children were away from home and my tea-time hours free, I became an ardent Bridge player; but as I could rarely spare whole afternoons to play what is called "private Bridge", I often played at clubs between tea and dinner time. I, like many other folk, was silly enough to try to pick up Bridge after having one or two lessons in the rudiments of the game. Bridge players, especially those who

Mrs C. S. Peel, O.B.E. 'Life's Enchanted Cup', 1933

play at clubs, dislike partners who are picking-up the game. They disliked me and did not hesitate to show it, for, with some notable exceptions, manners at these clubs were a trifle unrestrained. Soon I realised that auction is a game which needs considerable study if one would play it even moderately well; while contract is still more difficult — though to me far more interesting.

'I also began to realise that although I was playing for stakes which I could afford to lose, others were not, and in addition to the irritation caused by my mistakes, there was the irritation caused by losing more money than could be spared. I often wondered to what extent the housekeeping in many a home suffered after a run of bad luck at cards. Bridge became an obsession with many women. By three o'clock they would be waiting impatiently to begin to play. They drank their tea while they played, ate a light club dinner, talking Bridge meanwhile, were in the cardroom again directly it opened for the evening's sitting, and departed only when its doors closed, which, if they were willing to pay fines, might not be until a late hour.'

¶ These bridge-playing ladies talked an extraordinary language of their own:

A Foreign Resident.
'Society on the New
Reign', 1904

'In the inner vocabulary of twentieth-century smartness, a royal personage is designated a "man-man". If a lady wishes to intimate that the charges of her dressmaker are high, she speaks of that person, not as expensive, but as "expie". The robe, proper for the function, known to the Parisians as five o'clock tea, is not a teagown, but a "teagie". Another robe, donned at a later hour, is of course a "nightie". The epithet of "deevie", applied to these or other articles, signified that they are quite too delightful. The exclamation "fittums" is by interpretation, "What a capital fit!" The fair one, who has borrowed money of her friends with little prospect of repaying it, boasts of "lootin'" her pals; for of course no one with the slightest pretension to smartness could take the trouble to pronounce the final "G". Thus the daughter of a ducal house, like the humble maid-of-all-work, complains that some one has been "ratin'" her, by which she means finding fault. On the other hand, by that linguistic law expounded by the late Max Müller, as a compensation for the dropped "g", a superfluous "r" is affixed to words ending in a "w", so that smart lips give exactly the same sound to paw or pour. When, in addition to all this, certain old-fashioned critics hear that "diskie" means disgusting, they

40

are tempted to think that here at least is the proper adjective to describe the *patois* occasionally overhead in the drawing-rooms which one might have expected would be 'barred against it'.

¶ That 'ladies' should belong to clubs, especially gambling clubs, would have scandalized an earlier generation. But there was a new freedom in the Edwardian era which allowed them even to dine in public restaurants. It was the heyday of the palace-restaurant, and some of the entertainments given there were lavish in the extreme:

'The Savoy Hotel in London has certainly been chosen by the wealthy eccentrics for their freak dinner-parties more frequently than any other Hotel in Europe.

J. Rey. 'The Whole Art of Dining', 1914

'It was at the same establishment that the famous "Gondola Dinner" was given by Mr. George A. Kessler.

'With just a little more than twenty-four hours' notice, the manager and his staff accomplished a veritable "tour de force" of ingenuity and good taste on that occasion.

'The host expressed to the manager his desire of giving a sumptuous dinner to some of his distinguished friends, and wanted it to be something quite out of the ordinary and a thing to be talked about.

'After considering several schemes and suggestions from the manager it was decided that the dinner should be served in a floating Venetian gondola.

'The scene chosen for the dinner was the courtyard at the back of the building. This was made water-tight and filled with water several feet deep.

'Many scores of hands were busy throughout the night and the next day, transforming the old courtyard into a miniature panorama of Venice.

'They included engineers, carpenters, plumbers, upholsterers, electricians, and scene-painters. A score or more of tailors were also busy making costumes for the waiters who were dressed as Venetian gondoliers.

'The dinner-table was most artistically laid out inside the gondola; and this covered over with a canopy of white silk gauze.

'Several little gondola boats and a number of swans could be seen gliding on the water; and the Italian airs played by the troupe of Venetian mandolinists during the dinner were delightful.

'Both the table and the gondola, as well as the surroundings and the

41

suite of rooms for the reception of the party, were most magnificently decorated with carnations and white roses; whilst the effects of the coloured electric lights were suggestive of Fairyland.'

¶ Not all the hosts of such parties belonged to the *haut ton*. What matter, if they had money to burn? There was never any lack of *convives*.

W. MacQueen-Pope. 'The Melodies Linger On', 1950

'Jimmy White, the famous millionaire, when at the height of his fame and fortune, once gave a dinner party to a crowd of other very wealthy men. There was always a streak of mischief and malice in the make-up of the ex-bricklayer from Rochdale, and on this occasion he engaged the Brothers Egbert to act as waiters, giving them a free hand. Plates crashed round their ears, the rolls were of cement, the knives and forks of india rubber, the spoons collapsed, and the few who managed to consume their soup found sets of old false teeth at the bottom. The Brothers Egbert surpassed themselves.'

¶ The Edwardians spent a surprising amount of their time in the open air, especially in places where they could see and be seen. They strolled down Bond Street, they attended 'Church Parade' in the Park, they rode in the Row and, on Sundays, they went 'on the river'. The river, indeed, remained fashionable until the end of Edward VII's reign.

'The Graphic', July 8, 1905

'The Thames is now in the height of its glory. The river between Maidenhead and Cookham is particularly delightful, with wooded banks and shady backwaters. Boulter's Lock, just above Maidenhead, is the most popular point, if one may judge from the crowd of boats that pass through on Sunday afternoon. The scene afforded by the Lock crammed full of boats, in which are daintily clad ladies, are (*sic*) of the prettiest imaginable.'

¶ Even Royalty itself did not despise these pleasures:

'The Graphic', July 8, 1905

'Last Saturday the King and Queen took a launch trip on the Thames as far as Monkey Island, in the direction of Bray. Their Majesties were accompanied by Princess Victoria and the two young Princes Edward and Albert of Wales, and were attended by members of their suite. The Royal party, numbering seventeen in all, embarked in the Royal launch, and from Maidenhead proceeded to Monkey Island, where

42

they landed and took tea outside the hotel, remaining for an hour, and subsequently returning to Windsor Castle.'

¶ 'Henley was a social event of the first magnitude:

'A Glorious Henley'

'The Sketch',
July 13, 1904
'In spite of the King not being present at the great Thames carnival, as it had been rumoured that His Majesty would be on Thursday, Henley was brilliantly successful. Not for three years has the Regatta brought together so large and cheerful a company of noted folk all bent on enjoying the prettiest Society gathering of the year. The Isthmian, has alas, disappeared, but Phyllis Court and the Sports Club, to say nothing of the many delightful houses and gardens lining the river, were, as a consequence, fuller than ever of brave men and fair women. Then the house-boats made up in quality what they lacked in quantity, especially charming being the decorations, the wealth of bright blossoms, outlining the gay little *Cigarette*, the more stately *Viscountess Burg*, and the Eastern-looking *Ibis*. As for the racing, of course the greatest victory was the carrying off of the Diamond Sculls by a Canadian, Mr L. F. Scholes, of whom Toronto may well be proud. But the Etonians, always especially popular with the ladies who grace Henley with their presence, also did very well, the Ladies' Plate once more bearing the trophy of the Light Blue.'

¶ Gradually the river lost its exclusiveness, the gorgeous fringes of society replacing the *comme il faut:*

Cyllene Moxon in
'The Day Before
Yesterday', 1956
'My first Ascot Sunday must have been in 1910. Some years before this a famous author wrote: "Maidenhead too snobby to be pleasant, the haunt of the river swell and his overdressed female companion, showy hotels and those demons of the river, the steam-launches." By the time I knew it the river party on Ascot Sunday was no longer a society function, it had become almost entirely a theatre Sunday, a musical comedy outing. But there was still snobbiness, for the greater the star the greater the snob value.

'Those years before the first world war were the era of lavish spending on anything and everything that might be considered to be amusing. For Ascot Sunday much thought was given and money spent on clothes. What dress should be worn for the occasion? Not only had it to stand up to a long day, but also to the sharp eyes and searing criticism of

Henley, 1914.

'A Riverside Melody.' Drawing by Leonard Lindsell, 1903.

theatre friends. Boulter's Lock on Ascot Sunday has been described as a floating dress show, but I would say the real dress-show took place on the lawn of Skindle's Hotel, which is at Maidenhead, where everyone assembled before lunch to see and be seen.

'Much has been written of the lovely reach between Boulter's Lock and Cookham Lock. Cliveden Woods rising up from the water's edge in a harmony of blended greens, and high above the tree tops Cliveden Court looking down proudly upon the hoi polloi. Up there I knew, for I had been told so, there would be a large house party, but they would not come on the river for it was no longer considered fashionable. For in 1910 there was a sharp distinction between society and the musical comedy world, despite the many marriages there had been between the two. Not that distinctions of that sort troubled me, for I was mixing in the world of my choice, and would not have changed places with anybody.

'The ideal finish to Ascot Sunday was an invitation to dinner to one of the furnished houses taken by the stars for the season. These invitations were much sought after, and as a matter of course the invitation was extended to the escort. To the escorts there gatherings were sheer delight, for they belonged to the society world, and a theatre party was something different. Not that the set-up was really different from what they were used to in their own homes, for the stars knew what was what, and without ostentation could entertain their guests extremely well; but at the same time they could afford to dispense with convention in a way unknown in the environment to which the men belonged.

'What fun those parties were! What an enchanting ending to a perfect day! Frivolous, extravagant, gloriously silly, but so colourful and so gay to remember.'

¶ Even the Season was not entirely spent in London or its immediate neighbourhood, for the week-end habit had now become an established institution. It was the heyday of country house entertaining, and some idea of its scale can be gained from the extensive guest wings which some of the wealthier Edwardians thought it necessary to add to their already large country mansions. How large they were and how solidly built:

'All was warmth and security, leisure and continuity. An order of things which appeared unchangeable to the mind of nineteen hundred

V. Sackville-West.
'The Edwardians',
1930

45

and five. Why should they change, since they had never changed? There were a few minor changes, perhaps; no armourer was beating out a new pair of greaves for his young master; but in the main the tapestry had changed very little. The figures were the same, and the background was the same: the grey walls, the flag on the tower, the verdure of the trees, the hares and the deer feeding in the glades — even to the laundry-maid hanging out the washing.'

¶ In retrospect those who lived in the great houses, especially the older members of the family, have an air of antedeluvian monsters:

V. Sackville-West.
'The Edwardians',
1930

'The Dowager Duchess carried an air of solid assurance which belonged to a less uneasy age. That slightly raucous note of defiance was absent from her pronouncements. She did not protest; she merely ignored. Nothing unpleasant ever ruffled her serenity, because she simply failed to notice it. Darwin and the Labour Party alike had passed unnoticed under the bulwark of her mighty nose; the one in eighteen seventy-one, the other in nineteen-six. She remained unaware that the Americans were discovering Europe far more rapidly than the Europeans had discovered America. The only event that had ever been known to arouse her indignation was the death duty imposed by Sir William Harcourt in the Radical Budget of eighteen-ninety-four. She had been forced to take notice of that; because her son, Sebastian's father, had been killed in the South African war in nineteen-hundred when Sebastian was fourteen years old; and she had read in the *Morning Post* that the duty payable on the Chevron estates would amount to one hundred thousand pounds' benefit to the Treasury. On that occasion the Dowager Duchess had startingly and alarmingly emerged from her trance, had sent for her man of affairs, and had dictated a letter of protest to the Chancellor of the Exchequer.'

¶ It must not be supposed that the life of the guests in the great houses was one of easy relaxation:

Anthony Glyn.
'Elinor Glyn', 1955

'The clothes to be worn at these visits were formal and picturesque. In the daytime the guests would wear whatever was suitable for the time of year and the particular sport of the moment. It was not, however, correct to lunch in tweeds and ladies were expected to change into a frock. After lunch they changed back again into tweeds, if it was a shooting party, or put on a full length sealskin coat if they

46

were to go motoring. For tea they changed again into tea-gowns, seductive diaphanous affairs with low-cut bodices while the men wore brightly coloured velvet smoking suits. For dinner the guests wore full evening dress, the men in white ties and tails and the women in dresses with trains, carrying ostrich feather fans. Evening bags were never used, as cosmetics were at that time almost unknown in society circles and could only be bought at a theatrical costumiers."

¶ To us casual moderns such a life has an air of almost Chinese rigidity and etiquette.

'It must be admitted that a very large fraction of our time was spent in dressing and undressing. We were for ever changing our clothes, a custom which necessitated travelling with a mountain of luggage — at least one large domed trunk called a Noah's Ark, an immense hat box and a heavy fitted dressing case. Winter was the worst season for changing. You came down to breakfast in your "best dress," usually made of velvet, and after Church changed into tweeds. Another "change" for tea — those who possessed that specialised creation — into a "tea-gown"; the less affluent into a summer day-dress. However small your dress allowance, a different dinner gown was considered essential for each evening. Thus a Friday to Monday party involved taking your "Sunday Best," two tweed coats and skirts, three garments suitable for tea, your "best hat" — usually a vast affair loaded with feathers, fruit or corn — a variety of country headgear, as likely as not a billycock hat and riding habit, numerous accessories in the way of petticoats, stoles, scarves, evening wreaths and what not; and a large bag in which to carry about the house your embroidery — then the most universal "work" of the idle, for "reading aloud," that gentle entertainment now all but killed by wireless and television, was still much in vogue, and while one member of the house-party read nearly all the Shes would ply their needles.'

Lady Cynthia Asquith in 'The Day Before Yesterday', 1956

¶ Even more astonishing than the clothes the Edwardians wore was the food they ate — or rather the amount of food they ate:

'Most households were cheerfully resigned to breakfast — then a fabulous meal — going on till half past ten or so, and the little blue flames under the array of lidded, silver chafing-dishes kept piping hot the crisp, curly bacon; eggs (poached, boiled and fried), mounds of

Lady Cynthia Asquith in 'The Day Before Yesterday', 1956

47

damp kedgeree (made with salmon), haddocks swimming in melted butter, sputtering sausages and ruddily-exuding kidneys. First, the young men of the party would line themselves with porridge immersed in thick yellow cream. Next they would pile some of the contents of nearly each hot dish on to their plates. This course consumed, they would ram down scones, thickly buttered and topped with home-made jam, marmalade or honey. Fruit from the walls, nets or hothouses of the kitchen garden wound up this minor meal.

'Nor in those days did women sustain themselves for the wear and tear of a whole morning's idleness on nothing more substantial than a triangle of toast and some orange juice. Far from it. In the days of which I write, I remember no talk of banting; yet nearly every girl's waist measured less then twenty inches. For sportsmen even such a breakfast as I've described wasn't considered adequate. I remember my alarm one morning when, on coming down punctually to that meal, I found myself the only She among four red-faced fox-hunters, all devouring MUTTON CHOPS!'

¶ It is amusing to note that a writer just before the First World War — it is true he is thinking of hotels and not of country houses — not only accepts the lavishness of the English breakfast but is at pains to indicate that American visitors might take something different — but equally lavish and filling:

J. Rey.
'The Whole Art of
Dining', 1914

BREAKFAST MENUS

English Style	American Style
Tea, Coffee, Cocoa	Iced Melon, Grape-fruit
Chocolate, Malted Milk	Apples, Pears, Grapes
	Radishes, Olives, Water-cress
Fresh Fruit assorted	Creamed Oats, Boiled Sago
Stewed Fruit	Hominy, Force
	Cracked Wheat
Porridge and Cream	Shredded Wheat Biscuits
	Corn-on-Cob
FISH:	Grape Nuts and Cream
Grilled Mackerel	Buckwheat and Golden Syrup
Grilled Turbot	
Fried Soles	FISH:
Finnon Haddock	Panned Blue Points

48

Earl's Court, August 1903. Drawing by Frank Reynolds.

Aubrey: '*Look here, old chap, let me give you a piece of my mind.*'
Percival: '*Won't it be robbing you, deah boy?*'
Drawn by Frank Reynolds, 1907.

Kippers, Bloaters
Grilled Fresh Herrings
Kedgeree, Fish cakes

Broiled Whitefish
Grilled Salmon Steak
Planked Shad
Fish Rolls

Fried Eggs and Bacon
Plain Omelette
Ham and Eggs
Poached Eggs on Toast
Grilled Kidneys
Calf's Liver and Bacon
Grilled Gammon Rasher
Sausages and Mashed Potatoes
Grilled Tomatoes and Bacon
Grilled Mushrooms on Toast

Buttered Eggs
Poached Eggs
Parsley Omelette

Baked Beans
Scotch Pie, Irish-stew
Beef-Hash
Curried Mutton

TO ORDER

TO ORDER

Ready in 20 minutes
Mutton Chops
Chump Chops
Rump Steak
Lamb or Mutton Cutlets
Kidneys Vert-Pre

Ready in 20 minutes
Sirloin Steak and Fried Potatoes
Sheep's Liver and Bacon
Grilled Ham
Mutton Cutlets
Pork Chops

COLD BUFFET:
Roast Beef, Lamb
Mutton, Galantine
York Ham, Ox Tongue
Chicken, Pressed-Beef

Corned-Beef, Ox-Tongue
Veal and Ham Pie

Hominy Cakes, Hominy Fritters
Oaten Biscuits
Preserves

Muffins, Crumpets
Honey, Jam, Marmalade

Buttered Toast
Hot Rolls and Crackers

¶ Working-class menus were, of course, rather different:

'THE WORKING-CLASS TEA

The tea of the English working-class is the most eccentric of meals, and one of the greatest injuries a gourmet could possibly conceive (according to the ideas of Brillat-Savarin); for with the tea they partake of various kinds of salted meat and dried fish, such as "corned-beef,"

J. Rey.
'The Whole Art of
Dining', 1914

kippers, bloaters, red herrings, winkles, shrimps, pickles, watercresses, cucumber, lettuce, jam or marmalade, bread and butter, and cake. This incongruous kind of food may, no doubt, be quite nice and tasty for this class of people, but it must shock any one endowed with refined epicurean instinct.'

¶ Breakfast, of course, was only a beginning:

Noel Streatfeild in 'The Day Before Yesterday', 1956

'Stomachs have shrunk, for no one to-day could eat the meals that were swallowed as a matter of course fifty years ago. A solid luncheon was followed a few hours later by a tea of sandwiches of several kinds, toast or muffins, and a large choice of small cakes, and that was followed by a dinner of many courses. Even that was seldom the end, for sandwiches were served at about ten. If extra exertion of any kind was called for, whoever was about to exert themselves was usually offered extra sustenance. Soup at eleven, or an egg at tea time.

'I do not know if my grandfather was unusual, or whether it was a date when people took snacks. I can remember at eleven every morning a tray being brought to him with on it a glass of port and a plate of ginger biscuits. And on the piano in the drawing-room there was a china bowl kept constantly full of crystallised violets. The violets were, I believe, home-grown and crystallised in the kitchen, as were great stalks of angelica, but of course what I remember is eating the violets, as did everybody else feeling peckish. Nor at my grandfather's were violets our only between-meal snacks, for I seem to remember sweet biscuits at odd hours, and very rich beef tea at eleven in the morning. It was a wonder we did not burst, and indeed I was always having billious attacks, as they were called, which no child seems to have to-day.'

¶ Yet, by modern standards, the great country houses lacked many of the amenities we take for granted:

Lady Cynthia Asquith in 'The Day Before Yesterday', 1956

'Despite the lavish breakfasts and the general super-abundance of food and drink, few pre-war country houses could have been condemned as luxurious. For one thing, however comfortable, figuratively speaking, the atmosphere of a house might be, its actual temperature would strike people of to-day as extremely Spartan. A degree of cold greater than that inflicted on us by the long emergency of the Second World War was then cheerfully taken for granted. Electric fires being still undreamed of, and upstairs fires very rarely lit before evening, bedrooms, often huge and many-windowed, could be as cold as churches on week-days. I remember only a very few blessed exceptions, where, luxury of luxuries, you would be woken by the snapping of newly kindled twigs, the crackle of burning paper, and open your eyes on the pleasing spectacle of a smiling, becapped housemaid in a stiffly starched dress, matches in hand, on her knees at the hearth.

'Nor was there as yet any thought of running water in the bedrooms. Instead, a brown lidded can, in a turban of towel, was brought up morning and evening to your bedroom and placed on one of the two china basins on the washstand. Private bathrooms? No! You perambulated long, icy passages in search of the nearest bathroom, often to find it locked, or worse, not locked, but occupied by some careless wallower — who having neglected to turn the key yelled as you opened the door. Sometimes — very sharp practice — the possessor of a valet would be unscrupulous enough to send his "Gentlemen's gentleman" on in advance, unlawfully to annex — sponge instead of flag in his hand — the bathroom, and keep others out until his "master" was ready to occupy it in person.'

¶ There were, at least, plenty of servants:

'A phase of social history which has now disappeared in this country is the backstairs life of a large country house. At its zenith between 1880 and 1914, it never returned to its full splendour after the First World War.

Daphne Fielding in 'The Age of Extravagance', 1956

Some of the old servants who still remember Longleat in its halcyon days have told me how a large country house, such as this, was managed fifty years ago. The intricate hive which buzzed so busily below stairs led a complete life of its own; and its ritual and etiquette make a fascinating study. It was governed by the hierarchy of the steward's room, of which were the house steward and the housekeeper.

To-day Longleat is no longer used as a family home. The empty kitchens which once gleamed with burnished copper are almost as sad to see as the silent nurseries which have missed the care and attention of a whole generation of children.

Fifty years ago the Longleat staff numbered 43 and was composed of the following:

> One House Steward
> One Butler
> One Under Butler

One Groom of the Chambers
One Valet
Three Footmen
One Steward's Room Footman
Two Oddmen
Two Pantry Boys
One Lamp Boy

One Housekeeper
Two Lady's Maids
One Nurse
One Nursery Maid
Eight Housemaids
Two Sewing Maids
Two Still Room Maids
Six Laundry Maids

One Chef
Two Kitchen Maids
One Vegetable Maid
One Scullery Maid
One Daily Woman

In those days the kitchen staff led their own life apart from the rest of the household. They ate in the kitchen, and the daily duty of preparing breakfast absolved them from attending early morning prayers.'

¶ Lady Cynthia Asquith, whom we have already quoted, gives a charming picture of her visit as a little girl to a *really* big country house:

Lady Cynthia Asquith in 'The Day Before Yesterday', 1956 'At the age of five I remember going to stay in a country house, so much larger and grander than my own home, that there resided in it, not only an exalted being hitherto unknown to me called The Housekeeper, but also a mysterious dignitary called the Groom of the Chambers. Despite the promise of the magic word "groom," this majestic man turned out to have nothing whatever to do with horses, a great disappointment to me. What precisely his office was I failed to discover, but I believe he was responsible for the appurtenances of all the writing tables in the house.

'I remember the thrill of my first sight and whiff of the Housekeeper's Cupboard (in reality a small *room*) to which the bustling little housekeeper conducted me the morning after my arrival. I can

Blenheim Palace house party and Yeomanry sports, May 1911.

The Duchess of Somerset at Cowes, 1911.

*The Empress Eugénie with the Duke of Alba
at Cowes, 1912.*

*The Duchess of Westminster with the Marquess of
Shaftesbury at Ascot, 1908.*

still hear the jingle of the clustered keys worn at her waist, and savour the fragrance of crystallised apricots, lumps of ginger, almonds, raisins, and a hundred other delectabilities. This potent alchemist — she distilled rosewater, dried lavender, bottled fruit, made potpourri and "such sweet jams meticulously jarred" — had her own sitting-room, and presided as hostess in that state apartment mysteriously called THE ROOM, or in some very grand houses, THE STEWARDS' ROOM. Here, at ceremoniously-served meals, visiting ladies-maids and valets were entertained with great formality by the hierarchical HEADS of the household, whose subordinates ate in what was called The Servants' Hall.

'Though I had often heard that the custom of The Room was for visiting maids and valets to go into dinner (evening dress essential) in the order of precedence of the rank of their respective employers, then called "masters and mistresses," I had supposed this to be a mere legend, but answers to questions put to someone who in her day had banqueted in The Room, assure me that it was a solemn fact. This explains WHY on learning of my engagement to what she called "a commoner," my aspiring ladiesmaid burst into tears.'

¶ The rigid hierarchy of below-stairs was even more marked than that which reigned on the *piano nobile*:

'Down in the steward's room the butler offered his arm gravely to the Duchess of Hull's maid, and conducted her to the place at his right hand. Lord Roehampton's valet did the same by Mrs. Wickenden the housekeeper. Mrs. Wickenden, of course, was not married, and her title was bestowed only by courtesy. The order of precedence was very rigidly observed, for the visiting maids and valets enjoyed the same hierarchy as their mistresses and masters; where ranks coincided, the date of creation had to be taken into account, and for this purpose a copy of Debrett was always kept in the housekeeper's room — last year's Debrett, appropriated by Mrs. Wickenden as soon as the new issue had been placed in her Grace's boudoir. The maids and valets enjoyed not only the same precedence as their employers, but also their names. Thus, although the Duchess of Hull's maid had stayed many times at Chevron, and was indeed quite a crony of Mrs. Wickenden's, invited to private sessions in the housekeeper's room, where the two elderly gossips sat stirring their cups of tea, she was never known as anything but Miss Hull, and none of her colleagues in the

V. Sackville-West. 'The Edwardians', 1930

53

steward's room would ever have owned to a knowledge of what her true name might be. It is to be doubted whether Mrs. Wickenden herself had ever used it. Mrs. Wickenden and Vigeon the butler, between whom a slightly hostile alliance existed, prided themselves that no mistake had even been made in the Chevron steward's room, and that consequently no disputes had ever arisen, such as were known to have happened, most distressingly, in other houses. The household at Chevron was indeed admirably organised. For one thing, any servant who had been at Chevron for less than ten years was re-garded as an interloper; at the end of ten years' service they were summoned to her Grace's presence and received a gold watch with their name and the date engraved upon the back; a few encouraging words were spoken by her Grace and henceforward they were accepted as part of the establishment. But for this one, brief, intimidating occasion, the under-servants rarely came into contact with her Grace. It was to be doubted whether all of them knew her by sight, and it was quite certain that many of them were unknown to her. Various anecdotes were current; one to the effect that the duchess, meeting the fifth housemaid at the foot of a stair, had asked whether Lady Viola were in her room, and had been completely routed by the reply, "I'll go and see, madam; what name shall I say?" Then there had been that other terrifying incident, when her Grace, taking an unusually early walk in the park on a Sunday morning, had observed the black-robed, black-bonnetted procession setting off for church, and had descried a white rose coquettishly ornamenting a bonnet. The white rose had bobbed up and down across the grass. It was a gay little flower, despite the purity of its colour, and to the shocked eyes of the duchess it had represented insubordination. Mrs. Wickenden, sum-moned on her return from church, was equally scandalised. She explained the whole matter by a deprecatory reference to "those London girls," and the culprit had been discharged from Chevron by the afternoon train.

'It was, however, seldom that any complete stranger obtained a situation at Chevron. The system of nepotism reigned. Thus Mrs. Wickenden and Wickenden the head-carpenter were brother and sister; their father and grandfather had been head-carpenters there in their day; several of the housemaids were Mrs. Wickenden's nieces, and the third footman was Vigeon's nephew. Whole families, from genera-tion to generation, naturally found employment on the estate. Any outsider was regarded with suspicion and disdain. By this means a net-

54

work was created, and a constant supply of young aspirants ensured. Their wages might range from twelve to twenty-four pounds a year.'

¶ But it is time we left the great house — we are fifty years too late. Even contemporary guests were not expected to stay for luncheon on Monday:

'On the Monday morning they were all disposed of; the carriages came round to the front door, and they were all stowed away safely inside — the men into the station bus, with its fusty smell, its rattling windows, and the rumbling of its rubberless wheels on the gravel; the women into the rubber-tyred broughams, the windows making a frame to the pretty veiled faces and waving hands.' *V. Sackville-West. 'The Edwardians', 1930*

¶ Let us take a last look at 'The Season'. Its final term was Cowes:

'In the last year of King Edward's reign, a vast fleet of yachts gathered for Cowes Regatta. The *Victoria and Albert*, with her attendant battleship, dominated the roadstead. The Tzar come in his yacht *Standart*, the Kaiser in the *Hohenzollern*, and the King of Spain with his racing yacht *Hispania*. All three presented prizes. The King entertained twenty members of the R.Y.S. to dinner aboard the *Victoria and Albert* to be presented to the Tzar. Ashore and afloat there were dinner parties and balls. Steam launches, with gleaming brass funnels, and slender cutters and gigs, pulled by their crews at the long white oars, plied between the yachts and the Squadron steps. By day, the sails of the racing yachts spread across the blue waters of the Solent like the wings of giant butterflies, by night the riding lights and lanterns gleamed and shone like glow-worms against the onyx waters and fireworks burst and spent themselves in the night sky. And over this splendid scene presided the King — a genial, portly, yet always majestic figure.' *Anthony Heckstall-Smith. 'Sacred Cowes', 1955*

¶ Of course, not everybody could go to Cowes:

'The Castle at West Cowes was destined to become the clubhouse of the Royal Yacht Squadron and the most impregnable fortress ever held by the aristocracy of England against the storms and sieges of the combined forces of the rich merchants and the bourgeoisie.' *Anthony Heckstall-Smith. 'Sacred Cowes', 1955*

¶ Even Sir Thomas Lipton, who had spent a fortune on yachts and who was the friend of the King himself was not admitted as a member until the very end of his life. And perhaps he did not mind for the aristocracy came to *him*:

Desmond Chapman-Huston.
'The Lamp of Memory', 1949
'There is a good story told about Sir Thomas Lipton which, when I repeated it to the Empress Eugenie, she stoutly declared was untrue. The representative of a well-known London firm arrived on board the *Erin* one morning during Cowes week to transact some urgent business with the owner. When this was finished Lipton, with his air of genial dictator, said:

' "You must stay to luncheon."

' "Thanks so much, Sir Thomas, but I'm afraid I can't."

' "Can't — why not, why not?"

"Well, Sir Thomas, to be quite honest, you have such famous titled people aboard that I would be uncomfortable because I wouldn't know how to address them correctly."

' "Young man, aboard my yacht, you will always be quite safe if you say, 'Your Grace'." '

¶ It must have been wonderful while it lasted:

Anthony Heckstall-Smith.
'Sacred Cowes', 1955
'In those halcyon days, Cowes Regatta was the culminating function of the Season, and when it was over the Court retired to Balmoral. The aristocracy of England, who had, in theory, enjoyed one another's company since the previous May, went off to their grouse moors in Scotland and to their country estates. The visiting Crown heads sailed for their own countries, accompanied by their Arch-Dukes and Duchesses, and Barons and Baronesses. The last Blue Hungarian Band played its last Strauss waltz. The last exhausted hostess relaxed her eighteen inch waist from the tortures of whalebone and steel. The debutantes tied the little bundles of dance programmes, with white pencils attached, placing them sentimentally in the handkerchief sachet, and wrote in their diaries: "Another wonderfully exciting season has ended." The last tired lady's maid pressed out the last ball-dress from Mr. Worth or Mr. Paquin, before dispatching it to some poor relation in the country. . . The social top that had started spinning with the Court Presentations, gaining momentum with Ascot, Henley, Lord's and Goodwood, came to a standstill as the last rocket spent itself in the indigo sky of an August night at Cowes, which was the signal that the regatta was over.'

¶ Ehen fugaces!

56

CHAPTER III

DU CÔTE DE CHEZ MAXIM

THE BRITISH had been travelling abroad in increasing numbers ever since the Battle of Waterloo. But the Victorians, to judge by their memoirs, often went to the Continent in order to remind themselves how much preferable English life — and even English cooking — was. Gradually, at least among the upper classes, this attitude changed.

'During the anti-Russian Jingo fever of 1878, I recollect it being said by the pleasant gentleman who is today Lord Rendal that Lord Beaconsfield had taken John Bull to Cremorne, and that the old fellow rather liked it. Bull has developed a good deal since then; he may still wear his traditional hat. The rest of his costume speaks the *flaneur* of the boulevards. He has adopted the swagger of a citizen of the world. On the strength of that, he piques himself on living in the true metropolis of the universe and under the one and only cosmopolitan prince.'

*A Foreign Resident.
'Society in the New
Reign', 1904*

¶ Edward was certainly a cosmopolitan prince, and liked nothing better than to find himself on the other side of the Channel. Paris and its pleasures were an open book to him. The aristo-plutocracy shared his tastes, and the favourite resort of wealthy pleasure-seekers in the French capital was — Maxim's.

'Not to know Maxim's is to argue that Paris is a closed book to you. It is as famous as the Madeleine, as cosmopolitan as the Opera, as picturesque as the contents of the Louvre. It is celebrated in a thousand novels, and in that amusing comedy, "La Dame de chez Maxim," which has been translated into every language under the sun, barring Welsh. Redskins have probably penetrated to Maxim's; certainly men

*'Illustrated London
News', 1907*

of every other race and clime. You meet Indian Princes, Russian Grand Dukes — of course, they live there — English noblemen in disguise — or, as we should say, incognito — Chancellors and Court Ministers, Grand Viziers, and a long stream of semi-potentates and powers. Such is the fame of Maxim's that a man would blush to say to his friends: "I have been to Paris, and have not supped at the famous midnight restaurant in the Rue Royale." The situation stands for much in the peculiar *renommée* of the house. It stands on the edge of the great fashionable West End of Paris, where are gathered the wealth and elegance of the civilised world. It overlooks the magnificent expanse of the Place de la Concorde, the finest square in Europe; it neighbours the club of the Rue Royale, one of the most aristocratic that exists; it is in the near vicinity of the British Embassy and the Elysée, with the stately houses that belong to the Faubourg St. Honoré, and it is linked with the great bustling heart of the city by the short and famous street which forms, at the Church of the Madeleine, an obtuse angle with the world-renowned Boulevards.

'Let us push the swing-door of Maxim's to-night and pass through into this bright, new world of elegance, of gaiety, of *entrain* and *abandon* in evening clothes. A brilliant and fascinating sight meets the eye. Behind and in front of little tables spread with the finest napery, men and women, representing the last word in fashion, are discussing supper. The gilded necks of champagne-bottles emerge, at a comfortable and convivial angle, from ice-pails, and plates are occupied with the solid vestiges of succulent "ostendes" and "marennes vertes." The theatres and music-halls, the Opera and the concerts, have disgorged their world, and it comes here to while away an hour on feathery wings before departing homewards in swift Panhard or voiture de maître. If you continue past the buffet, with its elegant fringe of the *jeunesse dorée*, past the long line of tables to the end of the room, you will discover an open space at right angles, and more tables set therein. Continue a little further, up two steps, and you will discover another section set apart for supping, and commanding an excellent view of the lower floor. It is in this portion, especially, where Parisian gaiety bubbles and froths like champagne every night in the year. The best-dressed, wittiest, and prettiest women of the *monde* are supping here with their male friends and relatives, who are sure to be some of the smartest men in diplomacy and the world of affairs.

'As the night proceeds in the *chaleur communicative de banquet* —

58

to quote a phrase which had its vogue in Paris and its political allusion
— the music of the red-coated band becomes more exhilarating and
more alluring. It intoxicates the brain, it invades the feet; it invites
to the waltz. And presently there are couples swaying rhythmically,
with swishing feet, upon the floor. Some professional beauty, with
glittering eyes and marble throat, embellished with costly pearls, is
waltzing divinely in the arms of an American king of postage stamps.
It is an enchanting scene — this light-hearted, swift, and evanescent
fun, which never degenerates into vulgarity and never goes beyond the
borders set by discretion and good taste. If there is a moment in all the
year when it is a social duty to visit Maxim's it is on the eve of Christ.
mas Day. It is then the gayest spot in all the town. Laughter and merri-
ment hold undisputed sway, and the gloomy man or woman is
instantly shamed from melancholy. The air is charged with electricity
— electricity of the sort that gives off flashes of wit in pure joyousness
of living. Yes, *joie-de-vivre* is the "note" at Maxim's at Reveillon, as
Christmas Eve is called in France. At the midnight hour, when
everyone has feasted on turkey and the finest cheer, expedited by the
generous product of sunny Southern slopes, everyone solemnly
arises as to perform a sacred duty, and toasts his neighbour in the
brimming glass. This is one of the immemorial rites of chez Maxim.
To have been at Maxim's at Reveillon, to have toasted one's fair
neighbour, to have received a brilliant smile in answer, to have felt the
intoxication of the hour, the *ensemble* of captivation, is, surely, not
to have lived in vain.

All this is summed up in the fascinating idea of Maxim's, but it
means something more. One cannot visit the famous restaurant without realising the wonderful stream of gold that hourly flows through
its doors, for business is cash. The restaurant in France is not a mere
fashion, as with us: it is an integral part of the national life. Every
Frenchman of any consequence takes his meals at the restaurant. For
him excellence of cuisine is all-important, and at Maxim's he finds
this to perfection.'

¶ Never since the eighteenth century had the English upper classes
found themselves so much at home in France, in a society which, in
spite of superficial differences, was so like their own. On both sides of
the Channel there is an air of *haut ton,* and some of the contemporary
social gossip has all the charm of a faded *carnet de bal:*

'The dinners and receptions of T.R.H. the Duke and Duchess of Vendôme have been the *clous* of the spring Season.

'T.H. Prince and Princess Murat gave, for their children's friends, a dinner of fifty *couverts,* after which the young people *bostonned* [*le boston* was then the rage in Paris], while their parents gave themselves up to the delights of bridge.

'Luncheon followed by a reception given by the Comte and Comtesse Aimery de la Rochefoucauld in honour of the Comte and Comtesse d'Eu.

'Dinner followed by a reception given by the Marquis and Marquise d'Argenson in honour of T.R.H. the Duke and Duchess of Vendôme...

'Very elegant *Five o'clock tea* given by the Marquise deTalleyrand-Perigord...

'Very beautiful reception given by the Senateur of Morbihan and Comtesse G. de Gaulaine, née de Perrien, for the signing of the Marriage Contract between their daughter Yvonne and M. Charles du Pré de Saint-Maur, lieutenant in the 28th Dragoons, and son of M. and Madame René du Pré de Saint-Maur, née Bourbon-Busset. The display of presents was a joy to the eyes. The marriage was blessed in the Basilica of Sainte-Clotilde by M. l'Abbé de Sesmaisons...

¶ It sounds like a ceremony under the *Ancien Regîme,* as indeed, in a sense, it was. But the social chronicle includes an account of another wedding which would certainly not have been described in the same terms at any earlier period:

'The New Year began with a fashionable wedding: that of Baron Maurice de Rothschild, second son of Baron Edward de Rothschild and of the Baronne, née de Rothschild, with Mlle. Noémi Halphen, daughter of M. Jules Halphen and of Madame, née Pereire. An incredible crowd was packed into the vast Temple in the Rue de la Victoire, gleaming with light. The nuptial dais and the choir were splendidly decorated with camelias, roses and white lilac. M Alfred Levi, Chief Rabbi of France, before pronouncing the benediction, delivered an oration of the most elevated kind...

'The religious ceremony was followed by a great reception at the house of M. and Madame Jules Halphen in the Avenue Victor Hugo, where the innumerable wedding presents were on show. These included: a tiara with five emeralds and diamonds, another with pearls in a Greek design, a head-ornament with five kinds of pear-shaped

60

Above: Cosmopolitan Society at Deauville, 1906. Drawing by Simont from the 'Illustrated London News'.

Below: King Edward abroad with a discreetly obscured lady. Reproduced from 'L'Illustration', 1910.

Ostend, 1911.

diamonds, a necklace with three large diamonds, a necklace with five rows of pearls and a diamond clasp. . . furs, lace, fans, etc.

'Among the donors were: Baronne Guillaume de Rothschild, emerald necklace with a pendant of diamonds and pearls; Baron and Baronne Gustave de Rothschild, tiara in the form of a bird, with brilliants and sapphires; Baron James de Rothschild, two Sèvres vases and a piece of lacquer; Baronne Alphonse de Rothschild, butterflies of diamonds and rubies; Mlle. Miriam de Rothschild, brooch with pink pearls; Baron Albert de Rothschild of Vienna, sapphire and diamond pendant; Baronne Alice de Rothschild, diamond and sapphire brooch; Baron and Baronne Edouard de Rothschild, lady's watch and chain, jewelled umbrella handle, a pair of Sèvres vases; Lord Rothschild, bracelet; M. and Madame Leopold de Rothschild, necklace plaque in diamonds; Baron and Baronne de Rothschild, gold box with sapphires; M and Madame J. Halphen, necklace and grand piano; Duchess of Devonshire, smoker's compendium; Baron and Baronne Henri de Rothschild, gold watch and chain; Duke and Duchess of Gramont, blotting pad with gold binding; M. Rudolphe de Goldschmidt-Rothschild, sapphire ornament; Lord Dalmeny and the Hon. Neil Primrose, pair of cuff-links; The United States Ambassador and Mrs White, lapis-lazuli box, etc.

'Space is lacking for the enumeration of all these marvels of value, taste and elegance.'

¶ Wealth and Beauty seemed the most important things in life. It is amusing to note the beginnings of the Beauty Industry and of its clever publicity, still veiled (but how transparently) by this pretence of editorial comment:

'To succeed in life, one must be strong. One might add when addressing women: To be happy, be beautiful! Physical attractions constitute a real superiority by which it is easy to profit. . .'

¶ *Et comment!* But let us continue:

'It is about her complexion above all that a woman should worry. *'Les Modes', 1909* Its beauty is not easy to maintain, for the diaphanous pellicule which is the top layer of the skin is of an extreme delicacy. Like the reflecting surface of water it indicates all the movements of the organs [not perhaps very happily expressed!] and reflects the vibrations of the surrounding air.

'The complexion of a child is usually deliciously fresh to the eye and exquisite to touch. This is due to the abundant secretions of the subcutaneous glands. In many adults these secretions are less abundant and the skin becomes dry and scaly. How can this be remedied? Hear on this question the advice of that *Doctoresse ès Beauté*, the incomparable Madame Eleanor Adair:

' "The skin of the face is like a very fine tissue pierced by imperceptible holes. It is thanks to this porosity that the skin can breathe. The pores must be kept clear yet they are constantly being obstructed by dirt and poisonous germs and it is necessary to clear them by frequent ablutions.

' "The common error is to imagine that washing with pure water is sufficient. In quality neither water nor soap can perform this function properly. Quantities of microbes escape and remain buried in the skin like the wolf in the sheep-fold. Hence, faces congested, covered with pimples, rednesses, roughnesses, even ecsema and the whole gamut of skin diseases." '

¶ It is a frightening picture. Happily, however:

'*Les Modes*', 1909   'Madame Adair has not contented herself with drawing up a list of these painful afflictions. She has succeeded in curing them by creating a specific lotion which provides an elegant solution of the problem. This marvellous product has been named by its inventor *Tonique Diable Ganesh*. Its power is effectively diabolic, since it has the gift of reviving the bloom of youth on the most ravaged faces. Use it ladies! all of you! night and morning and you will be astonished to see your skin recover its diaphanous nature, and become as soft as satin and as pure as the lily. This lotion gives the sensation of a scented caress. We shall describe in a later article how the celebrated hygienist has succeeded in overcoming the most obstinate wrinkles, thanks to the curious properties of her *Huile Orientale Ganesh. . . Consultations tours les jours, 5, rue Cambon.*'

¶ The incomparable *Doctoresse ès Beauté* was, however, not without her rivals, and here, strangely enough, the English had an advantage, even in Paris:

'*Les Modes*', 1909   'One is astonished, and with reason, by the dazzling complexion of Englishwomen. . . and one is accustomed to say that when they take any trouble to be beautiful they are more beautiful than anyone else. . .

'Two women have accomplished the miracle of restoring freshness to faded faces. . . Mrs and Miss Earle are in fact English; they have come to us from Great Britain where they have had an enormous success, particularly in northern towns like Liverpool and Manchester [!!!], to establish, at 279 rue Saint-Honoré, an English Institute of Beauty to which all the beautiful women who wish to remain so, all those who have been beautiful and wish to be beautiful again, all those who wish to remedy Nature's parsimony with regard to themselves. *C'est plus qu'un succès, c'est une folie.*'

¶ Paris, of course, was only habitable during the Season, but there was no lack of other places where one could hope to meet personages of the highest *ton*. There was, for example, Dieppe, which was beginning to recapture something of the vogue it had enjoyed during the Second Empire when its habitués had included the Princess de Sagan, the Duchesse de Persigny, the Marquise de Galliet, the Duchesse de Fitz-James. the Duc de Grammont-Caderousse, the Rothschilds (yes, already!) and Arsène Houssaye.

'Since about three years ago there has been a revival. The importance of the racing on the pretty Rouxmesnil racecourse, the varied attractions offered by the Casino, golf, tennis, bathing; all these have attracted the élite once more and not merely for a few days but for the whole season. . . *'Les Modes', 1909*

'At Puy, Alexandre Dumas' villa was occupied by the Comtesse Robert de Mun and her children. . . In Dieppe itself lived the Comtesse Sala in her artistic and hospitable villa in the rue Aguado. . . and almost every evening, dinners of supreme elegance were given for neighbours and other friends. One met also the Comte and Comtesse de Pracomtal and their daughters, and little Princess Brinda de Jubal, engaged to the Maharajah of Kapurtala, the Duc and Duchess de Morny. . . Prince Francois de Broglie and his sons, Comtesse and Mademoiselle de Sainte-Aldegarde who were with Prince Philippe de Caraman-Chimay on his yacht. . . the marquis de Villeroy. . . Comte Georges de Montesquiou. . . the Duchesse de Lesparre, the Prince and Princess d'Arenberg One could believe, this year, that the great days of Dieppe had come again.

¶ Of course it was very important to go to places only at the right time, that is, during 'the Season'.

'*The Graphic*',
June 8, 1907

' "My life is all a 'season'," was said by a very fashionable English-man some thirty years ago, and the statement was fastened on by the serious-minded of the time, who used it as a text for many meditations reflections. There are hundreds of women in England today who could repeat the assertion, but the condition is comparatively so common that it would not occur to them to suppose the circumstances worth mentioning.

'There are the London season, from the middle of May to August; the German-Bath season, from August to the middle of September; the country-house season, from the middle of September to the middle of December; and the South of France season, from the middle of December to the middle of May. That programme regulates — more or less — the movements of several hundreds of men and women in England, whose main object, in this direction, is to keep apart from the majority — which brings to the front the matter the writer wishes to deal with. The London season is gradually being removed from the programmes as an "Unfashionable" item.

'Those who have such continual opportunities of meeting no longer depend upon the London season for the purpose. They affect to abhor crowds, and the town is crowded in June and July. . . The observant have noticed that there are many more houses to be let for the season than there were formerly, that there are each year fewer balls in Mayfair, and that every opportunity is seized by many to spend most of the time in the country. In June and July now thousands pour into London from the Provinces, the Colonies, the United States, and the Continent, but the tendency is for Mayfair to empty except when there are Court entertainments.

'The growth of cosmopolitanism throughout the world is an important and interesting feature of the time. The items in the pro-gramme which has been given in a previous paragraph show much of the year is spent abroad by the rich and prominent among us; the increasing inflow of visitors to London during the season from foreign countries proves that the development is not confined to the English. . . We are all exchanging our rich.'

¶ No one reflected the international world of pleasure with more verve than the French caricaturist Sem. His lavish albums form a series from the beginning of the twentieth century to 1912, and are a social document of the highest order. We see life (High-Life we should perhaps call it) in Paris, at Maxim's or the Palais de Glace. We attend

64

Above: Captain Dawson, President of the Tennis Club at Cannes, 1913.

Below: the Roulette Room of the Casino at Monte Carlo, 1902. Drawing by Reginald Cleaver.

Above: Mr and Mrs Winston Churchill with Millicent, Duchess of Sutherland, at Monte Carlo, 1913.

Below: The Duchess of Westminster in Switzerland, 1912.

garden parties with the famous dandy and spendthrift Boni de Castellane, or race meetings with Prince Troubetskoi. We drive in the Bois with Réjane, Prince Orloff, and King Leopold of the Belgians. With Polaire we watch the fashionable skaters, and rub shoulders with Liane de Lancy, Liane de Pougy, Jeanne Derval, Cléo de Mérode, la belle Otéro, and other famous beauties. We meet authors *à la mode:* Rostand, Alfred Capus, Hervieu, François Coppée, Porto-Riche and the veteran Catulle Mendès: famous actors like Mounet-Gully, Brasseur and the Coquelins, draughtsmen like Forain and Caran d'Asche, and actresses like Lavallière. Henri Rochefort, that old revolutionary, dines with Santos Dumont, the pioneer of motorcars and aeroplanes, the Princesse de Hohenlohe lunches with Consuelo, Duchess of Marlborough. We catch a glimpse of the interesting nose of J. P. Morgan; we meet the young Aga Khan and the equally young James de Rothschild, Solly Joel and Madame Paquin. At Monte Carlo, at Deauville, at Cannes, the same people foregather — authentic nobility and *nouveaux riches,* authors and artists and *grandes cocottes,* imprisoned for ever like flies in amber by the sinuous silhouette of Sem. There is a certain malice in the presentation, but Sem was no social reformer. He loved the life he depicted so well. In the preface to his first Monte Carlo album he writes:

'This album is consecrated to typical Monte Carlo figures, but one will find many Parisian silhouettes among them. Monte Carlo, in fact, is still Paris, but a Paris transfigured, renewed by the splendid light which magnifies everything, makes men look younger and women more beautiful, as every winter draws hither the rich visitor from every corner of the world to this delightful shore. For Monte Carlo is also London and New York, it is the High Life of the great capitals of the world, condensed during the Season on this splendid rock, in a fairy-tale of light and luxury. . .' *Sem. 'Monte Carlo', 1904*

¶ The Riviera was still regarded as a winter resort and the popular places continued to be Monte Carlo, Nice, Cannes, Menton, San Remo and Hyères. At Menton, 'the new casino is proving itself a great success in every way, and roller skating is much in vogue there just now' (1910). At Monte Carlo, 'several receptions and bridge parties have been held lately. . . "The Merry Widow" has been very popular'. At Hyères, 'golf, tennis and croquet are the order of the day and dancing, music and cards the order of the night'. At Nice, 'there was a good influx of visitors for Christmas, and the fashionable hotels are filling up rapidly'. But Monte Carlo was still the Queen:

'The Queen',
Jan. 21, 1905

THE FASCINATION OF MONTE CARLO
by Lady Helen Forbes

'There is no place on earth, not even excepting the Garden of Eden, which has attracted so much attention for its size as the Principality of Monaco. One would think that by this time the preachers and the novelists and the journalists must have exhausted the theme; they have preached and romanced and written about it so often. Yet still it fascinates. Over the "unco' guid" it exercises the fascination of a snake over a bird. They think, or say that they think, it a very wicked place, but they cannot keep away from it. It draws the British matron and the possessor of the Non-conformist Conscience as infallibly as it draws gilded youth and grasping age, the harridans with systems and the *filles de joie* from Paris. Over the student of human nature it exercises the fascination of his favourite study. He sees his subject there in its best and worst and most interesting lights, and if truly "the proper study of mankind is man", he could find no place in the world where he would be better employed. Over the lover of tongues it exercises the fascination of being the most cosmopolitan place in the world; over the lover of music that of producing all the newest operas; and even over the lover of food that of boasting the best *chefs* and most varied menus.

'Monte Carlo is like the Serpent of Old Nile, beloved, even though feared, and most alluring if most deadly; ageless, arresting, retaining always that which she has won. With such places and such women familiarity never breeds contempt. We return to them after years of absence, and find them the same; yet they never pall on us, for their variety is infinite. When far away we remember them always in their gayest moods, the women in laughter, the place in sunshine; and though the woman can frown and the place shiver under cold winds, it is not thus that they appear in our dreams.

'Even those who do not frankly love them are attracted. They hover near with a fearful joy. Their vanity is flattered by the idea that they are doing something wicked and daring, and they speak of their exploits with a self-conscious laugh. "Of course, it is a dreadful place, you know. I only went there to see how horrid it was." "Of course, she is an odious, designing adventuress. Let us go to see her and find out

66

who's there too." There is an element of treachery in their allegiance; but many good people think no shame of being false to their bread and salt. They take all they can get, but will not acknowledge their obligation.

'But as to the true lovers, they ungrudgingly glory in it, and with them the woman or the place will reign as a queen for ever.

'Such a place is Monte Carlo. And much as the preachers and journalists and novelists have scribbled and declaimed and woven stories about her, still they will go on scribbling, declaiming, and weaving as long as she lasts in the memory of mortal man. And they will always find people to hear, because, though the topic of Monte Carlo is old, yet it is ever new.'

¶ Certainly 'everybody' went to Monte Carlo, including ladies of the utmost respectability and high-mindedness:

'Monte Carlo was a glamorous place where money lost its normal value; the tables were piled with gold and silver pieces which came and went at the caprice of a whirling ball or the colour of a card. The days were made lovely by the sun, the sea, the great baskets full of carnations, stocks and roses offered for sale by sunburnt, smiling women, and the perpetual smell of freshly-ground coffee which came from the service door of the Hôtel de Paris, where a man in a blue blouse sat roasting it and singing a gay song, added to the fascination.

Mrs C. S. Peel, O.B.E. 'Life's Enchanted Cup', 1933

'Sooner or later all the world was to be seen in the Rooms, in the Square or on the Terrace; though there I never went because of the pigeon shooting. At Monte Carlo I saw for the first time Lady Randolph Churchill in the height of her dark, Southern beauty, lovely Miss Muriel Wilson, Mrs. Langtry, and a man whose face I have never forgotten. He was Mr. Carson, now Lord Carson. Often I have seen faces and found them again in portraits of men or of women of a former age, but never in any picture gallery have I seen a replica of Lord Carson's strange and compelling countenance. I think he invented his own face. He would sit at the tables, a "cartwheel" in his hand — I never saw him play high — waiting and waiting, on his sad, kindly face a withdrawn expression. Then, almost reluctantly, he would stake.'

¶ Every now and then some visitor would make a spectacular 'coup', and the Casino authorities were not at all displeased that it should receive the utmost publicity:

' "The man who broke the bank at Monte Carlo," as the newspapers called him at the time, was the host of a remarkable feast given some time ago at the Savoy Restaurant, Strand.

'*L'amphitryon* of this special dinner-party had won a large amount of money on the *roulette* at Monte Carlo, and *Rouge* had been the colour responsible for his good fortune.

'To celebrate his lucky event in an appropriate manner he invited thirty-six of his intimate friends to dinner, which was the talk of everybody, and commented upon in the Press.

'This feast was called amongst the people in the Hotel "*Le Diner Rouge et Noir*," but the Press referred to it as "The Red Dinner at the Savoy," for everything from the ceiling to the carpet in the saloon was red. Even the waiters wore red costumes; and their shirts, ties and gloves were also red.

'A magnificent display of beautiful and expensive flowers, and the electric lights were of the same tint. And the dinner, as much as it was possible, together with the wines, which were of an elaborate and costly character, were of the same colour.

'The menu was composed of "Prawns," "Queues de Langouste en Aspic," Créme Portugaise," "Saumon à la Nantua," "Mousse au Jambon," "Filet de Boeuf aux Tomates Farcies," "Choux-Rouges braisés," "Poularde à la Cardinal," "Canard Sauvage au Sang," "Salade de Betterave," "Mousse aux Fraises," etc.

'The table itself represented a huge roulette, built especially to accommodate the same number of guests as there are numbers on the real roulette. In the centre of it there was a suggestive decoration made of beautiful flowers. The covers were numbered in the same order as on a real roulette, and were separated by red and black silk ribbons parting from the centre of the table. The number on which the money was won, was to be seen everywhere in various shapes and ways in the room, and at this same number the host sat at the table.

'The saloon and the table presented a wonderful spectacle, and the cost of the feast, it was rumoured, reached over four figures.'

¶ No doubt the casino, in the sense of a palace where gambling could be carried on, was an institution of long standing, but circumstances now combined to give it a social significance it had hardly enjoyed before. Monte Carlo became the Mecca of European Society, of the rich Americans who could afford to join in its gaiety. Luxurious expresses were run from all the capitals of Europe. An especially luxurious one was the St. Petersburg–Vienna–Cannes express, which had card- and writing-saloons in addition to the dining car, where the cuisine was equal to that of a first-class restaurant. 'So very smart are some of the travellers,' remarks a contemporary newspaper, 'that they insist on dressing for dinner.' Indeed, so wealthy and extravagant were the majority of the passengers brought from Russia to the Riviera that it became the dream of every *demi-mondaine* to be kept by a Grand Duke.

The gaming-rooms at Monte Carlo were crowded all day, and attained a particular animation in the evening. They became a social promenade even for those who did not intend to gamble seriously. The most extraordinary mixture of clothes was seen in them, everything but knickerbockers being admitted, the ladies wearing smart day dresses or evening dresses with the addition of immense plumed hats.

The upper classes of Europe had succeeded in establishing for themselves a perpetual summer, and this fact was reflected in women's dress. There was a tendency to lightness of colour; the old dark shades, which might have been worn with both propriety and economy in a London fog were obviously out of place on the Cote d'Azure. A 'Fashion Forecast' describes 'a typical Riviera *toilette de promenade*':

'The material is cloth, of so fine souple a character as almost to resemble some silken fabric, and of that delicate neutral tint characteristic of the little champignon. It is a tone just removed from white, with a trend towards pink; but nevertheless, a true neutral *nuance*. At the foot of the plain skirt comes a broad band of skunk, the chief constructive efforts being reversed for the corsage which displays one of the many fancies now prevailing for scarf draperies — the single dependent end finished bell-rope fashion, with a large padded silk ball tied with silver cord. . . The crowning triumph of this toilette is a drawn silk chapeau exactly toned to the gown, plumed with skunk brown ostrich feathers, divided by a large, lightly pleated chou of dull pink velvet." *'The Queen', Jan. 9, 1909*

¶ The social commentator — member of a new profession — did not, however, always approve of what he, or she, saw:

'The attire in which people follow the simple life at Monte Carlo is mightily complex, and never have I seen fashions so formidable as those which have appeared this week on the Terrace and in the Casino. At the same time, I must confess that I have never seen Englishwomen *'The Queen', Feb. 27, 1909* compare so well with Frenchwomen, and I put it all down to their hats. Times have indeed changed that one may say that, and brave contradiction with a calm mind, for the Frenchwoman has hitherto, in my memory at any rate, held the palm for good millinery. Apparently she has for the moment gone mad. . . I saw one woman wearing a violet tailor-made, well cut and graceful, with a light green straw pudding basin, the largest size. Into this she had thrust her head as far as it would go, and round the edge she had wound a wreath of small roses of the brightest and most varied shades she could find.'

¶ Biarritz, owing to the continued patronage of Edward VII, was as fashionable as Monte Carlo, and there it was possible to combine the pleasures of country house life with the pleasures of being abroad:

'The Queen', *Jan. 9, 1909*   'In perfect weather the Biarritz and Bayonne Foxhounds met on Saturday in the grounds of the Hotel d'Angleterre. I was much struck by the turn out of the hunt, the Master, M. Fernand Dufaure, the huntsman, and three whips, all well mounted on bay horses of Irish breed, made a capital show, and the seventeen and a half couples of hounds looked a first-rate lot. Some sixty well mounted riders followed the chase. . . Among the spectators and others looking on in automobiles and carriages were the Grand Duke Alexander and his family, Prince Alexander of Oldenbourg, Princess Eugenie of Oldenbourg, the Duke of Leuchtenbourg and their suites, Sir Malcolm and Lady Morris, Mrs Cavendish-Bentinck, Mrs J. Tyrwhitt Drake. . . Mrs and Miss English, with a crowd of a hundred or more. . . .'

¶ The Riviera was, as we have noted, still regarded as a winter resort — it was only the French Middle classes who went to Nice in summer — but it was already obvious that the notion that one ought to go to a *warmer* climate in winter was breaking down owing to the new enthusiasm for winter sports. 'Wengen, the Alpine Resort, for the first time is receiving winter visitors' we are told in a lady's journal for 1910. Gstaad was also recommended but Grindelwald, the visitor was warned, 'gets no sunshine actually in the village for about a month. This has its advantages as well as its drawbacks. It keeps away consumptives and invalids, and the strong say that the absence of sun on the ice-rinks makes them much better than they would otherwise be.' Even children — rich children, of course — began to be taken away for *winter* holidays:

'SNOW BABIES'
by Mrs Aubrey Le Blond

'The heights of Switzerland in mid-winter would, at first sight, 'The Queen',
Nov. 26, 1904 seem quite the last place one would choose for one's children. Indeed for years it was considered, on no evidence beyond this restrictive notion, that to take babies or little ones to the Engadine after the snow was down showed gross selfishness on the part of their parents. Thus many who were ordered in winter to the Alps and did not wish to leave their families at home compromised with their doctors and went to the Riviera instead. . .

'More recently, however, the fallacy of this notion has become evident, and we find each winter in the Alpine resorts a large number of children looking the picture of health and enjoying themselves to their heart's content. . . Little tots of three already begin to learn how to toboggan, while there is always the spade and bucket familiar at English seaside resorts for which many interesting uses can be found. Snow is a delightful substitute for sand. . .

'When they enter the house their nurse's first duty will be to give them on the threshold a thorough good brush with a broom, so that no snow is carried upstairs. They will then be as dry as one could wish. . .

'Ski running is very popular amongst the children, though, of course, the exertion would be too great for the very little ones. It is not only the English children who are learning the use of ski, but also the Swiss. . .'

¶ If the last sentence sounds unbearably patronizing, we should perhaps remember that skis were in fact introduced into Switzerland by the British. It is amusing to find the same admirable journal in its *Answer to Correspondents*, replying to an enquirer:

'*Winter Sports in Holland* ("Nancy"). — I cannot name you a 'The Queen',
Nov. 26, 1904 winter resort such as you require. Skating can be obtained in various parts of the country, but not tobaganning and ski-ing, on account of the flatness.'

¶ The 'German-Bath season' stretched, as we have noted, from the beginning of August to the middle of September. The most fashionable places were Wiesbaden, Ems, Hamburg and Marienbad. Edward VII particularly favoured the last named:

Viginia Cowles.
'Edward VII and
His Circle', 1956
'Of all his journeys, the King apparently enjoyed his annual trip to Marienbad the most. Although the object of the visit was to take the "cure", which consisted of drinking the mineral waters and observing a stringent diet, the King refused to follow the prescribed routine too closely. He arose at seven in the morning and took a two-hour walk before breakfast but he insisted on lunch being the same substantial meal that it was at home.'

¶ The indefatigable Newnham-Davis gives us a hint of the scanty fare to be expected at Homburg by those taking the cure. It is a miracle that the poor things managed to survive:

Lt.-Col Newnham-
Davis and Algernon
Bastard.
'The Gourmet's
Guide to Europe',
1903
'A typical Homburg dinner is a very small affair compared to German feasts over which the doctors do not have control. This is a dinner of the day at Ritter's, taken haphazard from a little pile of menus, and it may be accepted as a typical Homburg dinner:

Potage Crécy au Riz.
Truite de Lac.   Sce. Genevoise.   Pommes Nature.
Langue de Veau à la Hongroise.
Petits pois au Jambon,
Chapons de Châlons rôtis.
Salade and Compots.   Pêches à la Cardinal
Fruits.   Desert.'

¶ Rich pleasure-seekers were pushing ever further and further afield. It was, for instance, quite usual to 'winter in Egypt'.

THE CAIRO SEASON

'The Sketch',
Jan. 21, 1903
'In spite of the cholera scare that threatened to frighten all sun-seekers away from Egypt, the season there is a big success. Cairo is very full, and, as it has had no case of cholera since the beginning of November, there is no need for anxiety. Of course, the Cairo of the international hotels, with their modern luxury and sanitation, is very different from the Cairo of the native quarter, where hygiene attracts no attention at all. The Delta Barrage, which is within twenty miles of the town, is a very popular place for excursions just now, and some point-to-point races have been held recently near the same spot. Many well-known people are wintering in Cairo or paying the city a short visit, including Sir Ernest Cassel, General Sir Archibald Hunter, Mr. Seligmann, of the great American banking house that offered to

settle the Venezuelan dispute, and Captain and the Hon. Mrs. Clive Behrens (Lord Rothschild's daughter). The dahabeahs on the Nile are doing a thriving business, so are the hotel-keepers. The weather is sufficiently fine and mild to permit open-air functions to thrive, and there is an unprecedented gathering of wealthy Americans, to the great delight of all who have anything to sell. Military bands are to be heard regularly at most of the big hotels, there are dances and social functions every day, and, altogether, there is little room for additions to the gaiety of life.'

¶ With that, perhaps, we may leave the delights of 'dear abroad'.

CHAPTER IV

GAIETY AND EMPIRE

THE GAIETY AND THE EMPIRE were two very different institutions but both bore, even in their names, a symbolic relation to their age. For the Empire still seemed to be built on unshakable foundations and gaiety had not yet gone out of fashion. Never before, or since, has England had a King-Emperor who was also gay. He *was* the Empire and he gave his personal approval to gaiety — indeed to the Gaiety. We must borrow the words of the most prolific and entertaining of theatrical historians to paint the scene:

W. MacQueen-Pope. 'The Gaiety was up, ready to open, and the cynosure of all eyes.
'Gaiety, Theatre of There it was, in grey stone, with strips of green marble around it, and
Enchantment', 1949 surmounted by its green dome or cupola, with the female figure in gold, on top, blowing a trumpet. . .

'They did not have long to wait. The old curtain had fallen on 4th July, 1903; the new curtain arose on 26th October of the same year. It was for so short a time as a bare four months that London was without its Gaiety.'. . .

'All the people who mattered, to the theatre anyway, went to the Gaiety that night, and George Edwardes and his manager, Edward Marshall, saw a succession of famous faces pass by them en route to stalls, boxes and dress circle. There was a real atmosphere of an "occasion" and a feeling of intense excitement. And then Mr. Edwardes hurried rapidly from the vestibule and was seen a moment later at the Royal entrance, bowing and ushering in a bearded gentleman in evening dress and a lady as lovely as she was Royal. For King Edward VII and his Queen Alexandra had arrived to see the new Gaiety Theatre open. It had been his favourite theatre when he was Prince of Wales; it was his favourite theatre when he was King; and it reached its zenith in the true Edwardian days. No higher compliment could have been paid to the Gaiety than that the King and Queen should attend its opening. That was a rare, most unusual and signal honour. But then the Gaiety was a most unusual and unique theatre. A Royal visit to its first night showed its position in the scheme of things as nothing else could have done.'

¶ Perhaps the 'gay' periods of history are always those in which aristocracy and plutocracy shake hands:

'The era of the Stock Exchange was in full swing. The institution now set every standard. Musical Comedy filled the theatres devoted to it, and this was its peak, the age of *The Merry Widow*. This play, first produced at Daly's on June 8, 1907, ran for over two years, during which time its music, by Franz Lehar, served as background to every meal in a restaurant, every dance, and every garden party that was given. . . . I remember being taken to see this piece during an exeat from Eton in the autumn of 1907: we sat in the stage box, and so I was able to watch the expressions of the members of the audience, reproducing in their own fashion the sentiment and humour that came to them from the stage.

I'm going to Maxim's

Where fun and frolic gleams;

The girls all laugh and greet me;

They will not trick or cheat me.

reflected the current ennui with the responsibilities of life to perfection; how marvellous, many of those seated in the theatre felt, to be able to say that, and to cast away your cares in this manner. And as, later, the banal, but in a way charming, waltz sounded out, and Miss Lily Elsie came down the stairs to her prince, and as the glare from the stage fell on those in the front rows of the stalls, on the stiff white shirts, flashing studs, white waistcoats, and self-indulgent faces, brown or white, on the noses, hooked or snub, and gleaming, pouchy eyes, of these members of the Cosmopolitan Bourgeoisie, I can recall con-templating them and wondering whether it were possible that in the future such entertainments or such an audience would — or could — be considered as being typical of their epoch, or providing a clue to it, in the same way that we looked back, past our fathers, to *La Vie Parisienne* or *Die Fledermaus*. I decided, then, that to adopt such a view would be to overrate both entertainment and spectators — but

Osbert Sitwell in 'The Age of Extravagance', 1956

75

I was wrong. It held a suitably designed mirror to the age, to the preference for restaurant to palace, for comfort to beauty, and to the idealization of Mammon. Mammon underlay the smudgy softness and superficial prettiness of the whole performance, as the skull supports the lineaments of even the youngest and freshest face. . . Nor was it only to the stockbroker that *The Merry Widow* appealed. So popular was it that, at its farewell performance, at the end of July, 1909, the theatre was besieged all day, the earliest arrival taking his stand at half past five in the morning. . .'

¶ George Edwardes did everything on the most lavish scale:

W. MacQueen-Pope. 'Gaiety, Theatre of Enchantment', 1949 'There were some magnificent dresses in *Our Miss Gibbs*. In the White City scene, the hats worn by the show girls alone cost sixty guineas each. They were brought down for every performance from the famous hat-shop, Maison Lewis, and experts from the shop put them on the girls, standing afterwards in the wings to take them off and re-pack and return them to the shop again, ready for the next day. No chances were taken. The effect of that fashion parade was superb. All actors in those days had a "wardrobe" of many suits which would fit most parts they were called upon to play. Many of these had been paid for by George Edwardes in the first place and "purveyed" by their wearers at the end of the run, on tour. They were called "God Bless" — a shortened form of "God Bless George Edwardes," the involuntary benefactor, who, of course, knew all about it.'

¶ But of course the chief attraction of the Gaiety was the presence of the 'Gaiety Girls' themselves:

W. MacQueen-Pope. 'Gaiety, Theatre of Enchantment', 1949 'The town was rich, so rich that it seems incredible today. There was leisure and time for appreciation of quality and beauty. Life was still in waltz time. And a surprising number of young men about town found their leisure permitted them the privilege of spending a great deal of it at the Gaiety. This period, from *The Orchid* up to the out-break of World War the first, was perhaps the peak of the Glory of the Gaiety Girl. Never had she been more beautiful or more adorable. Never had the show girls been more handsome, the dancers more delightful. For the chorus was in two parts, those who were there to sing, but chiefly to be looked at; and those who were there to sing and dance, and also to be looked at. The Gaiety stage door was, indeed, the gateway of romance. The Girls gilded the evening hours with loveliness as they approached it, and lit up the night, especially for their escorts, when they left it after the show. To know a Gaiety Girl, to take her out to sup, that was a cachet about town. The girls adorned the restaurants to which they were taken. Some of the most beautiful always had their own table reserved and were treated like queens.

'The story of the Gaiety Girls is sufficient for a book by itself; a most intriguing history it would be, too. There was Denise Orme, who appeared there in 1909 in *Our Miss Gibbs*. She became the Baroness Churston. She had married the Honourable John Reginald Yarde Buller in 1907, before she went to the Gaiety. Her real name was Jessie Smither. Her mother was a distinguished pianiste, and Denise herself became an excellent violinist. She was engaged by George Edwardes and first appeared at Daly's in *The Little Michus*. Her husband succeeded to the title in 1910, when Miss Orme left the stage.

'Sylvia Storey, daughter of that Gaiety star, Fred Storey, became the Countess Poulett. Her name was Sylvia Lilian Storey. She had started her stage career at the age of six in her father's production of *Rip Van Winkle*, at Kennington. She was at the Gaiety in *Havana* when she married Earl Poulett on 2nd September, 1908, at St. James's Church, Piccadilly. They were married very quietly, for the secret had been well kept. The bridegroom's mother and sister were at the wedding. When the news broke it was a sensation, for Earl Poulett was a very rich man, and his title dated from 1627. Olive May also married into the peerage. Her husband was Lord Victor Paget, heir presumptive to the Marquess of Anglesey. Olive May, whose real name was Meatyard, was a charming actress and dancer who delighted Gaiety audiences, and was a sparkling, vivacious soubrette. She died only recently, as Countess of Drogheda. The Gaiety had few more deservedly popular people than Olive May.'

¶ A French writer of the period expresses the inevitable Gallic astonishment at this state of affairs. What he couldn't understand was why the Peer had to 'marry the girl'. He dealt with this question in an article revealingly entitled:

'Petites Danseuses d'Outre-Manche

'I knew in London a troupe of English dancers, a troupe of the first quality, fêted, admired, who literally turned the heads of the young aristocrats of London. . . It was in October, 1906, when I had just arrived in London, that I was invited to dine at a Ladies' Club. The

Raymond Reconby. *'L'Illustration',* *Jan. 1909*

dinner was bad, which is not rare in London, even in Ladies' Clubs, but the conversation was charming. The young ladies present talked of nothing but the forthcoming marriage of a musical comedy actress, Miss Camille Clifford, to a future peer of the United Kingdom, the Hon. Lyndhurst Bruce. "All the lords are marying actresses," said one of the ladies, upon which a dowager remarked "Only in England would you see such nonsense. . ." We decided to go to the Vaudeville Theatre to see her, that very evening.

'Miss Camille Clifford appeared in the second act of the musical comedy; she sang the popular song "Why do they call me a Gibson Girl". She was dressed as a Gibson Girl herself; she wore a long dress of black velvet, moulding the figure, emphasising the hips and the smallness of the waist. These dresses, like the cover of an umbrella, were called: *Gibson gowns*. They were the rage that winter when everything was *à la mode* of the celebrated American artist.

'Miss Camille Clifford was no more than a link in a chain of pretty girls which an astute manager had offered to the English public and which had taken the town by storm. . . The dozen dancers called The Gibson Girls were young, fresh and charming. The *jeunesse dorée* of London, officers of the Guards, members of the most elegant and exclusive clubs like the Marlborough, and Whites, bought the three or four front rows of the dress circle every evening in order to applaud them. . .

'A well-known London critic said to me "Nobody is allowed behind the scenes in a London theatre. There is an absolute barrier between the audience and the actors." But in England, as elsewhere, something can always be arranged. Communication was somehow established between the aristocratic young men and the lovely girls. Suddenly it was announced that one of them, Miss Eva Carrington, was to marry Lord de Clifford. . . Scarcely was this first sensation over than a further announcement told the world that Miss Gates was to become the wife of Lord Ditton. Yet a third sensational marriage followed, then a fourth and a fifth. When the husbands were not lords they were at least millionaires. . . Miss Hilda Harris gave her hand to Mr Drummond, the rich banker; Mary Fairbairn, May Kennedy and Christina Humphries became the wives of three extremely rich Americans, Smithson, Peter Kelly and Anderson, Miss Eva Hillesdon changed her common name for that of Marquise de Florac. The Gibson Girls troupe grew smaller week by week. Only five were left, only four, only three. The *jeunesse dorée* (and to whom should such a phrase be applied if not to millionaires) strove to reduce the number still further. Barbara

Deane and Elsie Kay were married off (with intentions strictly honourable) by Basil Loder and Ronald MacAndrew, both extremely rich men. Kathleen Lawn, by her marriage to Mr Hardinge, became the ward of the Duke of Portland. . .

'Only one remained, the prettiest of all, Sylvia Storey. Who would pluck this last fruit on the branch? Eventually, she owed it to herself, to her contemporaries, to her theatre, to make a good marriage. A marriage with a barrister, a professor, a journalist or an actor would have been a real misalliance for the last survivor of the Gibson Girls. Sylvia Storey has just married Lord Poulett. . . Englishmen in every rank of society accept marriage with a frivolity which never fails to fill the French with astonishment.'

¶ The Gaiety Girls were models of respectability, but there were even more celebrated ladies of the theatre *qui, à force de tomber, se sont beaucoup elevées, et, à force de s'elever se sont beaucoup couchées* Among the most spectacular of these was Gaby Deslys:

'Gaby Deslys had appeared in London as early as 1903, as a dancer and soubrette in musical comedy, but it was not until she established herself as a vaudeville turn, singing slightly naughty French songs, doing somewhat acrobatic dances, and wearing fantastic clothes, that she came into her own. Gradually the flames of her reputation spread. There was never a greater fire in the forest. Gaby soon gained international attention as the mistress of the young King Manuel of Portugal, who had, indeed, spent a king's ransom on her and had given her a rope of pearls as long as herself. Newspaper stories of the day would have it that the Portuguese people revolted against the extravagances of their young monarch, whose bills for Gaby Deslys must have appalled his Treasurer. More than likely it was only the straw that broke the camel's back. Be that as it may, the actress severed her liaison with King Manuel after the loss of his crown and, taking her pearls, went triumphantly off to make her American debut. Contracts were signed with both Ziegfeld and the Shuberts, and her salary, from the very beginning, reached $18,000 a month, an astronomical figure in those days.'

Cecil Beaton. 'The Glass of Fashion', 1954

¶ If the aspiring young man-about-Town wanted to take the actress of his choice out to dinner or supper, the redoubtable Colonel Newnham-Davis was at hand to tell him how to do it:

79

Lt.-Col Newnham-
Davis.
'Dinners and Diners',
1904
'The happy thought came to me that I had better, as I wanted cheering up, ask Miss Dainty, of the principal London theatres, to be kind enough to come out and dine at any time and at any restaurant she chose to name. I sent my humble invitation by express early in the day, and received her answer by telegram: — "Yes. Romano's. Eight. See I have my pet table. I have been given a beautiful poodle. — Dainty. Be good and you will be happy."

'At luncheon time I strolled down to the restaurant, the butter-coloured front of which looks on to the Strand, and the proprietor, "the Roman", as he is called by the *habitués* of the establishment, being out, I took Signor Antonelli, his second in command, into my confidence, secured the table next to the door, sheltered by a glass screen from the draught, which I knew to be Miss Dainty's pet one, and proceeded to order dinner. Antonelli, who had all the appearance of a very well-fed cavalry colonel, led off with *hors-d'oeuvre*. I followed with, as a suggestion for soup, *crème Pink 'Un,* a soup named after a light-hearted journal which practically made "the Roman's" fortune for him. Then, as there were some beautiful trout in the house, the only question was as to the cooking of them. *Truite au bleu,* my first thought, was too simple. *Truite Chambord,* the amendment moved by Antonelli, was too rich; so we compromised by *Truite Meunière,* in the sauce of which the lemon counteracts the butter. *Cotelettes de mouton Sefton* was Antonelli's suggestion, and was carried unanimously; but I altered his pheasant, which sounded greedy for two people, into a *perdreau en casserole.* Salad of course, Then, taken with a fit of parsimony, I refused to let English asparagus go down on the slip of paper, and ordered instead *artichauts hollandais.* Vanilla ice *en corbeille* and *petits fours* wound up my menu.

'When the handsome lady arrived — only ten minutes late — she swept like a whirlwind through the hall — past the flower-stall, over which Cleopatra presides, where I had intended to ask her to pause and choose what flowers she would — in a dress which was a dream of blue with a constellation of diamonds on it, and as she settled into her seat at the table, not quite certain whether to keep on the blue velvet and ermine cloak or let it drop, I was told the first instalment of her news at express speed. I need not look a crosspatch because she was late, the pretty lady said. It was the fault of the cabman, who was drunk, and had driven her half-way down Oxford Street. What was a good name for a poodle? The one she had been given was the dearest creature in the world. It had bitten all the claws off the Polar

*Camille Clifford in
'The Prince of Pilsen', 1904.*

Carroll McComas

bear skin in the drawing-room, had eaten up a new pair of boots from Paris, had hunted the cat all along the balcony, breaking two of the blue pots the evergreens were in, and had dragged all the feathers out of the parrot's tail. Was Sambo a good name? Or Satan? Or what? Why couldn't I answer?

My humble suggestions as to a name for the poodle having been treated with scorn, Miss Dainty turned her attention to the *hors d'oeuvre*. There were no plain sardines among the numerous little dishes on the table, and the ordinary tinned sardine was what her capricious ladyship wanted — and got. The *crème Pink 'Un* was highly approved of, and I did my best to explain at length how the combination of rice with a Bisque soup softened the asperity of the crayfish, and that the particular colour which distinguished this soup from all others was difficult of achievement. . .

'The quiet person with a silver chain round his neck had brought our bottle of *St. Marceaux,* and the clean-shaven little Italian waiter in a white apron had replaced the trout by the cutlets *à la Sefton*. For these Miss Dainty had nothing but praise, which I echoed very heartily. . .

'I asked Miss Dainty if she knew who the pretty lady dining with a good-looking grey-haired man at the end of the room was. She did know and gave me a full account of the lady's stage career, and while the *perdreau en casserole* was being cut up we ran over the professions of the various diners who occupied the triple line of little tables running down the room. The two men dining by themselves were powers in the theatrical world. "May I ask them to come and take their coffee and old brandy at our table?" I asked, and Miss Dainty graciously assented. There were as well a well-known theatrical lawyer talking business with the secretary to a successful manager; a dramatic author who was proposing plays to a colonial manager; a lady with golden hair and a permanent colour to whom a small Judaic youth was whispering with great earnestness; a well-known sporting lord, dining by himself; a music-hall agent laying down the law as to contracts to a journalist; two quiet ladies in sealskin coats; and many others, nearly all connected with the great army of stage-land.

'A little too much onion with the *perdreau en casserole* we both thought, otherwise admirable. Salad good, artichokes good, though we preferred plain vinegar as a dressing to the *hollandais* one, and the ice delicious. Then Miss Dainty trifled with cherries cased in pink sweetness and sections of oranges sealed in transparent sugar, and our two friends from the table at the far end came across and took coffee and liqueurs with us, and talked of the old days when Romano's was but a quarter of the size it is now, when it was far more Bohemian than it is now, when there was a little aquarium in the front window into which the sons of Belial used to try and force each other late at night, much to the consternation of the goldfish, when everybody who took his meals there knew everybody else, when poor Bessie Belwood, the merriest soul that ever stepped the music-hall stage, always had a good tale to tell to her circle of cronies, and the chaff ran riot down the single tables, and when every Sunday morning a devoted but Sabbath-breaking band were led across the Strand by "the Roman" to see his cellars, "best in London", as he used to say.

'All of a sudden Miss Dainty, whom these reminiscences did not interest very much, remembered that the door of the parrot's cage had been left open. She was quite sure that the poodle would be trying to kill the bird, and she must go back at once to see to the matter.

'I put Miss Dainty, who said she had enjoyed her lunch, into a hansom, two brown eyes full of laughter set in a pretty face looked out at me as she told me to be good and that then I should be happy, the cabman cried "Pull up" to his horse, and the pretty lady was off to the rescue of the parrot.

'Then I went back and paid my bill: Two couverts, 6d.; hors d'oeuvre, 2s.; creme Pink 'Un, 2s.; truite, 2s. 6d.; côtelettes de mouton, 2s. 6d.; petit pois, 1s.; pommes, 1s.; perdreau, 6s.; salade, 1s.; artichauts, 2s.; glace, 2s.; champagne, 13s. 6d.; café, 3s.; liqueurs, 5s.; total, £2:4s.

¶ The proprietor of Romano's was a remarkable man:

André Simon.
'The Art of Living',
1929 'Alfonso Romano left the Café Royal, where he had been private room waiter, in 1878, and took over a moth-eaten little bar in the Strand with a dusty oyster or two in the window, which called itself the Café Vaudeville. Heaven's blessing descended upon the little place in the shape of a fire, which enabled Romano to rebuild the place to which he gave his name. It became the rendezvous of literary, sporting and theatrical celebrities and of the men-about-town who loved the company of celebrities. The *Roman,* as Romano was known to all his clients, has gone, but his old cellarman, Bendi, is still "below" and one of the "boys" he trained, Luigi, is among restaurateurs in a class by hinself — *hors concours.*'

82

¶ Of course, Romano's was not the only restaurant patronized by the men-about-town and the ladies of their fancy:

'Another Italian who played an important part at the time in the catering life of London was Sebastian Bongiovanni. He owned the Globe, in Coventry Street, a great supper-house for *demi-mondaines*, and the Solferino, in Rupert Street, where the dining-room was small but where private rooms were numerous and strictly private. His brother owned the Cavour, in Leicester Square, which eventually was acquired by Oscar Philippe, who had been head waiter there for some time.'

André Simon.
'The Art of Living',
1929

¶ Philippe was almost as colourful a figure as 'the Roman':

'Oscar Philippe, at the Cavour, in Leicester Square, was in a class by himself, the only successful London restauranteur to be illiterate. . . He had never been to school, but he knew food, more particularly meat, exceedingly well; he also knew where to get the best of every-thing. He did not understand wine, except Champagne, and the Cavour was a great champagne house in those days, patronized by the cream of the *demi-monde* as well as by many of the music-hall favourites. At the back of the restaurant, where there is now a "News" Cinema, Philippe had a little garden where he grew sorrell, chervil, parsley, tarragon, chives and such like, the cost of which, had the rental value of the ground been taken into account, must have been quite uneconomic. But when the sale of Champagne at the Cavour averaged one hundred dozens per month, Philippe could afford to keep his little garden going.'

André Simon.
'The Art of Living',
1929

¶ Then, of course, there was the Café Royal, whose proprietor, Daniel Nicols, had died in 1897 worth a quarter of a million sterling.

'Among the French houses of the time the most popular, after the Café Royal, was Kettners, in Greek Street. Kettner was an Alsatian and the chef; his wife was a Parisienne and the boss until, after her husband's death, she married Sangiorgi, their Italian head waiter.
'There was also the Café de l'Etoile in Great Windmill Street, the Café de la Regence at the corner of Coventry Street, and the Hotel Mathis, named after its owner, which stood where Lyons' Corner House now stands.

André Simon.
'The Art of Living',
1929

'There were, in the same neighbourhood, a host of other hotels and restaurants, more or less respectable, and the less respectable the more prosperous: such as Challis's Hotel, a noted rendezvous of sportsmen and jockeys; Previtali's, where opera singers congregated; the Provence and the Europe in Leicester Square; Epitaux, later known as the Pall Mall, in Haymarket; Pinoli's, in Wardour Street; The Helvetia, in Old Compton Street, Blanchard's in Beak Street; Verrey's, at the top end of Regent Street; and the Continental, at the lower end of the same thoroughfare. Then came the two brothers Monico, who opened a cafe-restaurant in Piccadilly Circus, which became at once very popular, and the two brothers Gatti, who transformed the Adelaide Gallery, at the back of St Martin's Church, into one of the most successful restaurants in London. Farther east, in and just off the Strand, Smith's Oyster Shop and Rule's, in Maiden Lane, were the haunts of bohemian and sporting crowds.'

¶ A survivor of the 'Old Pink 'Un Days' writes of these and other places in nostalgic vein:

J. B. Booth. ' *"Master" and Man, Pink'un Yesterdays'*, 1926 'In no instance, perhaps, has London changed more completely in the last twenty odd years than in the nature of its restaurants and music-halls.

'Many of the famous — or notorious — restaurants have been swept away. Gone are The Continental and "Jimmy's"; the Globe is a memory only. The American Bar of the Criterion, famous in music-hall song and sporting literature, is as dead as the Russian debt; Dieudonné's now houses the Eccentrics; the Avondale no longer fronts Piccadilly, the Strand has a different Tivoli, and the Haymarket has replaced Epitaux's. The Hotel de Paris no longer adorns Leicester Place, and in Leicester Square the shade of old Philippe no doubt contemplates a changed and renovated Cavour, and, late at night, haunts sadly the site of the famous little garden at the back, where he grew his vegetables for the sole purpose of boasting that they were reared in the heart of the West End.

'Challis's in Rupert Street is no more, and, if things ever attained their perfect fitness, a statue of Joe Lyons would replace the Piccadilly Eros. The Café Royal rears a new front and talks of music, the old bay windows of Verrey's are no longer seen from the Street of the Regent; Hatchett's remains, with a difference; gigantic stone palaces have replaced many of the old eating-houses, and the Trocadero threatens

Actors versus Actresses, at the Theatrical Garden Party, 1910. Mr Rutland Barrington, as umpire,
shields Miss Vane Featherston from the sun. From 'The Tatler', July 6th, 1910.

'The Café Royal.' Painting by Sir William Orpen, Paris, Musée d'Art Moderne.

to dominate the heart of the West End, from Shaftesbury Avenue to Leicester Square.

'The advantages of the changes are many and obvious, but there have been losses. Gone apparently for ever are the days of the amusing little coteries who lived a portion of their lives within the quarter of a mile radius of Eros, who met regularly at tacitly appointed times at their habitual rendezvous; who, at their invariable hours were certain finds in their usual bar, restaurant, music-hall or theatre. The new London is too big, too bustling for them; if they exist, they are pushed into corners of gigantic food palaces, or sit demurely in their stalls in the great new variety houses, entirely surrounded by chocolate-eating flappers. The habits have perforce changed; the supper hour — an elastic hour indeed — is no more, as it used to be understood; so-called supper and dance clubs are poor substitutes for men who wish to sup and chat as of old, and the middle-aged ghost has a rude shock when he attempts to replenish his cigar-case after eight o'clock.

'Let us, in imagination, put the clock back some twenty years, and spend an hour or two in that pre-war London which is rapidly becoming as mythical as the London of the Regency.

'A very good place in those days for lunch or for an undress dinner was the American bar of the Criterion, and there were men "who knew their town" who swore by the grilled pigs' feet to be had there for supper.

'In these days of rebuilt London, the great café-restaurant in the hub of the West End, whose gastronomic fame was a parable of our forbears, has like the rest of its surroundings suffered many changes. But the Criterion was a name when the Carlton and Prince's, the Cecil and the Savoy were undreamt of, when the Trocadero was a very third-rate music-hall, when the name of Lyons was unheard-of, when Oddenino's was a small Russian pastry-cook's, and the late Alfonso Nicolino Romano evidenced the excellence of his fare by putting legs of mutton in his tiny window.

'However desirable the Criterion's translation, the various processes of dismantling and change, which began in 1908, caused many a middle-aged beholder to carry a heavy heart, for the sake of cheery old days. Sad eyes watched the ruthless stripping of roofs, sad eyes watched the relentless wrecking of walls, and grey memories arose in abundance of cheerful gatherings in the departed American bar, of jovial suppers in its departed grill-room.

'Managers came and went at the big caravanserai in Piccadilly Circus, but for years the American Bar remained the same.

'In our round of the London of twenty odd years ago, let us in imagination drop in for a moment before lunch. We are "sure to meet someone" — that certainty of "meeting someone" was one of the charms of the smaller London.

'The American Bar never seems to change. The ceiling may be occasionally renovated, and the fine patriotic design of the eagle, with its talons full of forked lightnings, embellished with fresh gold leaf in honour of Presidential elections or the establishment of the gold standard, otherwise changes are few.

'There are the little carved cupids on the outside portals; the marble-topped tables, which are deftly covered with tablecloths by the waiters in the usual French garb of white aprons and short jackets when the meal-times approach; the partitions of ground glass, and brass rail; the marble columns, and, at the end of the room, the grill with a clock above it, where, shielded by a transparent screen, a stout cook in white stands and turns the endless chops and the steaks on a Titan's gridiron. The two janitors, both of mighty girth, who stands at the outer doors, look in occasionally to give a message, for from about twelve in the morning to midnight the American bar is as busy as a beehive, and each edition of the evening papers is anxiously bought and scanned by most of the habitués, who have, as a rule, a tinge of the racing man about them.

'It would be odd indeed if the Criterion, placed in the absolute centre of civilization, did not attract to one or other of its salons the most remarkable mixture of humanity of the quarter of the century ending, say, in the early nineteen hundreds. . .

'Let us in imagination order an aperitif, and glance at some of the "celebrities" here this morning, either sitting at the tables or standing at the bar, where the many bottles on the shelves make a fine show, where the lager-beer engine is surmounted by a silvered statuette, and three white-coated tenders seem continually employed in mixing drinks in tumblers half-filled with cracked ice. Foremost amongst them is a Mr. Cockburn, a florid man of distinctly sporting appearance, whose cheeks still bear the unsightly scars that their wearer got in the now forgotten brawl with cutlasses in a house in Munster Terrace, Regent's Park. Near him is a spare, dark man, dressed in grey, wearing his bowler hat very much over one ear. This is Saville, Cockburn's fellow-sufferer in the battle of the blades, who, when the chief assailant, a Mexican card-cheat named Tarbeaux (who went to penal servitude)

86

was about to return to the attack on Cockburn, made the extraordinary appeal, "That's enough; don't twice him!"

'There, sitting at one of the tables, is a burly fellow, broad of back and lavishly bestudded with diamonds, who is a redoubtable book-maker. Pitcher whispers that it is he who headed the Birmingham contingent at most of the prize-fights of recent years, and particularly in evidence were they at the Smith and Greenfield and the Smith and Slavin encounters at Le Vesinet and Bruges.

'Many eyes are turned at the entrance of a well-known Oriental banker, a gentleman of great wealth, and one of the last personages one would have expected to see lunching *solus* and in the plainest manner possible. That it is a favourite resort of his is apparent from the fact that he walked straight to a table at which a chair had been turned up, and the manager of the room himself came forward to proffer those few words of advice — generally of a semi-confidential nature — which relieve the diner of so much hazardous speculation. Yet other newcomers are a stalwart ex-major of the Royal Artillery, and Didcott, the music-hall agent, who in the halcyon past had half the proprietors of variety theatres in London at his feet. To each and all of them "Charlie," the well-groomed head barkeeper with the accurately parted and immaculately-plastered hair, has something of a paramount interest to impart, and he seems so bland that one wonders how he ever survived the friendly raids of the olden days when a certain festive youth and his companions were wont to take the place by assault, and on one occasion stormed the bar, took possession of the tills, and scrambled the shillings among the chronic needy.

'What wild extravagances were they capable of! It was here that the undefeated racing man who used to be known as the best-looking youth in London, and was to be seen daily in Piccadilly with a black poodle decorated with bows and yellow ribbons, once mixed for the entertainment of his friends his fearful and wonderful "fruit-salads" — generally a couple of sovereigns' worth of hothouse fruit steeped in the cognac of Justerini and Brooks, and *liqueurs variées* the effects of which the friends aforesaid found the greatest possible difficulty in sleeping off by dinner-time.

'A fresh arrival of guests, most of them on the way to Kempton, with their racing-glasses hung over their shoulders, include a young man, with the name of a philanthropist of a past generation, who at one time owned a property with two racecourses on it, and a gentleman who used to drive a yellow-bodied coach with four piebald horses, which he alluded to humorously as his mustard-pot and guinea pigs, who, having run through one fortune, seems likely to make another as an agent to a well-known whisky distiller. A sporting baronet, who takes an interest in yachting; a dramatist, who had written more than one racing play, and no doubt finds the American bar useful for his local colour; and a dozen less well-known people, form a solid mass before the bar, and occupy all the available tables.

'But we have finished our aperitifs, and it is time to move on. Old John Corlett and half a dozen more will be at Romano's; Phil May is likely to look in; there will be much talk about the new Gaiety piece, and the prospects of the Guv'nor's horse in the big race; the latest story that is amusing the town will certainly be told, and one will hear all the news — veracious and otherwise.

'It is one of those rarest of all days — a perfect London June, and as the hansom swings down the Haymarket the air is like champagne. The sun gleams and glances on the glossy skins of the horses; the brasswork of the harness reflects a myriad sparks of fire; the brisk clatter of hoofs, the jingle of hansom bells, the deep, soft rumble of innumerable wheels, the pulsing stream of flesh and blood, human and equine — this is London: London, the only city in the world.

¶ But it is time we turned to the Empire, that other of Edwardian gay life:

W. MacQueen-Pope.
'The Melodies
Linger On', 1950 'The Empire, a dream of blue and gold, was a most luxurious place. Its carpets were of deep pile, its hangings and upholstery superb. Its stalls were like armchairs in which one could recline with ease. . . a few can still be sat in for when the Empire closed they were placed in the vestibule and lounge at Drury Lane, where they are now. There was never any noise, or unruliness, except on Boat Race nights, and the Empire knew how to cope with that. Boat Race night at the Empire was an event, a tradition, but not all the young men kicking up a row in the Promenade had ever been to either of the Universities who had rowed that day — or to any other University, either. In the days when the Empire flourished, the occasion provided an opportunity to go mad at night. The management cleared all the bars of everything breakable and put all glasses, bottles, etc. out of reach; even tables and chairs were moved away. They let the youth of London, and of Oxford and Cambridge, have its fling within reason, and then they threw out the worst offenders. Buncle, the gigantic linkman, and his mate of equal

88

stature, could, and did, carry out four young men at a time; there were giants in those days.

'And over the milling crowd watched Mr. Hitchins, the perfection of managers. He knew that the ejected promptly went round to the side entrance in Leicester Street and paid five shillings to come in again. The Empire took a lot of money on Boat Race nights. But he was very watchful. When he observed a youth who was getting out of hand, he would approach him gently, a very imposing figure in his full evening dress, never flustered, never flurried, never bad-tempered. On those nights, he also wore white kid gloves. Going up to some very riotous youth, he would reason with him and then gently pat him on the shoulder. It was a cue. That young man was immediately ejected. He would run, or stagger (it all depended), round to the side entrance but it would appear that the touch of Hitchens on his shoulder was a magic one, for those so touched never gained re-admission. The secret was that the manager bore in the palm of his white kid gloves a small piece of chalk. And a young roisterer so chalked was outside for the rest of that Boat Race night.

'But apart from such occasions, the Empire was a quiet, orderly place, just the spot in which to spend a liesurely, peaceful evening, if you were a man. There was never any hustle or bustle, everyone moved as if eternity stretched around; always there was that air of rich calm which accompanies good living and good dinners. The liveried attendants were as efficient and soft voiced as the servants in one of the best clubs; indeed, the Empire was a Club. You paid the entrance fee every time you went there and there was no subscription, but nevertheless, it was a club, and it proclaimed itself one on its program-mes, The Cosmopolitan Club of the World. And that is exactly what it was. All nations and races went there. It was the first spot to which a Briton home from abroad, from some outpost of the Empire when there was an Empire all over the world as well as in Leicester Square, made for on his first evening in London. It was an almost odds on chance that he would meet a friend. They had dreamed of the Empire when overseas and they hurried to it. It never failed them.

'Snatches of overheard conversation were most intriguing:

' "Good God, old man, is it really you? I thought you had been killed at Magersfontein!" "Ah, so did everyone else, but here I am, you see, in the old Promenade again. Come and have a drink." That was actually heard there. All classes, all grades of Society, the wealthy, the well-to-do, those of moderate means, those who had saved up to pay a visit, all met at the Empire. It was the centre of London's night life when London was the centre of the world. Foreigners visiting this country made a beeline for it, they all knew about the Cosmopolitan Club. A great traveller who had reached the city of Vladivostok, very far off indeed in the 1890's, handed his papers to the Cossack officer in charge for investigation. The officer looked at him. "You come from London?" he queried and his eyes sparkled at the answer, "London, ah, yes," he sighed, "London — The Empire." It was as famous as that.' ...

'To the ultra-respectable and to the Puritan (no offence is meant by the use of that word which really stands for a source of Britain's greatness), the Empire Promenade was anathema, a cesspool of Vice. Few of them had been there to see, but those who had, the scouts sent to make reports, certainly saw an eyeful of the Ladies. There was no secrecy about it, there was indeed nothing to hide. The Ladies were there for all to see and a great portion of the world went there to see. They made no secret of their profession and did not pretend to be respectable (it was their living not to be) yet they comported themselves, when in the Empire, with great dignity and decorum. But the Promenade was a storm spot all the same and many attempts were made to get it closed down, to have the Ladies swept into the streets where, according to their ultra-respectable opponents, they really belonged. How far this accorded with the principles of the various religious denominations who assailed the Promenade was never apparent; there was scriptural predecent for a contrary course. But the Empire survived all the shocks and so did the Promenade.

'The most determined attack was that led by Mrs. Ormiston Chant in 1894. The battle raged furiously and cries of White Slavery resounded from the attacking party — though there was precious little slavery amongst the Ladies of the Empire. But violent as was the assault, it failed completely. All its leader achieved was to become the most popular Guy of the Year on the next Fifth of November. And the Fifth was a great day then, with processions of guys converging on a huge bonfire on Hampstead Heath or elsewhere. But, as a result of the attack, the Empire management made a gesture, and it put up some wooden trellis work, decorated with artificial flowers, to make the place not quite so open. Affronted young men-about-town at once pulled this down, and among the leaders was a young man who was destined to lead his country to victory through its darkest, but most glorious hour. He would stand no nonsense or hypocrisy then or

90

now. So the Ladies of the Town went on Promenading at the Empire.

'No other place could compare with the Empire in this respect, there was nothing like it anywhere else in the world. Other theatres of variety, other music halls had their Promenades but not even the Alhambra could match that of the Empire, it was always a peg or two below. For the women of the Empire were the aristocrats of their "profession". And they looked it. Amazing creatures, amazingly dressed, of all races and speech, blondes, brunettes, redheads, they moved quietly and slowly to and fro, with a rather feline grace. A tiger pacing its cage has such a gift of movement. They were unmistakable, yet their manners were excellent. They never accosted a man, at the most he might feel the soft touch of a hand against his or the faint pressure of a silk-clad body if he stood by the rail watching the show.

'There was never any loud chatter, shrieking laughter or bad language. These women might have had no character outside but they had one to lose in the Empire. One complaint to the management and they were barred. And that was, for them, tragedy, irrevocable loss of prestige and descent to the depths. There were all types for all tastes, from the regally majestic, to the quiet and demure; from the bold, flashing, merry eye to the modestly downcast eyelid. But there was allure everywhere. Some of those women met sad ends but, believe it or not, some of them married men they had met at the Empire in the way of business and settled down into truly excellent wives and mothers, the author knows of several such cases. And as they moved to and fro, with silken swish and gleam of jewels, the scent of frangipanni and patchouli would be apparent as a kind of aura, it lingers in many nostrils still. The Promenade was unique and the Empire was unique — and the Ladies of the Empire were unique too.'

¶ 'Ladies of the Empire' in another sense: the respectable wives of the men who were consolidating our over-seas possessions, were apt to look upon it with a different eye:

'I desired to see the promenade at the Empire Music Hall. Young girls did not go to music halls; but married women might go to a box or to the stalls of certain houses. I was allowed to hurry through the Empire promenade, my tall husband on one side and a tall cousin on the other. This place was nothing more or less than a meeting place for women of the town and men who wishes to enjoy their society; but for some extraordinary reason the Empire had become a National Insti-

Mrs C. S. Peel, O.B.E. 'Life's Enchanted Cup', 1933

tution, and when Mrs Ormiston Chant made her famous protest against it, she excited much opposition for daring to interfere with what some of the newspapers referred to as the Club of the Empire.'

¶ Such it certainly was:

*J. B. Booth.
' "Master" and
Man, Pink'un
Yesterdays', 1926*
'One "dropped in" at the Empire simply because one was certain to meet half a dozen at least of the men one knew, and, as often as not, some returned wanderer from the ends of Empire, who, with the creases of packing still in his dress clothes, had made, straight as a homing pigeon, for the old spot where a lonely man was certain to meet an old friend, or, at least, a former acquaintance. Far more interesting frequenters of the promenade than the pretty ladies were the lean, bronzed men in crumpled kit, whose eyes would suddenly light up at a cry of: "Great Scott, old man, where have *you* sprung from?" And then, in the manner of greetings would come phrases such as: "Landed at Tilbury late last night — nothing to do this evening, so just dropped in to have a look at the old place — felt sure I'd find someone!" '

¶ To be 'chucked out of the Empire' was part of the worldly experience of every gilded youth — it is amusing to reflect that this fate once overtook no less a person than Winston Churchill. The idea of the aristocratic young man with nothing to do but enjoy himself was still a popular one, so popular that there were many who tried to emulate him without having his resources. The type has been embalmed for ever in music hall songs:

*Christopher Pulling.
'They Were
Singing', 1952*
' "He's vurry well known is Algy, to the ladies on the stage,
    Such a jolly good chap is Algy, just now he's all the rage,
    And a ripping big favourite, Algy, with the barmaids at the Cri;
    He's very well known is Algy,
    As the Piccadilly Johnny with the little glass eye." '
'Pictures of her [Vesta Tilley] show her immaculately dressed in tailcoat and white tie; or frock-coat, silk hat, white spats, lavender gloves, gold-mounted ebony cane in hand, gardenia in button hole. She got her clothes from men's outfitters, and actually set men's fashions. One can still picture that dapper, swaggering little figure, strolling jauntily back and forth across the stage, every touch only slightly caricaturing the real-life type. And what tunes they were:

92

Vesta Tilley

The Promenade of a West-End music hall. Drawing by Dudley Hardy.

' "Playing the game in the West,
    Leading a life that's thrilling.
Out of the two-bob piece
    All I've got left is a shilling.
Strolling along the Strand,
    Knocking policemen about,
And I'm not going home till a quarter to ten,
    'Cause it's my night out!"

'Vesta Tilley had had a Burlington Bertie before Ella Shields, but
that had been the "straight" swell,

        ' "With the Hyde Park drawl
        And the Bond Street crawl",

who, we were told, would if necessary fight and die like an Englishman. Ella Shields' *Burlington Bertie* was a character-study of a
decayed man-about-town keeping up appearances at all costs. The
unquenchable optimism, the "never-say-die" perkiness, of this
languorous, seedy, half-starved figure, left a haunting memory:

' "I'm Bert. P'raps you've heard of me?
Bert. You've had word of me,
Jogging along, hearty and strong,
Living on plates of fresh air.
I dress up in fashion,
And when I am feeling depressed,
I shave from my cuff all the whiskers and fluff,
Stick my hat on, and toddle up West.

' "I'm Burlington Bertie, I rise at ten-thirty,
And saunter along like a toff.
I walk down the Strand with my gloves on my hand,
And then walk down again with them off.
I'm all airs and graces, correct easy paces,
So long without food, I've forgot where my face is.
I'm Bert, Bert, I haven't a shirt,
But my people are well off, you know.
Nearly ev'ry one knows me, from Smith to Lord Roseb'ry;
I'm Burlington Bertie from Bow."

'In the second verse she told us: "Cigars? I smoke thousands; I usually deal in the Strand. But you have to take care when you're getting them there, or some idiot may step on your hand." '

¶ But alas! times were changing and after the death of King Edward things were never quite the same again. Even the music was different — or beginning to be:

Christopher Pulling.
'They Were
Singing', 1952
'Ragtime had found its way over in 1911 with *Alexander's Ragtime Band* and the American Ragtime Octette, which Albert de Courville brought to the London Hippodrome, to be followed by Ethel Levey and *Hitchy Koo,* and *Everybody's Doing It* at the Empire. The Chicken Reel and the Bunny Hug were soon to have their turn. Syncopation was all the rage. People found they wanted madder music and stronger wine, though at the same time they were beginning to show a liking for sadder music and longer whines (songs like *Beautiful Garden of Roses*), which seemed likely to take the place of the native raciness in the music-halls.'

¶ Many were still unaware of all that was happening both at home and abroad:

W. MacQueen-Pope.
'Gaiety, Theatre of
Enchantment', 1949
'The world was still moving to waltz time, and it did not seem possible that it would ever change. The new idiom, musically, of ragtime was insistently knocking at the door, and people found it amusing. That it should ever become the standard idea of music was unthinkable.

'The Germans were getting bumptious and had started building ships as fast as Britannia herself. Some people foretold War, but few believed it. We were friends with France and, anyway, we could lick the Germans single-handed. We had the *Dreadnought*. There had been an outcry about this invincible battleship: the public of the Realm demanded not just one or two, but eight, so as to put the German Navy, that upstart organisation, where it belonged. "We want eight, we won't wait," they chanted. They wrote the slogan on walls, on pavements. The newspapers blazoned it. In the end eight were forthcoming, so the nation, appeared, went to sleep again, secure behind the shield of the Royal Navy.

'The Gaiety twinkled on, the Girls gave visions of beauty on the stage and equal visions of beauty off it. But when they were taken out

94

to sup now, and driven home afterwards, it was seldom in a hansom, but in a taxi. The motor was speeding up life, and more and more barriers were going down before the onslaught of wealth. Money was the passport now, being counted the equal, or even the superior of breeding. More and more people were living in flats, Continental ideas were being widely adopted. But still the golden life flowed on, still London was an English city, still a foreigner was an object of amused tolerance, and still we had the true Cockney slang and the true English speech. The cinema was on the way up as a method of enter-tainment. But it was silent — it did not shout in American. There were no cinema stars. Just one or two, such as Max Linder and John Bunny, had become known by name, but the cinema was still a small affair and very cheap, with a pianist pounding out tunes, suitable or otherwise to the picture, which flickered on the screen as the figures jerked along with staccato movement, apparently amidst downpours of tropical rain.'

¶ Even the Gaiety Girls themselves were not the same:

'There were no true Gaiety Girls now. In their place were clever *W. MacQueen-Pope.* efficient chorus girls, who worked harder maybe than their sisters of *'Gaiety, Theatre of Enchantment', 1949* old; but who lacked alike the distinction, allure, the individuality of their predecessors. Indeed, all true individuality had gone. One girl looked much the same as another. They all dressed alike; all did their hair the same way. There was no crowd of excited young men at the Gaiety stage door now, with golden sovereigns burning holes in their pockets to get out and gild the night for a Gaiety Girl. Such people as did haunt the stage door were other girls, stage-struck young ladies who commented audibly on their favourites as they emerged, and even called them familiarly by their Christian names. There were, too, crowds of youngsters with autograph books and written demands, with their names and addresses on them, for photographs.

'So the girls from the Gaiety just got on buses, scurried to the tubes, and went home to the suburbs, little knowing maybe what a grand time there had been when the generation before them came out of that same door — and its darker, smaller predecessor across the road. They were pretty, those girls, they were neat and well dressed, and without doubt very efficient. But they all resembled each other. Their hair was short, their skirts were short, and they lacked the essential feminity of the older days. They were the Gaiety chorus, which was a very different thing from being a Gaiety Girl. And they were not permanent, they changed with every show; so the magic of the Gaiety, which still lingered, never had time to invest them with its glamour. The door was there, but its atmosphere had changed.'

¶ The same lively author, a generation later, writes the epitaph of the Gaiety, and with that we may conclude our chapter:

W. MacQueen-Pope.
'Gaiety, Theatre of
Enchantment', 1949

'There may be ghosts in plenty in the old theatre now, as it stands empty, and, maybe, ghosts around its stage door, too. For so many of that gay throng laid down their lives between 1914–1918, in order that life in the English way might go on. And visiting the Gaiety stage door was a habit with English — and British — young men. Though they have come down in story as "Stage-Door Johnnies", "Mashers", "Swells", "Toffs" and "Knuts", they were men who proved themselves and their valour.

'There are no stage-door Johnnies now — that phase of life is closed. But then there is no Gaiety stage door, nor anything like it.'

Patrons of the British Drama. Drawing by Will Owen. From 'The Tatler', August 10th, 1904.

'Old Studio' sideboard, designed by Liberty's, 1903.

CHAPTER V

'ART NOUVEAU' AND NEW ART

THE AVERAGE EDWARDIAN, even of the cultivated classes, was blissfully unaware that an artistic revolution was taking place before his eyes. There were in fact two revolutions, one in the applied arts and one in what it was still the fashion to call the Fine Arts — in sculpture and painting, in short. It will be interesting to deal with the revolution in furniture first.

The first signs of the new movement were plainly visible in the Paris Exhibition of 1900. There were two principal pioneers, one Emile Gallé of Nancy, and the other an energetic little man named Sigfried Bing who came from Hamburg and who worked in Paris.

Gallé specialized in marquetry of various woods and he usually managed to include in his design some improving motto such as *Travail est Joie*. He was also fond of poetry, particularly the poetry of Baudelaire (of all unsuitable people) laboriously cut out in marquetry. The dominant decorative motif was the Egyptian water lily with occasional leanings towards the convolvulus. The ornamentation was always assymetrical.

The Paris school was slightly more abstract but followed the same writhing convolvulus line. This was seen in architecture also, the best known architect of the group being Hector Guimard who designed the stations on the Paris *metro*. The entrances to these stations, now so familiar, are pure *Art Nouveau* and must have been somewhat startling when they were first erected.

On our side of the Channel, *Art Nouveau* first manifested itself in Glasgow where the architect Charles Rennie Mackintosh was its chief exponent. He was also a designer of furniture and exhibited at the Arts and Crafts Exhibition in London in the late 'nineties a hall settle embellished with a panel of beaten brass bearing the legend:

'Art and Literature seeking Inspiration at the Tree of Knowledge and Beauty.' Perhaps his masterpiece was the decoration of the Willow Tearoom in Sauchiehall Street, Glasgow, and this was the inspiration of many tea rooms all over Great Britain.

Mackintosh's wife, who worked under the name of Margaret Macdonald, was, with her sister, especially noted for her decorative needlework. Her designs were full of the elongated willowy figures of weeping women waving expressive hands. Another lady of the school, Jessie Newbery, formulated her decorative principles in eleven maxims, of which one, perhaps, may suffice: 'I believe in everything beautiful, pleasant, and, if need be, useful.'

'If need be, useful!' But many of the *Art Nouveau* designers disdained any such concession and constructed chairs in which it was impossible to sit down, side-boards with niches of such peculiar shapes and sizes that only 'art pots' specially designed for the purpose could be made to fit into them, and vases so elongated that they could never have contained more than a single lily and were quite impossible to clean.

England stood somewhat apart from these developments, although many of the Continental innovators paid tribute to the influence of William Morris and of the whole Arts and Crafts movement. The French writer Jean Lahore stated that Ruskin and Morris were the precursors of *Art Nouveau*, but if so, England once more manifested its obtuseness and ingratitude.

Stephen Tschudi Madsen. 'Sources of Art Nouveau', 1956

'Only one English architect can really be said to have worked in Art Nouveau, viz. Charles Harrison Townsend. Among his principal works are the Bishopsgate Institute, the Whitechapel Art Gallery, and Horniman's Museum, all in London. . . Townsend's position, however, is that of a lone wolf in England: the leading artists and designers turned their attention in different directions. It is only in metalwork and the ornamentational mounting among the Arts and Crafts artists that we can find a decoration which really recalls Art Nouveau. . . Art Nouveau was, and remained, in Great Britain almost entirely a purely Scottish phenomenon.'

¶ In one department of the decorative arts, however, the swirling lines of *Art Nouveau* can be seen quite plainly during the Edwardian period, and that was in the art of dress. If the Edwardian lady could have been cast in bronze, or better still, beaten out from behind in sheet copper, she could have taken her place quite naturally as a lamp standard or as the decorative motif of a fireplace panel. It is hard to say whether fashion or interior decoration owed more to the other. Perhaps they were both part of the same climate of taste. At any rate, the twisted fall of the flowing skirt of the Gibson Girl is exactly echoed in *Art Nouveau* fireplaces and other decorative units. There is a mystery here which perhaps it would be out of place to pursue in the present volume.[1] Let us turn to the question of Fine Art.

The Royal Academy was, at the beginning of the reign of Edward VII, at the height of its glory. The opening of the yearly exhibition was a social event of the first importance, to be compared with Ascot or Derby Day. The pictures are taken very seriously, and it is amusing, in retrospect, to note the amount of space given in *The Times* to the Royal Academy Exhibition of 1910. Some of the critic's remarks certainly read a little oddly today:

'We are sorrowfully reminded of the two great losses that British art has lately sustained by the death of Sir William Orchardson and Mr Swan, and the contributions that bear their name will long remain in memory. Here, signed by the trembling hand of a dying man, is the portrait of Lord Blyth, which Orchardson rose from his sick bed to finish, and to which he had scarcely the time or the strength to put the final touches. . . Here, too, is Mr Swan's "The Cold North", the largest and most elaborate version of that favourite subject of his, Polar bears among their native ice. . .

'Turning now to the more general aspects of the exhibition, we may say that portraiture predominates, perhaps to excess, though the absence of Mr Sargent from this department makes a gap that is not filled. The place of honour is occupied by a full-length seated figure of the King, in Garter robes, painted for the Academy by the President, Sir Edward Poynter. . . The President's best portraits have been the outcome of infinite labour in the presence of the sitter; for among his many gifts that of the instantaneous grasp of a face and character can hardly be reckoned. Hence the portrait will meet with a good deal of criticism; but it certainly will be a fine possession for the Academy, and its highly decorative qualities will cause it to group well with the other Royal portraits belonging to that body. . .

'The best Herkomer is the very straightforward portrait of Sir

'*The Times*', *Apr. 30, 1910*

[1] But see, by the present Editor, *Style in Costume,* Oxford University Press, 1949, plates 29 and 30.

Julius Wernher in the costume of every day; Lord Burnham, in red robes, is at least a speaking likeness; but the painter has not succeeded so well with the features of the late Lord Ripon, nor do the rather violent green robes of a Chancellor of the University of Leeds lend themselves happily to artistic treatment. Sir Luke Fildes has five portraits, including one of a lady — a rarity in the present exhibition, where men are in a most ungallant majority. When ladies honour our Academicians, it is generally Mr Dicksee or Mr Shannon that they choose, unless, of course, Mr Sargent is available, as is now so rarely the case. . .

'If the Academy gave medals, that in the department of ladies' portraits would have been given to Mr Dicksee, not for his more ample and sumptuous picture of "Lady Inverclyde", but for the very exquisite picture of "Mrs Arthur Herz". Mr Dicksee, of course, is wilfully academical and old-fashioned, because to him "the old is better". Others, who cannot draw like Greuze and Ingres. . . very naturally prefer a more summary and slap-dash style; but if one can draw like these men — and Mr Dicksee can — why not do so?'

¶ Why not, indeed — if one can!

In 'a second Pilgrimage through the galleries' the same writer points out 'a good example of that careful painter of military subjects. . . *The Rear Guard,* a true rendering of an incident in Moore's disastrous retreat upon Corunna'.

'The Times',
May 16, 1910 'Further on is the chief work of Mr J. W. Waterhouse, two semi-classical damsels[1] gathering roses — a pretty, decorative performance, but somewhat mannered. . . Mr Stanhope Forbes's *The Pier Head* [is] as sound and attractive a scene of Cornish seaside life as Newlyn has ever produced.'

¶ The Paris Salon was taken with equal seriousness, but rather more critically:

'The Times',
May 2, 1910 'Depression overcomes you more at the Old Salon than anywhere else, simply because it contains more and bigger pictures than any other exhibition. All the world goes to see it or wants to hear about it from sheer force of habit, but there is never much to say about it except that it is like the Salons of the past, only more so. . .

[1] Semi-classical is a euphonism for semi-nude.

'It is difficult to be sure of the intentions of M. Alleaume's profligate dinner party in the open air. Both men and women are mere sophisticated animals without any animal dignity. . . There is more dignity in the revelling women and Centaurs of M. Clovis Cazes. . . even the great Doric temple in the background does not look like an anachronism. But in the startling work of M. Georges-Bergès everything looks an anachronism. Here there is a sunlit landscape, half primeval, half like a modern wild garden. . . On the lawn and among the rhododendrons is the nude and sleeping figure of a woman. . . the painter has merely brought together a number of things beautiful in themselves without imagining any reason for their combination. . .

'The child's funeral by M. Gaurdault does convince. It has less stern ugliness than the work of Courbet and less rude grandeur of design, but is moving without being sentimental. As you look at it you do not feel that the painter has taken an unfair advantage of you. . . There are tears, but they are not grossly insisted on.'

¶ But this complacent acceptance of the anecdotage of Art was soon to be rudely shaken.

Desmond MacCarthy has left an entertaining account of how the famous Post-Impressionist Exhibition of 1910 came to be organised:

'When Roger Fry proposed that I should go abroad and help assemble a representative exhibition of pictures by Cézanne, Matisse, Van Gogh, Gauguin, Seurat, Picasso and other now familiar French painters (incidentally he promised me a few days bicycling in France). I don't think he chose me because he had special trust in my judgement.

'Hearing that the Grafton Galleries had no show between their usual London Season exhibition and the new year's, he proceeded to convince them that they might do worse than hold a stop-gap exhibition of modern foreign artists. . . It was all settled in a tremendous hurry. I had just time to interview the director of the Galleries. He apologised for the smallness of my fee (a hundred pounds). But if — he added, with a pitying smile — if there were profits, I might have half of them. Neither the committee of the Grafton Galleries nor Roger Fry thought for one moment that the show could be a financial success. . .

'On my return to London I reported that several hundred interesting

Desmond MacCarthy. 'Memories', 1953

101

pictures were available (transit insurance probably £150)... What was the exhibition to be called? That was the next question. Roger and I and a young journalist who was to help us with publicity, met to consider this; and it was at that meeting that a word which is now embedded in the English language — "post-impressionism" — was invented. Roger first suggested various terms like "expressionism", which aimed at distinguishing these artists from the impressionists; but the journalist wouldn't have that or any other of his alternatives. At last Roger, losing patience, said: "Oh, let's just call them post-impressionists; at any rate, they came after the impressionists..."

'Soon after ten the Press began to arrive. Now anything new in art is apt to provoke the same kind of indignation as immoral conduct, and vice is detected in perfectly innocent pictures. Perhaps any mental shock is apt to remind people of moral shocks they have received, and the sensations being similar, they attribute this to the same cause. Anyhow, as I walked about among the tittering newspaper critics busily taking notes (they saw at once that the whole thing was splendid copy) I kept overhearing such remarks as "Pure pornography", "Admirably indecent". Not a word of truth in this, of course...

'The Press notices were certainly calculated to rouse curiosity. And from the opening day the public flocked, and the big rooms echoed with explosions of laughter and indignation... I hit on a device for calming those of the furious who stormed down in a rage to my sanctum beneath the galleries. To these I would first explain that I was, after all, only the secretary, so that I could not very well close the exhibition on my own initiative that very evening. But I would add, "Your point of view is most interesting, and if you will write it down and sign it, I shall be most happy to pin it in the entrance for all to read." This suggestion acted as a sedative. The indignant one would reply, "Oh, I don't know that I want to put anything on paper; only I did feel that what I have said ought to be said." Occasionally I did get a document to pin up. I wish I had kept them...

'Presently we began to sell pictures. The Art Gallery at Helsinki bought a very fine Cézanne for £800, I remember... Not only had the exhibition been the theme of non-stop correspondence in the papers and of pamphlet wars — all the best known painters were, alas, against us — but it also provoked lectures from mental specialists. Fry himself did not make one penny out of the exhibition... Indeed, by introducing the works of Cézanne, Matisse, Seurat, Van Gogh, Gauguin and Picasso to the British public, he smashed for a long time

102

his reputation as an art critic. Kind people called him mad, and reminded others that his wife was in an asylum. The majority declared him to be a subverter of morals and art, and a blatant self-advertiser.'

¶ The first hint the British public received of what was happening to art on the other side of the Channel was provided, in the summer of 1910, by an exhibition at Brighton organized by H. D. Roberts, the Director of the Public Art Galleries, with the help of Robert Dell, previously one of the joint editors of the Burlington Magazine. The exhibition was a general one and included work not only by the Impressionists but by artists like Corot, Coralus-Duran and Tissot. But to the critics the most interesting section of the whole display was —

'the gallery given up to the Neo-Impressionists by the side of whose ultra-modernity that of the elder impressionists appears primitive, nay, almost archaic. The new art, which little by little will no doubt creep over Europe and America — much as the elder did, and in the face of the same violent opposition — must be faced, seeing that from the art of the future it will in all probability become the art of the present, not, indeed, in its actual crude and outré phase, but in some more acceptable development upon the basis for which the Neo-Impressionists are now fighting. . .

'Daily Telegraph', July 1, 1910

'What we have to do, notwithstanding the bitterness of our regret that the beauty of art, even as the beauty of life, appears to be departing, is to be fair to the new movement, to seek to understand the main principles for which it is striving. . . If only the promoters of the exhibition could have made up their minds to exclude certain intolerable and outrageous rubbish, which impudently flaunts by the side of serious, though it may be, disconcerting expositions in paint of the Neo-impressionistic theory. This failure to discriminate between the true innovators and the *fumistes* confuses the issue, and furnishes a splendid excuse to those who in disdain and loathing would turn their backs upon the whole business. . .

'Of the new men of mark in the *avant-garde* there has not hitherto been seen in England so complete a group as is now gathered together. They are all here, the divinities and prophets of the new movement; Cézanne, Gauguin, Henri-Matisse, Valloton, Vuillard, Xavier Roussel, the pseudo-mystic Odilon Redon, and others. It is a pity that Cézanne, a man of vast power in the more serious manifestations of his art, should be represented only by a grotesque and caricatural portrait,

103

"M. Albin Valabrègue". In Paul Gauguin's work there is something "rich and strange", something of the creative element without which art has no right to exist. Especially is this noticeable in the splendid and wholly novel colour-harmony, "Fruits de Tahiti". Into his weird, uncouth painting, "Les Boeufs", he has, consciously or unconsciously, infused a flavour of the proto-Cretan or Mycenaean... It is this charm, this power of evocation, that is wholly wanting in the work of M. Henri-Matisse, the prophet and protagonist just now of the whole movement. He appears to us as a moderately clever painter, who has deliberately entered upon these tortuous paths, having very little to say, but saying that strangely and not without authority in his strangeness. One of his "Natures mortes" here is just tolerable by reason of certain trouvailles in the daring colour-scheme; the other is a mere exercise, clever no doubt, but such as a painter generally has the grace to keep to himself. No bells need be rung, no drums need be beaten, over the one or the other piece."

¶ *The Times* was slightly more favourable:

'The Times',
July 11, 1910 'Never before have works in the latest movement of French painting been publicly shown in any numbers, and Mr Bell is at some pains to explain the aims of this movement, which still arouses surprise and resentment even in France.

'It has not yet got any single name for itself, and indeed it really consists of several movements, some reacting against impressionism, some developed out of it. There are symbolists and primitives and intimists and neo-impressionists; and it is difficult to defend any of them. But of all it may be said that their aim is rather to present a mental image, more or less controlled by theories, than to set down a direct impression of a real scene... Perhaps, therefore, we should call them expressionists rather than impressionists, since they have given up the impressionist curiosity about new aspects of reality and new methods of representing than for a curiosity about new methods of expressing the emotions aroused by reality. This is an entirely logical development, but the results will surprise most people. At first sight they will take these pictures for the work, or rather the play, of charlatans or mountebanks, of men who paint thus because they cannot do any better, and who make a parade of their incapacity. Yet there is no doubt that Cézanne and Gauguin were, and that M. Matisse and M. Maurice Denis are, accomplished artists...'

¶ And the writer proceeds to a very fair appraisal of these artists, and of Othon Friess, and André Derain. Of the latter he says:

'All these painters tend to use colour rather as an equivalent of the force of light than as a direct representation of it. This method is carried to an extreme in M. André Derain's views of London. There are pink trees on the Embankment, the road is green, and the sidewalks pink; the traffic is blue and the sky yellow and green. One can see no clear reason, scientific or aesthetic, for the choice of these particular colours. But the picture has rhythm and movement; it is amusing, and it would look far less ugly on the walls of a room than most photographic landscapes.' *'The Times', July 11, 1910*

¶ But this was only at Brighton. The great public of London had yet to be introduced to these startling novelties.

Naturally enough, the public was completely bewildered, and *The Queen*, among others, offered a guiding hand:

'Twenty years ago the New English Art Club was a place where the ordinary sober-minded lover of art received electric shocks almost as violent as those which rack his nerves at the Grafton Galleries. . . Is the moral of this that the Post-Impressionist movement will also cease to startle, will beat down all resistance, and win our sympathies in twenty years from now? The plea is extremely plausible; and it is a vague fear of a future *volte-face* in their judgement that compels many people now, in spite of their inner consciousness, to persuade themselves, on the word of one or two prophets of the movement, that there is some beauty and significance in Post-Impressionist art. But we need not hesitate. . . Their art, if it advances, must become more jejune and barbarous, childish instead of childlike, till it touches imbecility. That is the case already with the weak imitators of Van Gogh and Gauguin; and with their work as an object lesson we can fearlessly condemn the whole influence of the Post-Impressionist movement.' *'The Queen', Dec. 3, 1910*

¶ As might have been expected, many indignant citizens sat down to 'write to *The Times*'. The name of one of them gives him immediate precedence:

'Sir, — So our dear old friends the "Impressionists" are already *démodés*, and a younger and more audacious and more modern generation has raised the *dernier cri*. *'The Times', Nov. 17, 1910*

105

'But a surprising thing has happened.

'The critics do not acclaim the advent of the "Post-Impressionists" with that whole-hearted enthusiasm one might have expected of them. There are even signs that the egregious collection of canvases at present disfiguring the walls of the Grafton Galleries are not being taken quite seriously by the Press.

'How is this?

'Are not these very works the direct outcome and logical sequence of the teaching and preaching of our critics in the newspapers, at home and abroad, through a long series of years?

'It is many a long day now since students have been seriously advised to ignore the wisdom and experience of the past, to despise correct drawing, to shun beauty in any form, and to seek their inspiration in the tavern and the gutter. Such advice could have only one result — the anarchy and degradation of art exemplified today by the "Post-Impressionists".

'But why have their critical sponsors deserted them in the hour of need?

'The catalogue contains a half-hearted and tentative introduction by a nameless apologist.

'I have read it through carefully twice, in the hope of extracting from it any meaning whatever beyond the astounding assertion that the man who can neither draw nor paint is, for some mysterious reason, in a superior position to the man who can.

'What does it all mean?

'One is tempted to suspect that it is a huge practical joke, organised in Paris at the expense of our countrymen.

'There is an "honorary committee" whom the anxious catalogue twice carefully exonerates from all personal responsibility for the selection of the canvases. It contains one name at least which had better have been omitted.

'That the Director of our own National Gallery should have been included among those who even remotely countenance such an exhibition as is now being held at the Grafton Galleries must be cause for regret to all who take art seriously or are jealous for its dignity. The deliberate lowering of standards should not be encouraged by any official *imprimatur*.

'I am, Sir, yours obediently,

Philip Burne-Jones.'

106

¶ At this distance of time it is perhaps of interest to give the names of 'The ladies and gentlemen of the Honorary Committee [who], though they are not responsible for the choice of pictures, by lending their names have been kind enough to give this project their general support':

> The Rt Hon. The Earl of Plymouth, P.C., C.B.,
> The Duchess of Rutland,
> The Rt Hon. Lord Ribblesdale, P.C., J.P.,
> The Rt Hon. Lewis Harcourt, M.P., P.C.,
> Sir Charles Holroyd (*Director of the National Gallery*)
> Sir Edgar Vincent, K.C.M.G.,
> Claude Phillips, Esq. (*Keeper of the Wallace Collection*)
> Herbert Cook, Esq., F.S.A.,
> James Paton, Esq. (*Director of the Glasgow Art Gallery*)
> Whitworth Wallis, Esq., F.S.A. (*Birmingham Art Gallery*)
> Count Kessler,
> Princess Von Wrede,
> Madame Cohen Gosschalk Bonger,
> Walter Butterworth,
> Clive Bell, Esq.,
> M. Paul Leprieur (*Keeper of the Louvre Pictures*)
> Le Comte Robert de Montesquiou-Fezensac,
> M. Alphonse Kann,
> M. Théodore Duret,
> M. Bernheim Jeune,
> M. Auguste Pellerin,
> M. Octave Mirbeau.

Even such a list as this, however, failed to reassure *The Queen:*

'I am told by Roger Fry (at least, rumour says that Mr Fry wrote the introduction to the catalogue) that the art of the Post-Impressionists is beautiful, serious and significant. Remembering how contemporary critics, almost without exception, hurled abuse at the Impressionists, one is compelled to give a respectful hearing to those who claim to be their successors. Shall we get used to the Post-Impressionists? For myself, having read three times the gospel of the introduction, and having three times visited the exhibition, I recall the Duke of Wellington's famous speech, "My Lords, I read the Bill once; I read the Bill twice; I read the Bill a third time; and, my Lords, I'm damned if I know what the Bill means".' *'The Queen', Nov. 26, 1910*

¶ Several other writers seem to have 'studied the catalogue' without being able to understand it.

'Morning Post',
Nov. 18, 1910 'Sir, — Before giving serious, if dubious, attention to the Post-Impressionists at the Grafton Galleries, I studied with care the introduction to the catalogue. The writer states that "the Post-Impressionists consider the Impressionists too naturalistic", that in Impressionist work "the 'treeness of the tree was not rendered at all; all the emotion and associations such as trees may be made to convey in poetry was omitted". With special interest I read of Gauguin, one of the high priests of the new cult. Gauguin, we are told "felt that modern art had to a great extent neglected the fundamental laws which abstract form and colour can exercise over the imagination of the spectator". . .

'In Gauguin's Tahitian pictures I can discover no beauty of form or colour or design. Anyone who can evolve the treeness of a tree, or the pigginess of a pig (I do not know what the animals actually are) from these Tahitian subjects must be one of the elect, a poet indeed. . .'

¶ And the critic pounced on the fact that one of Gauguin's works had been based on a drawing by Prud'hon. "The sole difference is that which lies between refinement and uncouth ugliness of execution.' He continues:

'Morning Post',
Nov. 18, 1910 'It is significant also that the only two pictures by Van Gogh which are really rhythmic and decorative in design are personal adaptations of a painting by Delacroix and an etching by Rembrandt. . .

'So much for the childish simplicity, the naive emotions and Byzantine outlook of Gauguin and Von Gogh.

'Apart from Manet and — *longo intervallo* — these two painters, the exhibition is worse than worthless, a collection of "hysterical daubs", as Sir William Richmond expresses it, exhibiting various forms of disordered mentality. . . The pity of it is that the British public should be misled by a flowery preface and a committee of imposing names into thinking that this is art; and that our students, our young students, should find on these walls, hung there under the auspices of men whose opinions they have been taught to respect, things that are a justification of their own worst endeavours.'

¶ *The Graphic* gave the exhibition a whole page, with pictures:

'A Criticism of the Exhibition which is drawing the Town to the Grafton Gallery.

'Whatever you may think of the exhibition of the "Post-Impressionists," there is no doubt as to the emotion — (and "emotion", we are told, is of the very essence of "post impressionism") — which it has aroused in the breast of every visitor. Let me give three typical pronouncements, made to me by three several and distinguished artists, not one of whom can be called an academical painter.

'The first writes to me as follows: "Good G-d, has it come to this? Will no one arise and stamp out this fungoid growth that has smothered French art and now is coming here — and will the Press go on encouraging it and destroying every young artist we have? Why, if this stupidity or lunacy is permitted in the graphic arts, is it not permitted in music and literature? I do not think Manet's influence in art is good, but it is a gross insult to him to hang that mass of insincere bosh and ignorant trash in the same gallery with him. The bits of sculpture are beneath contempt, gross examples of charlatanism. I felt so disgusted and angered that I felt I must write you a line to let off the steam!"

'The second — one of the ablest artists of the day, and one of the leading lights of the International Society — was leaving the gallery as I entered it. He volunteered the information — (a) that the exhibition was amusing and interesting; (b) that two or three artists were sincere, and the rest incompetent *farceurs*, who, aware of their own inability ever to do anything on their own account, thought it a capital notion to play the fool and imitate the others, as the only way of attracting attention. . .

'The third — like the last, a rebel in art, although a member of a Royal art society — sauntered up to me as I was examining a horrible work of the unhappy madman Van Gogh, who did himself to death by self-mutilation in the desire to send pieces of himself to his friends. "I am afraid," he said regretfully, "you do not approve." "Approve? One can only deplore the public exhibition of a diseased mind. The man, as we can see, was a lunatic." "Ah," was the reply, "I have the greatest respect for lunacy." That, I thought, explained a good deal in the professed admiration of a certain narrow circle for the new "school" that has arisen. . .

¶ Thus far the eminent critic M. H. Spielmann. But *The Graphic* carried another full-page feature a week later with a text by E. S. Grew of a much more sympathetic tone:

'The Graphic',
Nov. 26, 1910

'An eminent Academician, after surveying the pictures of the Post-Impressionists at the Grafton Gallery, hastened to write to the newspapers in order to express his "fierce feeling of terror lest the youth of England, promising young fellows, might be contaminated there." In this he was following on the heels of an eminent art dealer who had suggested that the pictures ought to be burnt; and he was succeeded by several eminent art critics who have called the painters charlatans, or rotten egotists. One of the results of their chaste con- demnation is that the public, young and old, reckless of contamination, is thronging to the Gallery to make up its own mind about the pictures, or, at any rate, to see them for itself. I am one of this public. I have been five times to see the pictures, and I blush to say that I am impenitent. I dislike the pictures less each time I see them. That is, perhaps, because of the unhealthy contagion of their morbid growth. It is, perhaps, because I am slowly beginning to realise what some of the painters were aiming at. . .

¶ After announcing his 'conversion' to Gauguin, the writer continued:

'The Graphic',
Nov. 26, 1910

'To me some of these pictures convey a good deal, and some of them convey nothing. But I am not such "a rotten egotist" as to believe, because I cannot always see what Cézanne or Van Gogh was driving at, that they were charlatans, incompetent painters, defective in mind. . . It has become possible for me to survey one of Cézanne's rough-hewn landscapes and see in it what he has tried to put there rather than what he left out — to perceive in it the architecture of the everlasting hills and not be troubled about the blades of grass. . . Let us, then be humble, rather than abusive in the presence of these pioneers, who are trying to find a new way of expressing themselves, rather than to make a profit in providing what the public wants. Cézanne, Gauguin, Van Gogh, all died poor. They "made nothing out of it", though their influence has permeated the young French School and the young German School. Some day it will permeate the minds of the other critics who have yet to grow up.'

¶ For 1910 this was pretty good.

110

The most amusing of the humorous attacks on the Post-Impressionists appeared in the *Westminster Gazette:*

'The Most Impressionists'

'*Westminster Gazette*', *Nov. 26, 1910*

'The special private view of the exhibition inaugurated by the committee of the British Most Impressionist Club will be held at the Levana Galleries early next week. . . We are privileged to quote from the unpublished introduction to the catalogue prepared by a member of the committee.

' "The term 'Simplicissimists'," says the author of the Introduction, "which has been applied to this group, does indeed express a quality underlying their diversity; and it is the principal business of this introduction to expand the meaning of that word which sounds too like the protest of a flustered goose to be a happy appellation."

'The movement which has resulted in Simplicissimism can be traced back to a former pronouncement made in connection with an exhibition of the work of more sophisticated painters, who in a tentative fashion adumbrated the truths which this collection establishes. "A good rocking-horse often has more of the true horse about it than an instantaneous photograph of a Derby winner." This fearless statement of a fact unpalatable to the hidebound criticism of 1910 revived in the minds of our most enlightened connoisseurs memories of a drawing that had attracted some attention at a recent sale at Messrs Froebel's last spring. It was signed "Gogo", a name destined to rank first in the short but glorious roll of the world's great pioneers. Gogo's drawing. . . embodies two of the first principles of Simplicissimism.

'The principles were not unrecognised by the more conventional Synthesists. Manet, as is well known, made the first step towards disembarrassing Art of chiaroscuro. The Synthesists completed this emancipation, and seized upon the functional importance of the black line which they put round their mental conception of an emotion. In Gogo the black line is reduced to its essential values. It no longer indicates actual form, as seen by the sophisticated eye of the draughtsman who has passed through the academies; it is consecrated to the more primitive and passionate task of enclosing the most elementary registration of an idea so far known to human expression. . .

'The emotions produced on the mind, not by the horse, but by the quintessential rocking-horse, finds its perfect expression. . .

'But in the work of Beybe we have the last word in Simplicissimism. He has not discarded the black line; he has never known it. Colour is his only medium. And it is applied with the hand, no intervening brush is allowed to raise a barrier between the artist and his means of expression. The colours, too, are of the most elementary nature, their range being restricted to those pigments which the young artist may, in moments of abstraction, convey to his mouth and suffer no harm. Only one work by Beybe is on view at the Levana Galleries. It hangs in kingly isolation on the end wall of the large gallery. Its discoverer named it — wrongly, we believe — *Omelette inachevée.* Tracing it back to the origins of the movement, we find in its greens and browns and yellows a transcription of the emotion consequent on prolonged exercise on the rocking-horse taken by one of limited experience and delicate digestion. It is Beybe's masterpiece, the chef d'oeuvre of the youngest artist in England, for Beybe is only eighteen months old, while Gogo is nearly six.'

¶ The writer could hardly have foreseen the serious interest which, fifty years later, would be taken in Child Art, and in *Tachisme.*

Punch, which made such excellent and sustained fun of the Aesthetes in the 'eighties, makes do with a single reference to the Post-Impressionist Exhibition of 1910. This takes the form of:

'Punch',
Nov. 23, 1910   *'A Sketch at the Grafton Galleries'*
'Time — *Saturday afternoon. Visitors discovered, some making irreverent remarks, but the majority conscientiously endeavouring to understand works which they have been assured by the only people who know represent the Apotheosis of French Art, and, incidentally, the annihilation of all previous artistic standards.*

Miss Pamela Sleyd (a young Art Student, who has not yet found herself,) to Mr Dryden Prewin, *a painter who has long since found himself, but has not, as yet, been discovered by anyone else — as they inspect* Manet's *Portrait of Mlle Lemonnier:* I like the modelling of the nose, but do you know (with some hope of impressing him by her anatomical knowledge), I can't help feeling that her right sleeve has no arm inside it.

Mr Prewin (languidly): And why should it have? Manet, whatever else may be said *against* him, was perhaps the first to introduce the principle of eliminating all detail that is not absolutely essential.

Miss P.S.: But *isn't* a right arm an essential detail?

Mr P: Not if it doesn't appeal to the painter. In that case he simply ignores it.

112

'A Green-eyed Woman.' Painting by Henri Matisse.

'Tahitian Women with Mango Blossoms.' Painting by Paul Gauguin, 1899.
New York Metropolitan Museum of Art.

Miss P.S.: I feel that *must* be right. (*As they pass to* Manet's *"Un Bar aux Folies-Bergère"*). Now this I really do like. Those oranges and the still-life on the counter are quite marvellously real! It isn't possible to put more truth into bottles than Manet has into all those, *is* it?

Mr P. (*pained*): Possibly not. And it is just that realistic treatment that we Synthesists are in revolt against. It is too hopelessly out of date nowadays. We have got so *far* beyond Manet *now*!

Miss P.S. (*an assimilative young person*). Ah, poor dear! Perhaps he was just a little—er— early Victorian.

Mr Ellis Dee (*a young City man with advanced views on Art, to Miss Nebula Mistley*): You may *like* this new style of painting or you may not; but I can tell you *this*: it's like the motor-car, it's come to *stay*. You'll see — everybody'll be doing it in a year or two!

Miss Mistley (*dubiously*): I *wonder*. A good many people don't seem to see anything in it at all.

Mr E.D.: No more they did in Turner or Whistler and all those chaps. And look where *they* are now!

Miss M. I *wish* I knew someone who could *tell* me about these pictures!

Mr E.D. (*hurt*): That is just what I am doing. Why, there are fellows in Johannesburg — fellows who *know*, you know — buying everything they can get hold of. And prices simply *bounding* up.

Miss M. (*impressed*): Really! Then there *must* be *some* thing in it!

Miss Sleyd (*before "Calypso" by M. Maurice Denis*). I *love* that. I do *really*! The colour-effect of those warm pink rocks against the green sea is *too* charming!

Mr Prewin (*drily*): *Much*. These attempts to represent Nature under a pleasing aspect are unspeakably offensive to the eye of all-the-more *advanced* Synthesists.

Miss S. (*feeling sorry she spoke*): Oh, I *quite* see that. And of course as *Art*, a thing like this is simply *nowhere*!

Mrs Molesey (*to Mr Rumbell Wetheram, an eminent Art critic, before some of* M. Gauguin's *Tahitian studies*): Yes, Mr Wetheram, I do feel the rhythm and the emotional significance and all that, but I *should* like to know why some of the figures are drawn with such hard black outlines.

Mr R.W.: Because, my dear lady, Primitive Art makes no attempt to draw what the eye perceives, but—ah—aims at putting a line round a mental conception of the object.

Mrs M.: I *see*. And they're Tahitians, too—*so* interesting! I must get a book about Tahiti and read it up. (*She stops in some stupefaction before a landscape in which the foliage is represented by irregular polygons of Indian red, chrome-green, salmon-pink, and Prussian blue, edged with ochre rims*). Now *really*, Mr Wetheram, I can't quite see why he should paint all his trees such odd shapes and colours!

Mr R.W.: That, dear Mrs Molsey, is purely a matter of *technique*, which, let me remind you, is entirely the Artist's own affair. The Public has no right whatever to dictate to a painter *how* he should render the "tree-ness" of a tree.

Mrs M.: You mean he must be allowed to paint trees as he thinks they *ought* to be?

Mr R.W.: Precisely. And Synthesists have passed from the complexity of the appearance of things to the geometrical simplicity which design demands.

Mrs M.: I *see*. Then of course it's all right.

Miss Platt (*a matter-of-fact young woman, to* Miss Dobbs, *another*): "Le Postier." But why have they given him a *green* beard?

Miss Dobbs. Perhaps he'd been dyeing it just before he was taken.

(*They pass on to a study of a black bottle and a chamber candlestick*). "Le Bougeoir!" Fancy giving it a title like *that*!

Miss Platt (*tolerantly*): Oh well, they *had* to call it something.

A Wife (*to her husband, with enthusiasm*): Oh, George, how I envy the possessors of these glorious things! Don't *you*?

George: Not particularly. They may *have* 'em for all *I* care. But I tell you what, Laura, if you're so keen on 'em I don't mind giving you one for your birthday present. Only mind, you must hang it in your own room.

Laura: It's ever so sweet of you, dear — but I can't let you be so extravagant. You shall give me that sealskin and chinchilla coat I told you about, instead.

Mr Askelon Gathborne (*a frank Philistine, to* Mr Prewin, *who has been trying in vain to evade him*): No! but I say — just look at that picture of a donkey there. Why, it's more like a *wooden* animal than a live one!

Mr Prewin: Possibly; but, as the introduction to the Catalogue very justly observes, "A good rocking-horse often has more of the true horse about it than an instantaneous photograph of a Derby winner."

Mr A.G.: Has it? I should be sorry to back it for a place, all the same!

Mr Prewin: My dear fellow, that's entirely beside the point. But, of course, if you only come here to jeer —

Mr A.G.: Not a bit of it, dear old man. This has opened my eyes, I do assure you. I quite see from the way all this has caught on that there's only one set of men whose work is going to count in this country.

Mr Prewin: I hardly expected you would say so, but you are perfectly right. If English Art is ever to be rescued from its present state of utter degradation, it will be by us Post-Impressionists.

Mr A.G.: I wasn't thinking of *you,* old fellow. I meant those chaps who exhibit on the pavement. But perhaps I'm wrong. Some of 'em *do* seem to have learnt to draw a bit!

[*Mr Prewin is about to reply that, to the Synthesist, Drawing is entirely unimportant in solving the problem of how the artist may best express his own temperament — but decides, on second thoughts, to reserve his pearls for a more appreciative recipient.*]

¶ It is as well to remind ourselves that the new painting created just as much excitement — and indignation — on the other side of the Channel as in England. Already in March, 1910, the *Salon des Indépendants* had offered to the Parisian public an extensive exhibition which included pictures the like of which it had never seen before. The well-known writer Henri de Lavedan, in his *Courrier de Paris,* the column for which he was responsible in *L'Illustration,* gives an amusing account of the impact of the exhibition on an imaginary friend Placide Le Grincheaux:

'It was Placide. Tall, upright, with an exaggerated calm, he entered like a sleep walker without any greeting, his face rigid as of one who has just been insulted, his lips tight, his cheeks pale. He sat down in a heap, tapped his knees three times with his finger tips, hurled away a poor little cushion that had done him no harm, and crossed his legs, one of which he agitated without ceasing, watching me the while with the fixed eyeball of a Japanese who is about to be tortured with needles. For some time he remained thus, prolonging the effect of false calm, until, in answer to one's questioning silence he replied in a voice which he sought to make indifferent: "I have just come from the *Salon des Indépendants*".

' "But, *bon Dieu,* Placide, what were you doing *there*? Is that the milieu for you? Did you have to venture into such a place? It was inevitable that you should come out in a state of collapse. You are unreasonable."

'L'Illustration', Mar. 26, 1910

'He shook his head and using his words deliberately said "I wanted to see. I wanted to see for myself. And for six weeks I have been building up my reserves of patience and sang-froid. Well, this morning, when I went to Cours-La-Reine I was armed, at all points, ready for anything. For anything!. . . And I was stronger than I thought possible. . . Parbleu I had Etna inside me, tempest and yellow fever and colic. I passed from apoplexy to dysentery — but no one, except myself, perceived it. I came and went among these six thousand vomits like a good citizen in the Louvre. . . I made suitable gestures of appraisal and approval. Occasionally I bent down and looked at the pictures, between my legs, to see if they were any better upside down. I pretended it was all quite natural. But now that I have *escaped*, I will allow myself to say that I saw things of which I cannot imagine that any human being would have been capable, or that any human being could be found to frame them, to hang them, to catalogue them or to expose them to public view. . . And now, when I think of them, my calm fills me with remorse. Is it possible that I was present without crying scandal and having myself thrown out. I have only one regret, immense and inconsolable — that I am not a critic. That would relieve my feelings — they overflow. I would say —

' "Go on. It would do you good."

' "I would say that it was the Salon of the Lunatic Asylum, and the Uffizi for Incurables. I would say that the pictures were mediocre placards, brothel frescoes, wallpapers fit for the Boudoir of a Hottentot, Kanaka Rubenses, Art for cannibals and monsters fit only to throw negroes into delirium, nightmare pictures that infect the air, the light, the eyes in one's head. . .'

'*L'Illustration*',   Henri Lavedan takes the part of the reasonable man who ventures to
Mar. 26, 1910 suggest that a *few* of the pictures had something to be said in their favour, but "Placide Le Grincheux" will have none of it. And he threatens that to the next *Salon des Indépendants* he will send a picture himself. "And they will accept it!" "I don't doubt it. What will the subject be?"

' "I don't know yet. But it is of no importance anyway, for picture won't represent anything. No one will ever know what it is. No one! Ever!"

' "Shall you give it a title?"

' "Yes, but it doesn't matter what. *Humanity, Nirvana, Smile on the Pacific, A Wind in the Wood, Apocalypse.* And I shall sign it with

116

'Blackfriars.' Painting by André Derain, 1910. Glasgow, City Art Gallery.

A donkey painting a picture for the Salon des Independents, and, below, the result as exhibited.
From 'L'Illustration', 1910.

a foreign name — the name of a fjord. And the lovers of the incomprehensible will not fail to discover great beauties in it. X., the famous critic of the *avant-garde* reviews will write as follows: '*Smile on the Pacific* by Kryüs Mnzcsötskp is a revolution which leaves us speechless with admiration. Vibrant son of Norway, Kryüs Mnzcsötskp, hitherto unknown, looks upon the world with infinite compassion. He is an Apostle. He paints with his great heart' — and similar twaddle. Then I, having lapped up all this like a cooling drink, will take up my pen and I will write to X. . .

'Monsieur et eminent maître,

It was not with my big heart that I painted *Smile on the Pacific* about which you have said so many obliging things. No. The picture was painted by me, blindfold, with pots of jam and squashed fruit. I paint out of the jampot. And under the very French name of Kryüs Mnzcsötskp is hidden the name of

Your obedient servant
Le Grincheux'

' "Placide, you will not perpetrate this art student's joke."

' "Indeed I will. I will show them up."

'He left without my having persuaded him to listen to reason. But I hope that a year from now. . .'

¶ It would have been strange if so fertile a suggestion had fallen on stony ground. The very next month the magazine carried an account of a joke perpetrated by persons unknown of which the paper *Fantasio* published an hilarious account. It had indeed been in preparation before Henri Lavedan's article appeared, for some weeks previously a manifesto had been issued in the following terms:

'Excess is itself a force, it is said, the only force. The scene is never too hot, the sky too green, the distant sea too red, nor darkness dark enough. Let us ravage our absurd museums and tread underfoot the disgraceful routine pictures of our painters of chocolate boxes. . . No more lines, no more gradations, no more craftsmanship! Something startling, at all cost!

Joachim-Raphael Boronali.!

A week later a picture entitled *And the Sun went to sleep over the Adriatic* formed part of the *Salon des Indépendants* and passed unnoticed among the crowd of equally surprising canvases. The promotors of the joke then revealed the fact (which they had taken care to have witnessed and recorded by a Commissioner for Oaths) that the picture had been painted — by a donkey. A brush charged with colour had been held to its tail and it had been induced to wag its tail in the proximity of a canvas. *L'Illustration* published a photograph of the picture and another one of the donkey painting it. Delight of all those who thought that all the new painting was just a bad joke. And the moral — if there is one — is that a considerable number of the pictures which caused such hilarity in London and Paris in 1910 are now the treasured possessions of the great museums of the world.

The 'Norseman' Bedroom Set, advertised by Hewetson's, 1905, together with two rush-set chairs, for £11 10s.

CHAPTER VI

INTERNAL COMBUSTION

IF ANYONE had informed an inhabitant of these islands at the close of the nineteenth century that in fifty years time it would be possible to walk about all day in London and never see a single horse, he would have been set down as a madman. No-one had any idea of the extent of the revolution which was about to commence. The bicycle, of course, was already well known, and was regarded as a dangerous innovation, since it made parental control almost impossible. The possibilities of the motor-car were hardly taken seriously. It is interesting to find Alfred C. Harmsworth, later Lord Northcliffe, apologizing for the word Motoring. 'Motoring (he says) — for the word will have to be accepted and recognised — is. . . sport.' The sentence occurs in the anthology, *Motors and Motor-Driving*, which he brought out in 1902. It formed part of the series known as the *Badminton Library* which is itself sufficient evidence that the sporting possibilities of the motor-car were uppermost in everybody's mind, for the *Badminton Library* was devoted entirely to sports of various kinds.

The provisions of the 1861 Locomotives on Highways Act which laid down a maximum speed limit of four miles per hour and required that a self-propelled vehicle on the roads must always be preceded by a man with a red flag were not repealed until 1896, so it is not surprising that progress (in both senses of the term) had, before that date, been extremely slow. The petrol engine, however, had already been developed, especially in France, and in the following year there had actually been a road race from Paris to Bordeaux and back, the winning vehicle covering the ground at an average speed of fifteen miles per hour. *The Autocar*, the first English motoring journal, was founded in November, 1895, and then *The Automotor and Horseless Vehicle Journal*. The interest aroused was not purely theoretical:

119

'An exhibition of motor vehicles was held at the Imperial Institute, London, in 1896. At the same time companies having prodigious capitals were floated and when, on November 14, 1896, motor vehicles were allowed to run on the roads, popular enthusiasm had been thoroughly aroused, and the start of what was virtually a race from London to Brighton on that day was witnessed by an enormous crowd."

¶ Hopes ran high. It was all very well to travel by train; you might even pass through beautiful country, but you were still obstinately tied to the rails on the track originally constructed.

'The motor-car may become a land yacht with more variety of scenery than its marine prototype, and an absence of the frequently disconcerting motion peculiar to the sea.'

¶ A sport itself, motoring was going to be useful for other kinds of sport also. There were, for example, the 'advantages of a motor for fishing'.

'If you have driven a long distance the horses must have rest, and very often have been put up at a farm some way from the water, whereas the motor is left on the road at the spot nearest the stream, and should you decide in favour of some other kind of sport, or a return home, you can change the rod for the gun, or rejoin your wife, go back to your garden, or possibly to "bridge" or "ping-pong".'

¶ For shooting, the motor was even more convenient; it was even possible to shoot (not from the saddle but) from the driving seat:

'As to wildfowling, you can go to your punt more rapidly in the morning, and an extra ten minutes in bed will be welcomed by anyone who has had experience of early punting. You can also, when the opportunity presents itself, shoot your Golden Plover from the motor-car without any chance of your horse suddenly bolting at the discharge, and wood-pigeons and cock partridges later in the season can be brought down from the road after a little practice with the greatest ease, without rising from your seat. Rabbits and hares at night will run sometimes for a quarter of a mile before your acetylene lamps, and you can pick them off in the same way with your gun;

120

oftentimes with your car you will unintentionally run over panicked rabbits or hares who dash frantically under your wheel. It is always worth while stopping to see whether you have secured your quarry; and although the mode of killing may result in the hare being more fit for soup than for roast, at times you will be lucky, as I have been, and a head that its mother would not know is the only damage done.'

¶ The same enthusiast had his doubts, however, about the petrol engine for 'Town':

'I am inclined to think that for town work electricity or steam will be the main propulsive agents. . . and as broughams and landaus are largely used for night work, the same power that produces the motion will produce also a most brilliant light for your lamps, light your cigarette, and heat your foot-warmer.' *Hon. John Scott Montagu, M.P. ibid, 1902*

¶ Even if he was wrong about 'propulsive agents', the Hon John Scott-Montagu shows himself singularly prophetic in the second half of his paragraph.

The *usefulness* of motors had already made an impression on wide-awake journalists like R. D. Blumenfeld:

'I saw Claude Hay, brother of Lord Kinnoul, in Dover Street sitting in a large motor-car with a tonneau body. He informs me he is off to Leicestershire to help a friend in the election, and has adopted this novel vehicle as a method of taking people to the polls. A motor maker tells me that he will not be surprised if motor-cars are used in future as much as horses. The *Daily Express* has issued a warning on the dangers of motoring, for these machines are not to be handled on a casual acquaintance.' *R.D.B's 'Diary', Oct. 1, 1900*

¶ The motor-car, indeed, was generally regarded with suspicion. Its excessive speed caused grave misgivings:

'Lord Carnarvon is becoming a public nuisance as a motor scorcher. He was summoned again to-day. Clouds of dust as high as the neighbouring trees, said the police witness, rose up as his car whizzed along the road. By careful timing and measurements the superintendent calculated the speed at a mile in two and a half minutes, or twenty four miles an hour! *R.D.B's 'Diary', Oct. 1, 1900*

'Frank Butler, the hon. secretary of the Automobile Club in Piccadilly, is very angry with the police. They hauled him before the New Romney magistrates yesterday for scorching in his new Panhard, at eighteen miles per hour; but he got off.'

¶ The Highest in the Land began to take an interest in the new contraption:

A Foreign Resident.
'Society in the New Reign', 1904
'In 1896 the motor was introduced to the English public at an international show of horseless carriages at the Crystal Palace. The novelty, the complexity, and, above all, the costliness of the new invention, soon secured for it acceptance at Court. In his youth, Edward VII, and his friend, the Duke of Sutherland, had often acted as amateur engine-drivers on English railways. The warm welcome given by the Sovereign to these latest apparitions on his own highway implied therefore a sort of return to a first love. Whether in town or country, the motor has become as much a part of a courtier's baggage as is the cigarette case. The secret of the thing's popularity is its intricacy, quite as much as its expensiveness. The King not only knows all about the mechanism and the working of the locomotive himself, but he expects his fashionable subjects to be able to discuss its internal arrangements with the same knowledge that they once possessed or affected of the pedigree of the royal thoroughbreds.'

¶ The King's enthusiasm was contagious:

'The Sketch',
Jan. 21, 1903
'Another Royal Convert to Automobilism
'The Prince of Wales, who has hitherto seemed somewhat indifferent to the charms of the horseless carriage, is reported to have changed his mind, for he has ordered a motor-car of exactly the same size, pattern and horse-power as that which was built to King Edward's order some time ago. Those interested in the great new industry should feel very grateful to the many Royal personages who were among the first to recognise the value of horseless vehicles. Among these Royal personages our Sovereign stands easily first; still, in this, as in so many other matters, His Majesty has always shown sound sense, and he does not belong to the group of motorists who would like to see the horse as extinct as the dodo. Hitherto the Prince of Wales has been an enthusiastic cyclist, and, unlike most sailors, he is quite at home on horseback. Yet, none of the Princesses have followed

the Queen's example and invested in a horseless victoria, but the time may come when even Princesses will regard horses as unattainable luxuries.'

¶ It was plain that the reigning monarch liked the horseless carriage more and more:

'The King, in his capacity of leading the fashion, has given an order for a new all-British automobile of nearly double the horse-power of his present carriage, in which he has travelled more than once between Marlborough House and Windsor as fast as it is done by train. The new carriage, which is to be made by Daimler, is to hold six people, with room beside the driver for a footman. It is to be of the double phaeton type, and will cost somewhere in the neighbourhood of £1,000.'

R.D.B's 'Diary', Dec. 23, 1901

¶ Edward VIII had every right to be known as 'The Motoring Monarch'.

'The King usually had the Mercédès sent ahead when he went to Marienbad or Biarritz. Although he suffered many inconveniences in the shape of minor breakdowns, his enthusiasm did not cool, and finally, in 1905, he solved the problem by engaging his own 'motor engineer', a Mr Stamper, who sat on the front seat with the chauffeur ready to leap out if anything went wrong. Whenever the King successfully completed a journey, no matter how short, he always stepped out saying "A very good r-run, Stamper, a very good r-run, indeed!" '

Virginia Cowles. 'Edward VII and His Circle', 1956

¶ Certainly the driver of a car in those early days needed to be something of a technician:

'A prime difficulty of the establishment of a motor-car is the chauffeur or engineer. The perfect motor servant should be a combination of gentleman and engineer. He is a new type of man, and will require the wages of other engineers. I do not think that a competent cool-headed, skilful, well-mannered engineer will ever be obtainable for 30s. a week.'

Alfred C. Harmsworth, in 'Motors and Motor Driving', 1902

¶ It wasn't everybody who approved of these developments. *The Sketch* published an illustrated interview with a bus driver, in which the old jarvey expressed himself as follows (one cannot help feeling that what he actually said must have been somewhat expurgated):

'The Sketch',
Oct. 19, 1904

'As for motors, jest cast yer eye over that blinkin' arrangement! Cross between a perambulator and a steam roller; that's wot I call it. Give me a 'orse any day of the week. This off-side un's a bit of a jibber, but when he drops unexpected 'e don't need a injun-driver to start 'im again. . . Ah well, Sir, the business 'll last out my time, and then I'll make room for the lady bus-drivers, an' airships, and wot not. The papers'll make good reading them days.'

¶ All the horse-bus drivers were of the same opinion:

R.D.B's 'Diary',
Dec. 4, 1901

'I had a prolonged chat with an omnibus driver all the way from the City to Sloane Square. The old man must be over seventy, but looks quite young. They now have a 'Busmen's Union', and they are beginning to agitate for a day off now and then without being fined for it. They work 365 days a year, and think that too much. Besides, the pay is bad — never above £2 a week, including extras. Out of this rents have to be paid at an average of 7/6d a week, and food, so that there is not much left over for beer.'

¶ Most of the cab-drivers, too, hated the new-fangled contraptions:

R.D.B's 'Diary',
Dec. 15, 1901

'My hansom cab-driver who calls for me every morning at two o'clock after we have sent the paper to press informed me that his brother, who is also a cabman is taking lessons in automobile driving in the hope that some day he will be able to drive a horseless cab. I told him it would be a good idea if he, too, took lessons, but he shouted through the opening at the top that he wasn't going to waste his money on such foolishness.

' "Them automobiles," he said, "are all right as playthings, but you can't depend on 'em. Besides, they are dangerous, and you can't guarantee getting your fare to the place he wants to reach. You'll never beat my old 'orse."

'I wonder if he is right.'

¶ Few people in the first decade of the century had any notion of the transformation which was taking place before their eyes:

James Bone in
'The Age of
Extravagance', 1956

'The whole appearance of the London street suffered a change more sudden and more drastic in Edward the Seventh's short reign than any change in a generation in London's long history. When he was

124

bove: King Edward,
hen Prince of Wales,
in Lord Montagu's
? h.p. Daimler, 1900.

elow: King Edward
vith Wilbur Wright.

A lady in Hyde Park, 1906.

crowned the horse was as necessary and pervading a part of the capital as it had been at any time since Boadicea had driven her team across Londinium. When Edward's reign ended the horse bus had almost vanished and the hansom cab and fourwheeler lingered as curiosities while the cart-horse and van horse were a dwindling remnant of their old strength.'

¶ The same author notes:

'The hansom cab lingered much longer, indeed a magnate of the Cable and Wireless Company had a smart one in the last years of the Second War when petrol restrictions were at their worst, and elderly Londoners would cock their ears as they heard the old clip-clop, clip-clop, jingle jingle, arising on the streets again. But in 1912 there were only four hundred of them in London of the 7600 that pervaded the town at the turn of the century. Half a dozen stragglers were on the cab rank opposite the Café Royal in Regent Street in the 'twenties, and later and on rainy nights a hansom would wait outside the Garrick Club in Covent Garden, in case Sir Squire Bancroft thought of driving home to Albany. *James Bone in 'The Age of Extravagance', 1956*

'The drivers were a stiff-necked, sporting class of men, and had they accepted the taximeter they might have made a long fight of it as the Paris fiacres drivers did, but prudence was not their style. "Toss you for the fare — double or quits!" was a challenge they rarely refused. Some of them learnt to drive motor cabs but most of them went down, so to speak, with their whips flying.'

¶ It was not that the 'Powers that Be' gave the early motorists any encouragement. The authorities, especially the Local Authorities, were distinctly hostile, What seems now the very reasonable proviso that all motor vehicles should be 'registered' was much resented by the devotees of the new sport:

'The Motors Act of the present year and the Local Board Regulations by which the Act is to be administered have left the automobilist few weapons wherewith the combat his numerous foes. But, either by malice aforethought or by an oversight, the draughtsman of the Act has left one loophole, which I would suggest that automobilists should not neglect to take advantage of. . . The Act of 1903 sets forth that the car owners must register their cars with *a* County Council or Borough *'The Sketch', Dec. 9, 1903*

Council but does not specify that the registration shall be made with the particular County Council or Borough Council in whose area they reside. Here, at least, is a weapon ready to our hands. Within the next few days every car in the country will be registered. Let their owners see to it that not one halfpenny of those fees passes into the hands of the Councils of such counties as Surrey, Hunts, Sussex, and others upon whose roads and by whose instructions automobilists have suffered most virulent persecution in the past. I would suggest that cars should be registered with the Councils who have behaved well towards motorists, as the London County Council and those of Kent, Notts, Herts, and Hants, among others.'

¶ Truly the early motorists were hardy and determined fellows:

The Rt Hon. Sir John H. A. MacDonald, K.C.B. in 'Motors and Motor Driving', 1902

'For the sake of any readers of Badminton who have never tested the fascinations of autocarism, I should like to recount some incidents which show that when the motorist's blood is up he will go through hardships equal to any that the most ardent votary of any sport will face. Mr. Rolls, driving a car from Paris in 1900, [had] the following mishaps: joints of waterpipe gone, bad junction to be replaced, bad cut in tyre of off front wheel; chain loose, burst of back tyre, mackintosh loose and wound up in shreds on pump, leaking cylinder, whole upper ends of cylinders red-hot, pump jammed, leaks in radiator pipes, ignition tube burst twice, oil on the brakes, another tyre burst.

'These were surely trials enough to break the back of resolution, but what the Anglo-Saxon and the Gael will do and dare can be appreciated when I mention that all these troubles were encountered in mid-winter, sometimes in blinding snow and always in well nigh Arctic frost, most of them happening between dusk on one day and six in the morning of the next day, with icicles hanging from hair and beard.'

¶ The machine itself was still far from perfect. Even accessories like tyres were in the experimental stage:

C. L. Freeston. in 'Motors and Motor Driving', 1902

'With all its drawbacks, however, the pneumatic tyre is almost indispensable for most types of motor-carriage. In speed, in comfort, in saving the mechanism from pronounced concussion, and in facility of steering, there is no question as to the superiority of the air chamber as compared with solid rubber. The curious fact, moreover, remains

126

that in the very circumstances which emphasise the weak points of the pneumatic tyre the solid would be even worse. High speed and a heavy car form a combination which tests the pneumatic tyre severely, but the solid tyre in like circumstances can with difficulty be kept on the wheel at all.'

¶ Some of the devices of the early designers sound today more ingenious than safe. For example:

'*The Sprag.* — This is an adjunct fitted to most cars. In the early stages of driving, it is as well always to leave this down when ascending steep hills, so that in the event of the novice missing his change of speed, or if through any other cause the car tried to run backwards, it would be arrested in its early movement and damage obviated.   *S. F. Edge and Charles Jarrott. in 'Motors and Motor Driving', 1902*

'It should be borne in mind, however, that the sprag should be dropped before the car actually starts to run backwards; otherwise the momentum on the car may induce it to jump the sprag to the danger of the passengers and the great annoyance of the chauffeur, who finds that before being able to proceed he will have either to detach the sprag or cut it away. We remember seeing the owner of a large motor carriage in this predicament. After taking the precaution of having a solid sprag fitted, he spent some hours beneath his car in an endeavour to cut through a solid inch and a half of iron with a very blunt hack saw.

'Immediately the necessity for the use of the sprag has disappeared, it is as well to pull it up at once by the cord.'

¶ Useful advice was given on

'*Using the Brakes.* — A very good rule to follow is that under ordinary circumstances the brakes should not be used with such violence as to cause the wheels to skid, or to occasion a jar to those driving in the carriage. If this is carefully observed the vehicle will last much longer.'   *S. F. Edge and Charles Jarrott. in 'Motors and Motor Driving', 1902*

¶ And advice less useful — indeed, suicidal — on

'*Going round Corners.* — Always keep to your right side, remembering that in all probability you will find some other vehicle coming towards you from the opposite direction.'   *S. F. Edge and Charles Jarrott in 'Motors and Motor Driving', 1902*

¶ The cyclists who, for a decade, had been monarchs of the road, were a great nuisance:

S. F. Edge and Charles Jarrott (Source?) 1902
'Lady cyclists are or used to be a great danger, for when a motor was heard approaching them from behind, they usually fell off their bicycles, apparently in terror; but this distressing spectacle is now comparatively seldom seen.'

¶ Some ladies added considerably to the dangers by their own attire:

R.D.B's 'Diary', Oct. 2, 1900
'Ladies who persist in riding bicycles in long skirts must expect to get hurt. I saw a handsome Junoesque figure today dressed in laces and flounces, riding on a bicycle in Sloane Street. Her skirt became entangled and she came down with a crash. My tailor tells me that women flatly refuse to wear short skirts for fear of exposing their legs.'

¶ Pedestrians — and horses — were equally tiresome:

Rt Hon. Sir Francis Jeune, K.C.B. (Source?) 1902
'The old people seem to manifest more curiosity than the young. The school children, it is true, usually line the road and utter shouts of which I have never been able to discern the significance, or seek the delight, to me, I confess, wholly unintelligible, of throwing their caps under the advancing car. But when a car stops old people invariably surround it with criticism and inquiry. The witticism, "Seems to me, measter, your horse can't get on without drinking any more than ourn", never fails, and many an old lady gladly accepts the experience of a ride to the end of her village and back again. I wish I could add that horses in the country manifested more indifference than their owners. But I am afraid it is just the old agricultural horse, who looks wise enough to know better, that exhibits an unexpected excitement, unless indeed he is standing unlooked after by his master, in which case his indifference to the passing car is usually beyond all praise.'

¶ The equine race certainly found the early manifestations of internal combustion most alarming:

R.D.B's 'Diary', Oct. 29, 1900
'Accidents due to horses shying at motor cars are far too frequent. Many motorists refrain from slowing down or stopping their engines when they approach horses on the road. . . Sir Walter Gilbey, who drives about the Essex roads in the Stansted district in a phaeton, with

Above: Irish A.C. Trials, 1908.

Below: Tourist Trophy, Isle of Man, 1905. Drawing a car to the starting point.

Above: A typical landaulette of 1906.

Below: Miss Ridge Jones at Brooklands, 1908.

outriders, complains bitterly that his horses run great risks whenever a motor comes along. He never drives on the main Cambridge road now for fear of meeting a motor car.'

¶ An Irish gentleman who was both an ardent motorist and an M.F.H. was ready, however, with a solution:

'There was sound wisdom in the recent decision of a court of justice in Paris, where it was held that it is the duty of owners of horses to have them trained to meet motors.

Hercules Langrishe, 'Master of the Kilkenny Foxhounds', (Source?) 1902

'The difficulty which has presented itself has been how horse-owners may obtain opportunities of training their horses to meet motor vehicles. The Automobile Club has already given demonstrations at the Ranelagh and other clubs near London of how horses may best be made tractable, and has advertised these opportunities. If any owner of restive horses will apply to the secretary of the Automobile Club, that gentleman will doubtless be able to arrange that some motorist in the neighbourhood will drive his car to the horse-owner's establishment and there train the restive animals. Members of the Club have done this over and over again, and motorists generally are most anxious to assist in this direction, thus overcoming prejudice.

'A well-known nobleman took the precaution to send his horses to Coventry, in order that they might reside in the centre of motordom, and they quickly became used to cars.

'The process of training is extremely simple: the horse should be stood in a paddock and the motor vehicle driven round it in gradually decreasing circles.'

¶ The motorist still had many troubles. One of the difficulties was to see the road in wet or misty weather, the windscreen wiper not having yet been invented:

'For station work in the country I would rather recommend — and I am supposing myself writing for those who have now a stable of some half a dozen horses — a covered as well as an open motor, or perhaps a motor which can have a top fitted on to it when the weather is bad. Ladies do not like arriving at tea-time with their fringes out of curl, or the feathers in their hats drooping or facing the wrong way; but always remember that the driver should be quite free, and that nothing is more dangerous on a misty day, and especially at night,

Hon. John Scott-Montagu, M.P. (Source?) 1902

than a glass frame on which the rain will fall and eventually almost obscure the road from his gaze. The man who drives the motor must always have the best possible view of the road, just as on the footplate of a locomotive every driver knows that in times of mist or rain the difficulty of seeing through the windows of the cab is immensely increased, and careful drivers prefer to have their heads round the edge.'

¶ The open car was certainly a menace to ladies, especially when they were clad in the elaborate clothes of the period:

Lady Jeune.
in 'Motors and
Motor Driving', 1902
'In most of the sports and pastimes of women the dress they assume is arranged with a view to adding to their charms, and in nearly every case it can be both pretty and serviceable. In croquet, lawn tennis, skating, hunting, driving, or bicycling, the dress worn by women may be excessively becoming, as it can be made to show off the figure, and the hat or headgear is generally a delightful frame to the face — indeed, the fact that the athletic costumes of women are so picturesque is possibly one of the reasons which have made out-door sports so popular among them.

'In the case of motor-driving or riding there are two things only to be considered: how a woman can keep herself warm in winter and not be suffocated by the dust in summer without making herself very unattractive.'

¶ There could be no doubt about it, lady motorists needed to be both hardy and determined:

Lady Jeune.
in 'Motors and
Motor Driving', 1902
'Alas! if women are going to motor, and motor seriously — that is to say, use it as a means of locomotion — they must relinquish the hope of keeping their soft peach-like bloom. The best remedy is cold water and a rough towel, and that not used sparingly, in the morning before they start. There is one other, the last, but perhaps the hardest concession a woman can make if she is going to motor, and that is that she must wear glasses — not small dainty glasses, but veritable goggles. They are absolutely necessary both for comfort and the preservation of the eyesight; they are not becoming, but then, as I have tried to point out, appearance must be sacrificed if motor-driving is to be thoroughly enjoyed. Those who fear any detriment to their good looks had best content themselves with a quiet drive in the Park,

130

leaving to the more ardent motorist the enchanting sensation of flying along the lanes and roads of our lovely country.'

¶ Was motoring good for the health? The question was earnestly debated, and eminent physicians were brought in to give their opinion:

'I am asked to write concerning the relation to health of driving motor vehicles. Personally, I have found my drives to improve my general health. The easy jolting which occurs when a motor-car is driven at a fair speed over the highway conduces to a healthy agitation; it "acts on the liver", to use a popular phrase, which means only that it aids the peristaltic movements of the bowels and promotes the performance of their functions; thus accomplishing the good in this respect which arises from riding on horseback. Horse-riding has, however, the advantages of necessitating exercise of the muscles of the legs. This is one of the disadvantages of motoring, but I have found that it may be to some extent overcome by alighting at the end of a drive of twenty miles, and running smartly for about two hundred or three hundred yards. I make this a practice in relation to my motor drives. Remaining seated in one position, with little or no opportunity of moving the lower limbs, renders them very liable to stiffness or cramp, especially in the case of elderly drivers, whose joints are less mobile and flexible than those of the young. The exhilaration which accompanies driving in a motor is particularly helpful to people who are somewhat enervated. I have known instances of ladies suffering from defective nerve power who have derived great benefit from the invigorating and refreshing effect of meeting a current of air caused by driving in an automobile.'

Sir Henry Thompson, Bt., F.R.C.S. in 'Motors and Motor Driving', 1902

¶ The Edwardians, given as they were to habitual over-eating, were conscious of another danger — the danger of 'putting on weight':

'Now let me give a few words of caution. The vigorous man who has been used to take exercise on horseback, on his bicycle, or on his legs, must beware less the fascination of motoring lead him to give up his physical exercise. Unless he systematically maintains habits of muscular exertion he may find that he is putting on flesh, becoming flabby, and generally losing condition. Whether he possesses a motor or not, he must use his muscles regularly and sufficiently if he desires to preserve his health. The eyes also should be carefully protected by

Sir Henry Thompson, Bt., F.R.C.S. in 'Motors and Motor Driving', 1902

glasses with silk attached to them partially covering the cheeks, whereby the small flies and dust which accompany road travel in the summer-time, and the cold winds of winter may be excluded.'

¶ The far-sighted saw that the coming of the internal combustion engine had set in motion the wheels of a real social revolution.

Virginia Cowles.
'Edward VII and
His Circle', 1954
'The feeling of change was apparent everywhere. The invention of the internal combustion machine had brought revolutionary ideas in its wake. Soon they would affect the factories, the land, the world forces. Already they had made an impact on the social world. The drawing-room of 1909 had a very different look from the Victorian setting King Edward had inherited from his mother. The motor-car was establishing "the week-end" habit as a national institution. The carriages in Hyde Park were thinning out and the Sunday church parade threatened to become a thing of the past.'

¶ It was natural that old-fashioned people should regret these developments:

V. Sackville-West.
'The Edwardians',
1930
'Standing upon the refuge waiting to cross Park Lane, he had seen her drive out of Stanhope Gate in her victoria with the smart, high-stepping cobs and James the tiger sitting very straight with folded arms upon the box, and his heart had swelled with emotion as he took off his hat. A nice turn-out, that, he had thought, watching the carriage bowl down Great Stanhope Street; and what a pretty thing it is, he thought, to see a lovely woman drive in London behind a well-matched pair. Lord Roehampton had no use for the motors that were beginning to invade the streets. He crossed into the Park and continued his walk, feeling that all the creases had been smoothed out of him. The Park was bright with tulips and the lilac-bushes near Rotten Row were all in flower; people were strolling or sitting under trees, watching the carriages go by; it seemed to Lord Roehampton that everything was specially animated and gay, that the women were like moving flowers in their light frocks, and that the men in their black coats were an admirable foil, their spats whiter than usual, and their top-hats more than usually glossy.'

¶ It was a pity, of course, that motoring could not be reserved for the Upper Classes. The general public was beginning to be interested, as can be seen from the music-hall ditties of the period:

132

A veil fitted with spectacles.

A close-fitting mask.

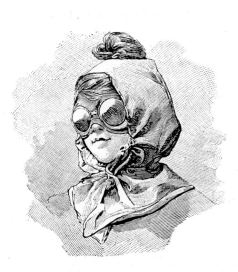

A combined mask and hood.

'La plus jolie femme de Paris.'

MOTOR FASHIONS IN PARIS 1903

Above: M. Guillon prepares to make an attempt with the Guillon and Clonzy aeroplane on Epsom Downs, April 11th, 1907.

Below: The Hon. C. S. Rolls in his machine on the Aero Club's ground at Eastchurch, 1910.

'There were many songs, of course, from the start about the *Christopher Pulling.* *'They Were Singing',* 1952 "horseless carriage". *The Motor-car,* set to the well-known tune *Funiculi, Funicula,* was sung in 1897:

' "The other day we had a short vacation,
    I and Mamma, also Papa;
We fixed on Brighton as our destination,
    By motor-car, by motor-car.
We started off from Camberwell 'hooraying',
    With loud 'hurrah!' also 'ha-ha!'
The people in the road stood still, and saying,
    'Oh, there they are! a motor-car!'

' "Puffing, snorting, so peculiar!
People shouting, 'They don't know where they are!'
They laughed at us — they laughed at Pa!
They laughed at me — they laughed at Ma!
When we went to Brighton on our famous motor-car!" '

'And for another ten years or more there were few about; they were still in the experimental stage, and if you set out on a journey in a motor-car you might get there or you might not. Indeed, as late as 1914 the song *He'd have to Get Under, Get Out and Get Under,* seemed still quite normal. You wrapped yourself up, if you were a man, in heavy coat and peak-cap, complete with goggles and leggings; the ladies wore long dust-coats, with large veils right over their hats, and tied beneath their chins.

'In 1901 there was *Oh, Flo!* ("the great motor-car song"), by Harry Dacre, author of Daisy Bell and scores of other successes:
' "Oh, Flo! Why do you go riding alone on your motor-car?
There's room for two, me and you, on your elegant motor-car."

¶ But what did all this matter when the convenience of the new mode of locomotion was becoming increasingly apparent?

'A British householder living in the middle of Kent — say thirty *J. St. Loe Strachey. (Source?)* 1902 miles from the coast — is going to take his family to the seaside for the usual three weeks. If it were possible for the householder to engage a light motor-car for himself and his wife and eldest daughter, a motor-brake for the children and servants, and a light steam-van for the lug-

133

gage, bicycles, buckets and spades, and perambulators, which would load up, not against time, but quietly at the front and back doors, and unload at the hotel or lodgings, what a vast deal of fuss and worry would be saved!'

¶ Besides, there was still the sporting element to be considered:

The Rt Hon. Sir John H. A. Macdonald, K.C.B. in 'Motors and Motor Driving', 1902

'And now, as a last word, let me say what I believe will be said by all who have enjoyed this new sport: that we value it for two reasons. The one is that it will open up to the community many advantages both social and commercial. The other I feel very strongly. It is that it extends in a delightful manner the range of one's personal friendships, and promotes pleasant social intercourse of both sexes, in healthy enjoyment of fresh air and cheerful surroundings. May we continue to be a friendly guild. Pioneers must always keep close together. Union overcomes difficulty, and our motto should be:
"Double the pleasure that friendship doth divide."'

¶ So much for motoring, but the Devil of Internal Combustion was not content to conquer the roads; he aspired to conquer the skies. Many of the pioneers of motoring were pioneers of aviation also. We catch a glimpse of one of the most eminent of them in a note by Blumenfeld:

R.D.B's 'Diary', Dec. 7, 1901

'This morning I met the Hon. Charlie Rolls, inseparable from his autocar, on his way to the Crystal Palace, where he is to fly this afternoon. . . Mr Rolls told me that the Automobile Club are going to propose that they will no longer oppose the compulsory fixing of indentification numbers or letters on autocars provided that the absurd twelve mile limit is abolished.'

¶ The same admirable observer had been watching developments from the beginning of the century:

R.D.B's 'Diary', Oct. 3, 1900

'I had a whole hour with old Sir Hiram Maxim at lunch today at the Café Royal. The old man drank water and ate some sort of fancy bread that he had in a paper bag. Every now and then he would suck away at a glass contraption which he called his anti-asthma pipe. He said he had spent £17,000 in trying to make a flying machine, but the thing no sooner rose from the ground than it fell down. As for navigable balloons, he agrees with the late Duke of Argyll that man can never overcome the natural laws that condemn all buoyant bodies to an inertia that makes them useless. He does not think Count Zeppelin will have much success with his forthcoming experiments.'

¶ As early as 1894 Hiram Maxim had constructed an aeroplane which would probably have been successful if he had been able to obtain a light engine. He was compelled to use a steam engine. Later, with petrol engines, he was more successful. The internal combustion engine indeed was the necessary tool the world was waiting for. The power plant which finally did the trick was a 4-cylinder, 12-horse-power petrol motor. It was fitted to the machine which Wilbur and Orville Wright had been constructing and which was launched into the air at Kitty Hawk on 17th December, 1902. 'The flight lasted only twelve seconds', wrote Orville later, 'but it was, nevertheless, the first in the history of the world in which a machine carrying a man had raised itself by its own power into the air in full flight, had sailed forward without reduction of speed, and had finally landed at a point as high as that from which it started.'

This epoch-making event created singularly little interest:

'In the United States, of all countries, one would have supposed that the invention of the practical aeroplane — the true inauguration of the air age — would have been heralded by the biggest "ballyhoo" of history. Far from it. What happened, or rather what did not happen, seems to us now quite incredible. To start with, well-meaning but completely misleading reports found their way into the newspapers; reports written and rewritten by men who had not witnessed the flights. The Press and public dismissed the reports as just so many more crackpot items amongst a host of routine absurdities in a bustling and exuberant epoch. One can hardly blame the disillusioned editors. They had heard too many stories of flying-machines which would not fly; and they had been told on the highest scientific authority that it was impossible for men to ascend in powered heavier-than-air machines.' *C. H. Gibbs-Smith. 'A History of Flying', 1953*

¶ Even three years later 'the respected magazine *Scientific American* made uproarious fun of reports they had received of the Wright's flying; but sent no one to investigate'. It was not until 1908 that the world really awoke to what was happening.

C. H. Gibbs-Smith. 'A History of Flying', 1953 'The year 1908 was the "annis mirabilis" of world aviation, for the Wright Brothers flew in public for the first time. While Orville astounded his countrymen at home, Wilbur caused a sensation in Europe. . . With poetic justice, the European, not the American, public saw the first flight. Wilbur accepted from Léon Bollée, a motor-car manufacturer, an offer of factory space to assemble his machine at Le Mans, some 125 miles from Paris. . . The Paris Press played a "dare" game, and accused him of bluffing. But Wilbur refused to hurry. "Le bluff continue," cried one paper. However, on 8 August, having transported his machine to the nearby Hunaudières racecourse, Wilbur prepared for his first flight. Everything was strange to the onlookers: Wilbur in his cap and stiff collar and tie; the biplane which looked like the glider the French aviators had copied four years before; and the launching rail and derrick. Then Wilbur took his place alone on the machine — it was the two-seater built in 1907 with upright seating positions on the wing — and pulled the release wire. The *Flyer* slid down the track and was off into the air. With the greatest of ease Wilbur banked and circled, and came in for a perfect landing on his skids. The crowd could scarcely believe its eyes; the sceptics were astounded and confounded, and the enthusiasm was uproarious.'

¶ Wilbur Wright had many visitors, among them the brother of the founder of the Boy Scout movement. Major B. F. S. Baden-Powell was farsighted enough to say: "That Wilbur Wright is in possession of a power which controls the fate of nations is beyond dispute".

Early in the year when the Wrights were operating near the Spanish frontier they were visited by no less a person than the King of Spain:

'L'Illustration', Feb. 1909 'Alphonso XIII's passion for sport — for every sport — is well known, and as soon as Wilbur Wright established himself at Pont-Long, near Pau, it was announced that the young sovereign intended to pay the aviator a visit. It happened last Saturday. About nine o'clock in the morning, an automobile took the King to the aerodrome and Wilbur and Orville Wright were presented to him. Alphonso XIII was in travelling clothes, Wilbur in his usual outfit of jacket and cap. He and his brother uncovered respectfully. The King also took his hat off and, bareheaded, engaged them in conversation. Alphonso XIII followed with the greatest interest the explanations given by the admirable inventor, bombarding him with questions concerning his

136

machine. It was plain that his dearest wish was to take his place in the
aeroplane for a few moments of flight but he had promised his royal
mother to abstain from that experience. He contented himself with
sitting in the seat on Wright's left while the American aeronaut
explained the mechanism. Then Wilbur Wright rose in the air, without
the King, and flew with his accustomed skill around the field, passing
over the carriages of those who had been invited. The horses were
scared by the unexpected noise from the sky. Then Alphonso XIII
retired, enthusiastic, and cursing the grandeur which kept him chained
to the earth.'

¶ To the highest and the lowest it was now plain that flight was now
an established fact.

'Flying was "in the air". It was five years since the Wright brothers *Christopher Polling.*
in Dayton, Ohio, had conquered the air. Blériot's cross-Channel *'They Were*
flight was still a year ahead. Another Frenchman, Santos Dumont, *Singing', 1952*
who made the first official flight in Europe, was the name in 1906,
when Lily Burnand was singing of flying-machines in the music-halls:

> ' "There's a wonderful time coming soon,
>   For they tell us we're all going to fly!
> And we'll take daily trips to the moon;
>   What a picnic for both you and I!
> When we're tired of the worry and whirl
>   Of the earth and all earthly things,
> To our friends we will cry,
>   'Will you come for a fly?'
> And when we have put on our wings —

> ' "Up we'll go! Up we'll go!
>   Flying amongst the stars.
> Up we'll go! Up we'll go!
>   Having a day with Mars.
> Oh! what a sensation,
>   To fly like a fairy queen!
> Mister Dumont, send me along
>   A beautiful flying-machine." '

¶ The success of the Wrights was only the beginning of a rapid
development:

Algernon E. Berriman, 'Aviation', 1913. 'July, 1909, was the greatest month of the history of aviation, for it witnessed the crossing of the Channel by Blériot on Sunday morning, 25 July. The event was not only one of epoch-making importance in itself, but the incidents associated therewith are of unique interest. Early in the month much excitement was aroused by definite announcements on the part of various more or less proficient pilots, that they would compete for the *Daily Mail* prize. Principal attention, however, centred around the preparations of Hubert Latham, who was the first to make any actual move. Having taken his Antoinette monoplane to Sangatte during the second week of the month, he patiently awaited a favourable day, which did not arrive for more than a week.

'His famous first attempt took place on Monday, 19 July, the start being made at 6.20 a.m. When from 6 to 8 miles out from the French coast, however, the engine began to miss-fire, and ultimately stopped, so that the pilot was faced with no other alternative than that of descending on to the water, which, fortunately, was calm. A well-executed glide terminated in very gentle contact with the sea and the peculiar construction of the machine, which was built with very thick wings and a boat-like body, enabled it to float when partly submerged. Latham himself did not even get his feet wet, and when rescued by a French torpedo destroyer, he was calmly smoking his inevitable cigarette.

'It was a splendid failure, but before it had even ceased to be the topic of public conversation, Blériot suddenly arrived on the scene, and without delay made his historic flight. A few days previously he had completed a very successful cross-country journey of 25 miles between Etampes and Orleans, and it was probably this achievement that determined him to try for the great event while fortune wore a smiling face — for it is not always that the Fates are favourable to the flyer. He chose Baraques as a starting point, and left the French shore at half-past four on Sunday morning, 25 July, arriving in England at 12 min. past 5, where he landed in the Northfall meadow behind Dover Castle. Allowing for the difference between French and English time, the journey occupied approximately 40 min., and as the course followed was far from straight, it is estimated that the speed was at least 45 miles an hour. One of the interesting minor points about the flight was that Blériot lost his way, and did not land on the spot that he had previously selected for the purpose; in consequence, the crowd awaiting his arrival was disappointed, and the only actual witness of his arrival was, so far as is known, Police Constable Stanford, who happened to be on duty in the vicinity.'

138

¶ Blériot was almost unique at this period in preferring the monoplane to the biplane. The public ignorance was as great as its interest, and experts came forward to explain:

'The technical difference between a monoplane and a biplane, however, is merely that a monoplane, in common with the bird, possesses only one pair of wings, while the biplane is provided with two main supporting surfaces, one situated above the other. *Algernon E. Berriman. 'Aviation', 1913*

'The presence of the two main planes as the distinguishing feature of biplanes is apparent at a mere glance and any confusion as to type, should, therefore, be impossible to anyone who has once appreciated the simple distinction that exists between biplane and monoplane. The appropriateness of the term "wings", when applied to the supporting members of monoplanes, should also be sufficiently self-evident from the pictures to call for no further comment. Moreover, after previous explanations it should be unnecessary to remark that the wings do not flap.'

¶ Even yet intelligent people were unable to realize that flying the Channel was not just a stunt but was the beginning of the end of England's immunity as an island:

'Last week M. Blériot flew the Channel in half an hour — thirty-three minutes to be exact. Mr H. Latham has tried it twice and failed. The first time he fell into the sea and was rescued by following vessels. I agree with Shackleton that these things represent a foolish waste of money. Besides, flying across the Channel means nothing after you have done it. You can't carry goods or passengers.' *R.D.B's 'Diary', Aug. 25, 1909*

¶ But the pioneers of aviation were not to be daunted. Perhaps it is well to remember who these pioneers were:

'The first British subject to fly was Mr Henry Farman, who is by birth an Englishman, although he has become a citizen of France. Mr A. V. Roe was the first Englishman to fly in England, and Lieut-Col J. T. C. Moore-Brabazon, after Farman, was the first Englishman to fly anywhere, but he made his first flight in France.' *Major C. C. Turner. 'The Old Flying Days', 1927*

¶ How recent all this is! Lord Brabazon (as he has now become) is still with us, yet he was in the business of flying from the start.

Major C. C. Turner,
'The Old Flying
Days'. 1927.

'At Leysdown, on October 30, 1909, Mr Moore-Brabazon, on the second machine built by Short Brothers, fitted with a 60 h.p. Green engine, won the *Daily Mail* prize of £1,000 for a circular flight of a mile on a British machine. He, by the way, was granted the first aviation certificate issued by the Royal Aero Club, and is sometimes familiarly known as "No 1".'

¶ It may be of interest to give the list of the first ten aviator certificates issued by the British Club, with the dates:

1. J. C. T. Moore-Brabazon   March 8, 1910
2. Hon. C. S. Rolls   March 8 1910
3. D. Rawlinson   April 5 1910
4. Cecil Grace   April 26 1910
5. G. B. Cockburn   April 26 1910
6. C. Grahame-White   April 26 1910
7. A. Ogilvie   May 24 1910
8. A. M. Singer   May 31 1910
9. S. F. Cody   June 7 1910
10. Lieut L. D. L. Gibbs, R.F.A.   June 7 1910

The famous names leap to the eye:

C. H. Gibbs-Smith.
'A History of
Flying', 1953

'Practical aviation in England had made a wavering start in 1907, with the work of the romantic Samuel Franklin Cody, an American who dressed like a mid-Western sheriff, and who later became a naturalised Englishman. He should not be confused with "Buffalo Bill" Cody. . . In 1907, Cody made and flew what he called a "power-kite", which is exactly what she was, and in her he made the first short aeroplane flight in England, at Farnborough. But it was on 5 October, 1908, that he made the first official powered aeroplane flight in England when, after a number of earlier and shorter flights, he covered 496 yards at a height of 50 to 60 feet. . . The machine was called "British Army Aeroplane No 1", and was compounded of kite-shapes and Wright-shapes. He won considerable fame and success, especially in his 1910 machine, nicknamed *The Cathedral*. . . In 1909 he could stay up for over an hour. He was killed flying his latest machine — his seventh — in 1913.'

¶ The early aviators — or aeronauts, as they were then called — certainly took their lives in their hands. The Bournemouth meeting of 1910 was marred by the death of one of the most famous and popular of the early fliers, the Hon. C. S. Rolls:

140

'The Sport of the Century.' Mr Wilbur Wright in flight, with the Comtesse de Lambert. From 'The Sketch'.

'The accident happened just in front of the grand stand. Rolls had *Major C. C. Turner.*
accelerated higher than was expected, probably to allow himself a *'The Old Flying*
longer glide down so that he could steer more easily for the landing *Days', 1927*
spot. . . At a height of seventy feet he stopped his motor and began to
glide down at an angle of about 40 degrees, relying on the wind to
help him to avoid a long run on the ground; but to check the descent
he brought the elevating planes up very sharply. The machine was at a
height of 50 feet when the left side of the tail-plane broke away with
part of the left of the rudder. There was a sound of splitting wood, and
the elevating plane swung back. The head of the machine turned
sharply towards the earth, then back, and so crashed upside down
from a height of about 30 feet. The crash, witnessed by thousands of
silent and horrified spectators, was followed instantly by a loud report
in the engine. Rolls was found lying clear of the machine, and apparently unscathed. He was, however, lifeless, and the doctor said that
death had been virtually instantaneous from concussion.'

¶ Most of those who had ambitions to fly were happily unaware of the
dangers involved:

'In 1910 one went to Hendon and got a flight as a passenger on *Major C. C. Turner.*
machines which to-day would be refused a certificate. They were *'The Old Flying*
unstable, uncontrollable, and structurally unsound; but the risk was *Days', 1927*
not realised. There were many machines which the crack flyers of
to-day would simply refuse to go up in, and if they went up would find
extremely difficult to manage. A typical sentence from reports of those
days runs: "At times the aeroplane was estimated to be flying at a
height of 25 feet"!'

¶ On the other hand aeroplane speeds were still low and there was no
need for a long runway either for take-off or landing. Sir Frederick
Handley-Page once told the present writer that, breaking a strut on
one of his flights, he 'came down in a field, cut another strut from the
branch of a tree, and went on'. Such happenings were frequent:

'In May, 1911, Captain Pixton competed in the Brooklands-Brighton *Major C. C. Turner.*
race, arriving last owing to losing his way and landing at Plumpton *'The Old Flying Days', 1927*
racecourse. This was his first cross-country journey, and the compass
fitted was entirely unsuited for aircraft, the card revolving round at
such a rate that it made him feel dizzy. As a sidelight on the way things

141

August Bank Holiday at Brooklands, 1910.

were done in those days the following incident may prove of interest: As he was starting up at Plumpton the village helpers pressed heavily on the fuselage, breaking the rudderpost in half. However, it was quickly repaired by cutting a stake out of the hedge and making a splint for the damaged part! A day or two later Mr. Pixton made a really sound job of it by contriving a new rudderpost out of a broom handle!'

¶ Flying, interesting to relate, was still cheap.

Major C. C. Turner. 'The Old Flying Days', 1927 'The price of a machine, including the motor, may be anything from £400 to £1,200; and there is no longer any reason to look askance at the lower end of the scale. Unless the purchaser desired an aeroplane that will travel at a speed of over 60 m.p.h., with two up, he need not anticipate an initial outlay of more than £600 or £700; he can even do it on less. The cost of learning to fly, including insurance, is £75 at most of the schools. . . The cost of flying as regards fuel and oil is easily reckoned. In the case of the most extravagant engine of 150 h.p., the consumption, perhaps, amounts to about 13s per hour. . .

'Accidents will happen even to skilful flyers, and bad landings are a thing to be reckoned with. These should be provided for in advance by a fund for the purpose; it is, indeed, already possible to insure against them. The principal thing to bear in mind at the moment is that the damage done to aeroplanes even in bad smashes, costs comparatively little to repair. It is very uncommon for a smash to exceed £20. Most mishaps involve the flyer in no greater expense than a sovereign or two, the reason being that the motor, which is the most expensive part of the machine, is rarely injured when the aeroplane is reduced to matchwood. It would be easy to instance scores of accidents in which the planes and the body have been broken and the motor has escaped without a scratch. The bill for tyres is negligible.'

¶ That 'the bill for tyres is negligible' is a wonderful thought!

Major C. C. Turner. 'The Old Flying Days', 1927 There was no question then of long and elaborate training:

'Lieut Spenser Grey learned to fly in the summer of 1911. He learned to fly at his own expense and in his own time; in fact, he had only seven days' leave when he went to the Hewlett and Blondean School at Brooklands; and he made the stipulation that he should be allowed to have a try for his "ticket" at the end of the week, whatever

142

state his training had reached by that time, a sporting proposition that was accepted. He succeeded in passing the tests in the time at his disposal. Proud of the achievement, he presented himself at the Admiralty in the hope of being taken as a flying officer, only to meet with a rebuff. Undiscouraged by this, he proceeded to purchase an aeroplane of his own, a Blackburn monoplane, and fly over the fleet at Weymouth. . . We find him eventually taken on as a flying officer at Eastchurch. . . On September 2, 1913, he took Mr Winston Churchill for a flight, and then Mrs Winston Churchill. . . and he afterwards gave Mr Churchill lessons in flying.'

¶ So Churchill was 'in the air' already in 1913. He must have been one of the first statesmen to see the possibilities of the new invention. Meanwhile aviators were becoming more and more daring:

'In 1913, Bentfield Hucks flew upside-down and looped-the-loop at Buc, the first Englishman to do it, and on return to England he was met at Charing Cross by other aviators and "chaired" upside down! This was followed by exhibitions at Hendon of upside-down flying and looping-the-loop. *Major C. C. Turner. 'The Old Flying Days', 1927*

'I have before me the menu of the "Upside-Down-Dinner" at the Royal Automobile Club given in celebration of the upside-down flying and looping by B. C. Hucks and Gustav Hamel, following Adolphe Pegoud's demonstrations. The cards of invitation were printed upside-down, with an aviator shown standing on his head, and the whole of the programme was ingeniously adapted to the occasion. I do not credit the story that the subsequent proceedings were even more realistic.'

¶ Major Turner does not tell us enough, so perhaps the following account of this strange affair may be of interest:

'Never was there such a topsy-turvy affair as the "Upside-down" dinner given on January 16th, 1914, by Hendon airmen at the Royal Automobile Club, in London, to Mr. B. C. Hucks and Mr. Gustave Hamel in honour of their "looping the loop" and "upside-down" flying. *J. Rey. 'The Whole Art of Dining', 1914*

'The usual order of dinner was reversed, and the meal ended with the Hors-d'Œuvre, the menu being as follows:

Fine champagne et Liqueurs variees
Café. — Pegoud

Savoury. — Canapés a la Chanteloup.

Entremet. — Souffle Hucks.

Legume. — Asperges renversées. Sce. Gnome.

Salade. — Blériot.

Roti. — Bécassines Hamel.

Entree. — Vol-au-ventà la Hendon.

Grosse Piece. — Baron de Pauillac à l'Aviation.

Poisson. — Looping Lobsters a l'Aerodrome de Londres.

Consomme. — Essence de Volaille Grahame-White.

Hors-d'Œuvre. — Caviare a la Morane.

'Everything was upside-down. The two guests of honour sat under large mirrors which reflected them "upside-down" at a table which was weirdly in the form of a loop. The table legs pointing upwards helped the idea.

'The most remarkable feature of this original dinner was that at the end of it nearly all confessed that they felt hungry. Some even suggested the plan of following the "upside-down" dinner with one "right-side-up".

'When dinner was over many of the guests tried to describe their feeling on the back of their menu card. A guest of honour wrote: "The dinner requires even more practice to enjoy, than flying".

'When Mr. Hucks responded to the toast of his health he began with "Lastly" and went on "Thirdly", and finished up with a sentence which began "Firstly". '

¶ The machines themselves were improving rapidly. One of the best of the early models was that devised by Farman:

Algernon E. Berriman. 'Aviation', 1913 'To mention all the successes that have been obtained by the Farman aeroplanes would be impossible, but to English readers one event in particular must always stand out very prominently, and that is the occasion of the London to Manchester flight. When the *Daily Mail* offered the extremely generous prize of £10,000 for a flight from London to Manchester everyone thought it would be years before the event could possibly be accomplished. A sum of this magnitude, however, is no mean incentive to effort, and within a very short time there were evident signs that someone or other was likely to at least make the attempt. Two pilots in particular, Claude Grahame-White and Louis Paulhan, speedily made up their minds on the subject, and

144

Hanriot's aeroplane crashes in the River Wey after a flight from Brooklands on August Bank Holiday, 1910.

Above: Adolphe Pégoud with Blériot after 'looping the loop,' September 25th, 1913.

Below: Gustav Hamel (facing the camera) with his machine at Brooklands, 1911.

this remarkable event almost started as a race. Both competitors used Farman biplanes, but in those days Louis Paulhan had had very much more experience in the air than Grahame-White, who, comparatively speaking, was then a beginner. His pluck however, was of an uncommonly well-seasoned kind, as many incidents in his attempt went to prove. Paulhan, as history has recorded, succeeded in accomplishing the journey and in winning a thoroughly well-deserved prize. His success formed another notable step in the progress of aviation, and it served in consequence as a great stimulus to future effort on the part of all who were engaged in the subject.'

¶ Flying "Meetings" continued to be arranged and to meet with increasing public response until 1914. Then (to borrow once more the words of Major Turner):

'On August Bank Holiday, 1914, I attended the Flying Meeting at Hendon. Already the shadow of the great catastrophe was falling. The weather was fine, yet looking back to that dim-remembered day it seems to me the very sky was darkened. There was but a small attendance. . . The programme was carried out in a half-hearted way, and some of the French pilots had already left for their own country, whilst there were significant absentees from the British list. . . M. Salmet arrived on his Blériot on his way to France, and announced the prohibition of his flight by the Home Office, and the conjectured commandeering of his machine; and when M. Pierre Verrier landed from a flight across country he was promptly accosted by a police inspector and asked to give an account of himself."

Major C. C. Turner. 'The Old Flying Days', 1927

¶ The First World War had come.

CHAPTER VII

CLOTHES
AND THE ORIENTAL DREAM

THE EDWARDIAN EPOCH is now sufficiently removed from our own for us to be able to admire the clothes of the period if not yet to imitate them. One of the influences in bringing them back into favour has been the genius of Mr Cecil Beaton who, temperamentally at home in a world of elaborate *toilettes*, has dressed a whole series of dramatic revivals in clothes which could not fail to capture the enthusiasm of the audience. Yet Edwardian women's dress was fantastically different from our own:

'Taste and Fashion',
1937
'The essential lines of female costume remained the same from the beginning of the century until 1908, and in some particulars even until 1910. These lines are easy enough to determine, for the characteristic of the period lay in the shape of the corset, which, while introducing a vertical line in the front of the body, had the effect of throwing the bust forward and pushing the hips back, giving every woman an S-shape swan-like appearance.'

¶ Jean Worth had tried to impose a similar fashion in 1888 under the name of *Corsets Louis XV*. In doing so he had been inspired by the writings of a certain Dr Frantz, who complained that the accepted form of the corset, with its all-round downward pressure, deranged the position of the internal organs and led to many ailments. Worth's attempts, however, were unsuccessful, and it was not until the opening of the new century that any important change appeared. Gaches-Sarraute invented a corset which supported the abdomen from below, the front of the bodice being made absolutely straight by a rigid busk. There was something to be said for this innovation from a medical point of view, but fashion cares little for health, and soon the straight-

146

fronted corsets had been exaggerated to such an extent that they too had become a danger. The abdomen had ceased to exist, all the fullness being thrown upward into the chest, and there was a violent bend in the body at the back — how violent we may see by studying any corset illustration of the period. With the so-called princess robe no corset was necessary, as this was already sufficiently boned, but it produced the same deformation of the female figure. The effect was heightened by the popularity of a new kind of skirt: Dr Willet Cunnington has described this with scientific accuracy:

'The term "Edwardian period" has become so well established that it would be an affectation now to attempt to avoid its use. Nevertheless. it is misleading, and it would be more correct to describe the period 1900–1908 as that of the "flared skirt".

C. Willett Cunnington. 'English Women's Clothing in the Present Century', 1952

'In the history of Costume here was an important innovation. Hitherto the outline of the skirt, as worn, had been either straight-sided or convexly domed; at any rate the sides and especially the front had never presented concave surfaces, any such curve being confined to the lower part of the back of the skirt when trained. A concave skirt-front would have seemed impracticable, and liable to interfere with walking. The essential of the flared skirt was that *every aspect* of it presented a concave curve; that, in fact, it was bell-shaped.'

¶ The appeal of the Edwardian silhouette was extremely subtle and sophisticated:

'In the art of Costume the excessive use of the curve tends to give a somewhat sensual effect, but this applies only to the convex curve, not to the concave. The Edwardian design seems to have taken particular care to avoid the crude configuration which had made

C. Willett Cunnington. 'English Women's Clothing in the Present Century', 1952

famous the Victorian "bosom". By means of the straight fronted corset the shape of the breasts was completely merged into a sculptured figure, veiled by hanging drapery or by the cut of the garments, so as to present an impressive but innocuous outline.

'The famous shape of "the Gibson Girl", with thorax pouched and protuberant so as positively to overhang the regions below, was an artist's daydream blocked out by the corsetière, whose task was to emphasise the curvature while denying the components of that region.

'Indeed, all through that period the floppy pouching of blouse or bodice by day, and the lace valance protecting the décolletage in the evening, composed a refined denial of anatomical facts. The whole spirit of the Edwardian design was, as we shall see, to combine suggestion with concealment. A natural result of this was that Edwardian fashions tended to favour the mature form of the matron rather than the more youthful outline.'

¶ Another characteristic of the fashion of the period was the falling Russian blouse:

'*Taste and Fashion*',
1937 'It was considered essential to have a kind of pouch of material hanging over the waist in front, reaching perhaps its extreme of exaggeration in the years 1902 and 1903. The general effect was as if the female body had been cut in two at the waist, and the pieces put together again after the upper portion had been pushed several inches forward, so that the whole looked like a ship's figurehead, carved to fit the prow of the vessel. The form of the corset made it almost essential to throw the head back in order to balance the carriage of the body, the bust being thrust upward and forward. The wax dummy figures in old-fashioned hairdressers' shops still show the essential lines of the figure at this period. It had the advantage, from a mature woman's point of view, of allowing the bust to be very big without distracting from the impression of elegance.'

¶ Elegant Edwardian fashions certainly were — and extravagant, too:

*C. Willett
Cunnington.
'English Women's
Clothing in the
Present Century*',
1952 'The coronation of King Edward the Seventh encouraged fashions to take more expensive forms, on the plea that extravagance was both loyal and good for trade. The "new look", based upon the shape immortalised by the American artist, Charles Dana Gibson, and supported by the new straight-fronted corset, was to be the ideal of perfect womanhood. "The feminine silhouette has a decided downward droop; the line from collar to shoulder is prolonged half way down the arm; the trailing skirt follows the same downward billowy line. Slimness is still the order of the day. We must be tall and slim would we belong to the type admired at the moment. Present-day fashions require for the ideal figure an upright poise of the shoulders, long sloping bust with straight front line, and a graceful curve over the hips. The waist held in well below the figure; the chest carried well forward and the shoulders down, the waist long in front and short behind."

Men's clothes are dead, but women's are alive. Drawing by Harrison, 1904.

NET RUFFLES, LACE and CHIFFON NECKWEAR.

PRINTED RADIUM SCARF (*as sketch*), white grounds, with reseda and rose, reseda and sky, and reseda and violet designs.
3 yards long, 21 inches wide.   Price **12/-.**

CHIFFON SCARF (*as sketch*), in black, white, navy, brown, wedgwood, fraise, sky, mauve.
3 yards long, 20 inches wide.   Price **5/11.**
3 yards long, 40 inches wide.   Price **10/6.**

Sent
on
Approval

Sent
on
Approval

CREAM TAMBOUR LACE SCARF,
2¾ yards long.   Price **7/11** and **12/9.**

REAL LIMERICK LACE SCARVES,
3½ yards long, 22 inches wide.   Price **58/6.**

ILLUSTRATED CATALOGUE,
POST FREE.

SMART RUFFLE (*as sketch*), in Ivory Ring Net, edged white or black chiffon or in colours to order.   Price **21/-.**

NEW RUFFLE (*as sketch*), in Ivory Ring Net, edged black bébé ribbon velvet with ribbon velvet ends.   Price **25/6.**

DEBENHAM & FREEBODY,
WIGMORE STREET, LONDON, W.

Advertisement by Debenham & Freebody in 'The Play Pictorial,' 1906.

"Everybody has rushed into the straight-fronted corsets, often with the most deplorable results."

' "The dressmaker's art is very rapidly reaching the topmost pinnacle of perfection. We have cultivated the picturesque in form, and now it is the picturesque in colour that is to influence us. Everywhere there is a desire for beautiful blending of tones. Dress grows more perplexing and bewildering every season. There is more liberty of choice, more scope for individual taste. . . The dress of to-day is certainly charming, but it has the drawback of being excessively expensive. Englishwomen over-dress more and more every day." '

'An essential element of Edwardian fashions was Edwardian affluence with its distinguishing air of serene luxury; and the expense of living up to those fashions was a point persistently commented on by writers of the time, in terms of surprise, envy or disapproval, according to the outlook of the writer.

'Advertisements such as "petticoats at all prices up to £50 each", or "evening confections at £200" (figures which must be at least doubled to give them their modern equivalents) tell their own story, and are even more convincing than the sermons on "The Sins of Society" which Father Bernard Vaughan used to thunder out against the luxury of his day.

'Those past splendours are just the items which catch the eye in museum cases or collections of fashion plates, recalling the ephemeral glories of the Ascot gown, of the confections designed for the Côte d'Azur, or for Melba nights at Covent Garden. They suggest that the Edwardian woman of fashion was extraordinarily artificial. In a sense this was true.

'There was that striking coiffure built up on pads and wire contraptions, and reinforced by "switches", hairframes and transformations, all with the effect of adding to the height; and the varieties of head-gear seem designed to float, as it were, on those billowy structures sometimes wave-tilted forward, or keeling over to one side, but never backwards. Hats and toques were rival monarchs of all they surveyed, for the bonnet had not survived the Nineteenth Century.'

¶ Fashion commentators of the period become quite lyrical on the subject of blouses:

'Most bewilderingly interesting is the demi-toilette blouse, a scheme *'The Queen',*
of tender pink chiffon, gold, spangled net and fine appliqué lace *Mar. 4, 1905*

lightly diamanté. A cleaving line is imparted to the figure by the shaped plastrons of lace, carried down the centre front, flanked, either side, by clusters of pink chenille fringe sparkling with diamanté, beyond which comes the folded fichu of fine French lace, the now requisite colour of the figure maintained by a folded belt of pink satin ribbon.'

¶ Another fashion writer of a couple of years later tells the same story:

'Les Modes', 1907 'Dress has become more luxurious than ever. Investments have sagged all along the line; taxes have increased and multiplied [the present Editor may, perhaps, be permitted here to insert a rueful mark of exclamation!], but there is still plenty of money in some quarters, and the cost and elaboration of attire today is one of the ways in which this interesting fact reveals itself. It is the lavish use of embroideries that accounts for the enhanced expenditure on dress. The rich and beautiful brocades, the fine velvets and lustrous satins which made the highest ideal of a costly court train of ten or fifteen years ago, did not cost nearly as much as the elaborate hand em-broideries of the moment's ambition. It is impossible in either words or black-and-white pictures to give an adequate idea of the beauty of these embroideries. The flowers depicted by the needle are as effective in the mass, as delicate and dainty in minute detail, as their natural prototypes. From a distance evening gowns seem a mass of silver, opalescent gold, or moonlight sequins.'

¶ There was another very important item of expense in the toilettes of the well-dressed woman:

'Taste and Fashion', 'More striking even than the embroidery was the quantity of lace
1937 which was considered necessary. Perhaps not since the days of William III had so much been used. Lace collars and collarettes, lace sleeves, lace plastrons, only to be glimpsed occasionally, but requiring, none the less, the finest workmanship — there was hardly any part of woman's dress which was not adorned with this most expensive form of decoration. Real lace in such quantities was often unobtainable, and machine-made lace being still somewhat despised, a compromise was discovered in Irish crochet, for which there was a considerable vogue, specially in the year 1907. Both Parisian and London dressmakers, we are told, regarded it with the highest favour. For light evening bodices or for dressy "afternoon blouses" there was nothing more fashionable.'

150

¶ Extravagance being the order of the day, those who pushed it to extreme lengths were sure of fame and even of a kind of immortality. Such was 'the fabulous Mrs. Lydig':

'She never ordered one thing of a kind, but duplicated each item by the dozens, with only slight variations in material, lace, or design. It was not unusual for twenty-five copies of one coat to be made. Mrs. Lydig's adoration of clothes was not for purposes of display, but because they gave her the satisfaction of a work of art. In her own bedroom she would wear, as a dressing-gown for her own pleasure, a circular skirt made from one piece of seamless eleventh-century lace. The price she paid for this garment was nine thousand dollars.

Cecil Beaton. 'The Glass of Fashion', 1954

'Her wardrobe included black velvet dresses for day; low-cut, bare-backed evening dresses; jackets and coats made of rich and rare materials and worn with velvet skirts by day or satin culottes for evening; nightdresses and underclothes trimmed with medallions incorporating classical figures in lace as delicate as the skeleton of an autumn leaf; black lace mantillas as light as gossamer; heavy lace tunics that appear like armour; blouses of embroidered batiste, needlework, or bobbin lace with the exaggeratedly high collars; cobweb-thin stockings with rare lace insertions; rose-point petticoats, small sable hats, fezzes of unborn lamb, and an umbrella stick of platinum with the name "Rita" set in diamonds on top.

'Although she walked very short distances, Mrs. Lydig possessed at least three hundred pairs of shoes, shoes that have never been seen before or since. These were made by Yanturni, the East Indian curator of the Cluny Museum, a strange individual with an extraordinary gift for making incredibly light footwear that was moulded like the most sensitive sculpture. The conditions under which he would supply a few favoured customers were somewhat unusual. Yanturni demanded a deposit of one thousand dollars, from which he would subtract the price of each shoe or boot supplied, though delivery often took two or three years. Once he had agreed to work for a customer, he made a plaster model of both feet, on which he would then work and mould his materials until they were as flexible as the finest silk. Mrs. Lydig's shoes were fashioned from eleventh- and twelfth-century velvets, with variations in long pointed toes or square-ended toes and correspond-ingly square heels. Her evening and boudoir slippers utilized brocades or gold- and silver-metal tissue. Some were covered with lace appliqué and leather spats that fitted like a silk sock. Mrs. Lydig collected violins expressly so that Mr. Yanturni could use their thin, light wood for his shoe trees. With its tree inside, each shoe weighed no more than an ostrich feather. She preserved these shoes in trunks of Russian leather made in St. Petersburg, with heavy locks and a rich cream velvet lining.'

¶ Underclothes attained a degree of luxury hitherto unheard of:

C. Willett Cunnington. 'English Women's Clothing in the Present Century', 1952

'Meanwhile increasing attention was being paid to "those garments not intended for a public career" (to wit, underclothes). "Petticoats are more elaborate than ever, and the amount of frou-frou from the knees downwards is immense. There is something very attractive about the elaborate petticoat with its frou-frouing mysteries. Our countrywomen realise at last that dainty undergarments are not necessarily a sign of depravity." The age of fascinating lingerie had begun; the Victorian Era was indeed dead."

¶ Dr Cunnington has analysed this development with his usual acumen:

C. Willett Cunnington. 'English Women's Clothing in the Present Century', 1952

'We must always criticise Edwardian fashions as a form of rococo art, shunning the simplicity of Nature. It was in this spirit that anything approaching nudity was regarded as indelicate, and it is to be noted that Edwardian décolletage in evening dress was far less daring than had often been the fashion in Victorian times. Instead, the veiling by lace and chiffon provided an exercise for the imagination, and if we frankly examine the Edwardian technique in sex attraction we realise how much of it was artificially constructed.

'The most striking innovation, in this respect, was a new attitude towards underclothing. The breach with Victorian tradition was fundamental. Undergarments became "lingerie", and their primary function was — to attract the other sex. We find them being frankly called "seductive" (though the meaning is somewhat equivocal), and it is significant that to mark their new function many of the old names were changed. Drawers became knickers, a chemise became a slip, and the petticoats, in common parlance, "frillies".

'The immense importance of "frillies" as an instrument of sex-appeal cannot, of course, be appreciated by a generation which has practically discarded that weapon, and is content that undies should be merely "amusing". The Edwardians took them very seriously indeed.'

¶ Gone was the notion, if it ever existed, that women's clothes were designed for decency and warmth:

'Fashions were distinctly orchidaceous; we read of "the temptatious teagown which absolutely defines the figure in a manner which is insinuating"; and the modes of the moment are labelled "this Season's Seductions". We are also told that "in ordinary dress there is very little difference between the frock of 1901 and 1902, except the colour. We are devoted to light colours. The skirt is a shade longer while the sleeve expands at the end. The bell and the bishop sleeves are engaged in mortal combat; I prefer the bishop with a tight top and a baggy base. The pouching of the sleeve at the wrist has reached the limit of exaggeration."

' "The questionable morality of the 'Pneumonia blouse' as a subject of conversation may be said to be threadbare. A transparent blouse of muslin and lace with next to no collar is neither sufficient, appropriate nor becoming."

'We are also informed that "home-dressmaking is becoming too difficult for these elaborate dresses; the cost of the material is as nothing compared to the making of a gown". '

C. Willett Cunnington. 'English Women's Clothing in the Present Century', 1952

¶ 'We are devoted to light colours.' Everything, indeed, was in 'pastel shades', the kind of tints which a few years later were to be ridiculed by Paul Poiret as 'nuances of nymph's thigh, lilacs, swooning mauves, tender blue hortensias, niles, maizes, straws: all that was soft, washed-out, and insipid'. We must return to Poiret's revolution later. For the moment it is sufficient to note that even the Stage confined itself to pastel shades:

'The leading lady's gowns were inevitably made by Lucile and were masterpieces of intricate workmanship. It was the fashion for women to wear high-waisted Directoire dresses, falling straight to the floor, where the wearer's feet would be encumbered by bead-fringes and possibly clinging trains. Lucile worked with soft materials, delicately mingling them with bead or sequin embroidery, with cobweb lace insertions, true lovers' knots, and garlands of minute roses. Her colour sense was so subtle that the delicacy of detail could scarcely be seen at a distance, though the effect she created was of an indefinable shimmer. Sometimes, however, she introduced rainbow effects into a sash and would incorporate quite vivid mauves and greens, perhaps even a

Cecil Beaton. 'The Glass of Fashion', 1954

touch of shrimp-pink or orange. Occasionally, if she wanted to be deliberately outrageous, she introduced a bit of black chiffon or black velvet and, just to give the *coup de grace,* outlined it with diamonds.

'In private life Lucile was Lady Duff-Gordon and a sister of the romantic novelist, Elinor Glyn. She had suddenly developed her own utterly personal *métier.* Nowadays her work is sometimes disparagingly referred to as "boudoir lampshade stuff". All fashionable dresses become costumes in time, however, and in her heyday Lucile's artistry was unique, her influence enormous. She was the first Englishwoman to create a name equally well known in London, Paris, Chicago, and New York. Until Lucile's advent the Paris dressmakers had displayed their clothes on mannequins of no particular looks. These models wore black satin "maillots", with high neck sand long sleeves, over which went the evening dresses of Doucet or Worth. It was considered shocking to see a lady's skin in daylight. Lucile discarded the black under-garment and employed beautiful young women as mannequins for her clothes. The fame she brought to the outstanding Hebes and Dolores is legendary. Drian, the painter, has described these tall women mincing about in their turbans and trailing trains as looking like impertinent lobsters.

'Just as ladies' costumes were limited to sweet-pea colourings, so their make-up was of a more restricted palette: lips were touched with coral instead of carmine, complexions were peaches and cream. Hair was pale nut-brown, and I remember that the yellow or peroxide hair which we now call blond was, at that time, considered unfortunate. Perhaps, in comparison with today, the art of physical embellishment was somewhat naïve; yet there was a dancer in *The Merry Widow* and *The Dollar Princess* who knew a thousand tricks of make-up.

'Gabrielle Ray was not a talented actress, not even a good dancer, but her parakeet features were not without possibilities. By sheer cleverness she was able to fascinate an audience and make it susceptible to her self-created prettiness. She metamorphosed herself into a sort of Maude Goodman nursery-picture-book unreality, with masses of soft, silky curls falling about her raised head and a straw hat hanging over her shoulder from a ribbon. The effect was as though butter would never melt in her mouth, yet there was an intriguing perversity about such excessive prettiness.'

¶ Even before the death of King Edward a change was foreshadowed. In dress the 'Russian Revolution' had already begun:

'Bearing evident witness of its Parisian inspiration comes the Rus- *'The Queen', 1910*
sian tunic suit to us to-day. It is a charming vogue, and one which is
having a great following in quite exclusive quarters. There is a marked
distinction in it, despite, or perhaps, because of, its simplicity, while
the subtleties of its cut make imitation quite impossible.

'Rinking is the order of the day, and nowhere is the Russian tunic
suit seen to better advantage than on wheels. Indeed, some quite
irresistible examples have already made their appearance at Olympia
on Sunday afternoons, where most of the fashionable world is to be
seen, victims to the charm of the ball-bearing skate. For such wear
black velvet seems to have put in an uncontested claim, and never is
it seen to better advantage than in the service if such a suit as this,
with chinchilla or sable as the edging. Coloured velvets with suitable
fur — old rose, peacock, amethyst, what you will — also fashion quite
irresistible suits; nor must the claims of corduroy be overlooked, not
that such rigid fabrics are in any way a *sine qua non* for the suit,
for cloth of various makes is a charming medium, and one which
will commend itself to many for practical purposes, rinking quite
apart.'

¶ But what really changed everything was the new wave of orientalism
largely due to the impact of the Russian Ballet:

'The year 1908 witnessed the first invasion of Western Europe by *W. A. Propert.*
the Russians, and their prompt capture of Paris. London, unaware of *'The Russian Ballet*
their existence, was at that time agitated by the rival claims of Miss *in Western Europe',*
Isadora Duncan, who interpreted Gluck, and Miss Maud Allen, who *1921*
introduced the long-suffering Salome to the music-hall stage. It was in
1909 that we saw the forerunners of the Diaghilev Ballet. In the
Coliseum programme, as announced in the "Times" of June 28, we
read the laconic entry, "Russian Dancers, 9.30". It meant nothing to
us. We had heard no word of that wonderful company that had just
roused Paris to such enthusiasm. I can find no comment in the "Times"
on their dancing. It was merely a music-hall turn, though the name of
one of the dancers was Thamar Karsavina.

'Such of us as do remember that brief season can only realize its
success by the fact that the spring of the following year, 1910, saw
the cult of Russian dancing become general, and no music-hall programme considered itself complete without its representative pair or
little company. . . Finally, in June, 1911, Diaghilev brought his whole

155

Company over to Covent Garden, and London had its first experience of what a stage setting could and should be.'

¶ It was the artist-decorators employed by Diaghilev who set the tone:

W. A. Propert.
'The Russian Ballet
in Western Europe',
1921
'In 1909 Diaghilev, returning to Paris with ballet as well as opera, brought forward three new painters — Alexandre Benois, Korovin, the official painter of the Marie Theatre, and Léon Bakst, whose name was destined to eclipse the others, and whose work came to be regarded as an essential ingredient of the Russian Ballet, and in a sense the hallmark of its authenticity. Certainly from 1910 to 1914, the most important of the new productions originated with him, so much so, that the public, always shy of new men, almost resented the announcement of any other name. . . The best of Bakst was a very delightful thing, and "Scheherazade" and "Thamor" were of his very best.

'Two untranslatable French words give us the keynote of his work — *volupté* and *luxe* are written all over them. Was there ever seen such a riot of colour as in "Scheherazade", such mountains of cushions, such enormous golden lamps and such a breaking of the Ten Commandments? Time moves quickly, but in 1911, if Londoners found it exhilarating, they also, undoubtedly, found it shocking. We have, since then, grown used to an even more generous display of unclothed humanity on our own stage, and the love affairs of painted Orientals no longer shock us.

'But leaving aside the moralities, it was a revelation to us then of the possibility of assembling and interweaving a multitude of sharply contrasting tornados of colour — scarlet, orange, purple, rose and blue, made more vivid by the brown and gold and silver of the slaves, and set against a background of green curtains.'

¶ The impact of this single stage production was enormous:

Cecil Beaton.
'The Glass of
Fashion', 1954
'*Scheherazade* was Bakst's great moment and to this day is the one ballet of Orientalism that is still successfully performed, though lacking the splendour of the original production. With the excitement engendered by the dance and the vivid colours, a whole debased and bastardized spirit of Orientalism was let loose. Costume parties and fêtes followed in the wake of the new sultan's dream. Society women gave *tableaux vivants* dressed as Eastern slaves, with gold bangles on

Original fashion drawing from the Worth Collection.

'The Brown Veil.' Painting by Sir William Nicholson, 1905. City of Birmingham Art Gallery.

their ankles and headache bands over their eyes. Baron de Mayer took photographs of ladies in Paris and New York in a flash of gilt tissues and the metallic brilliance of the Orient. London's society beauties were caught by the objective lens of less romantic cameras doing nautch-girl poses, with metal cymbals on their fingers and bells on their toes. A fashion world that had been dominated by corsets, lace, feathers, and pastel shades soon found itself in a city that overnight had become a seraglio of vivid colours, harem skirts, beads, fringes, and voluptuousness. Later there would be bright futuristic scarves of checkered or harlequinade triangles and squares, all of which could be traced back to Bakst.'

¶ Paul Poiret was always annoyed when people gave the Russian Ballet credit for these developments. Naturally enough, in his reminiscences, he claims to have been the innovator, and is at pains to demonstrate that his reputation was already made before that of Bakst, common as it is to consider all Poiret's characteristic gowns as being ultimately inspired by the designer of *Scheherazade*. Certainly Poiret always refused to execute dresses from Bakst's designs, and this was not jealousy on his part, but a very proper pride in his own creations. Poiret appears to have been an Orientalist from the very beginning, even when, as the humble assistant of an umbrella-maker, he purloined pieces of silk in order to dress a doll, now as a piquant Parisienne, now as an Eastern Queen. Cecil Beaton attempts to hold the balance between the rival claimants:

'Whatever the reason may be, Orientalism had in 1909 affected *Cecil Beaton.* European fashion many times before it again struck at the heart of *'The Glass of* London, Paris, and New York, This time it was to come via Russia, *Fashion', 1954* with the young Diaghilev and his artist Bakst as the spearheads of the invasion. A rising Parisian couturier, Poiret, was to filter Balst's imaginative *élan* down to the public itself; or, acknowledging that Poiret may have been the innovator when he claims that his personal Orientalism preceded that of Bakst, we may say that Paul Poiret exploited a parallel vein to the fantastic Orientalism which the Russian Ballet was to foster. As a matter of fact, Poiret's obsession with the East continued to impose itself on the world of fashion for a long time after the influence of Orientalism had waned. It is a tribute to his stubborn genius that he sent women off to the races wearing turbans and padded kimonos embroidered in gold peacocks and perversely made them accept his taste when time had already by-passed the spirit that animated it.'

¶ Poiret was certainly an innovator in the manner of presenting his clothes. His mannequin parades became themselves fashionable occasions, which had certainly never happened before in the history of dress:

'Taste and Fashion', 1937 'People went to a fashion parade as their forbears had gone to a play or to a private view of pictures. They expected a luxurious decor, soft lights, music, a procession of beautiful mannequins, and, what is even more important, they expected something startlingly new and original in the clothes presented before their eyes.

'To the man of the right temperament such circumstances provided an additional inspiration and incentive, and Poiret was not the man to fail to make use of them. He set the fashion of removing his business from the ordinary streets favoured by the dressmakers and showing his creations in a luxurious private house. His rivals prophesied his ruin, but the fashionable public, avid of novelty, flocked to his door. He employed the best artists of his day to decorate his salons; he chose his mannequins with infinite care. He was careful to admit only those whose presence might lend *cachet* to his exhibitions, and in addition to all this his clothes had an originality which began by shocking but ended by conquering the town. His house became the centre of a new religion, or rather of a very old religion which had now found its appropriate shrine, and of which he had constituted himself the high priest.'

Cecil Beaton. *'The Glass of Fashion'*, 1954 'To enter Poiret's salons in the Faubourg St. Honoré was to step into the world of the *Arabian Nights*. Here, in rooms strewn with floor cushions, the master dressed his slaves in furs and brocades and created Eastern ladies who were the counterpart of the Cyprians and chief eunuchs that moved through the pageantries of Diaghilev.

'Poiret had no respect for "good taste". He forced his victims to wear chin straps of pearls, slung them with white foxes, stabbed them with fantastic ospreys, imprisoned them (as one hobbles the forelegs of a horse to prevent him from running away) in harem skirts. Wired tunics like lampshades were hung round the ladies' hips, heavy capes enveloped them, and they were laden with tassels and barbaric jewels. This violent Orientalism, which shackled and bound some of Paris' most respectable women, was even more extraordinary when one considers that Poiret himself had at the time never been out of France.'

¶ An Englishwoman, visiting Paris in 1910, has left us an account of a visit to Poiret's establishment. There had recently been disastrous floods in the French capital which had left many people homeless and she was not at all sure that she ought to go:

'It was strange to find oneself wafted into a world of beauty, ease, and luxury, and for a moment or two the Puritan in me rebelled; but very soon reason told me that various elements are necessary to make the social ball, as it now stands, go round, and I ended by thoroughly enjoying myself. . . A friend of mine. . . had arranged to have a gown fitted at Poiret's and felt it as much her duty to keep her appointment there as to continue her help for the *sinistrés,* for, as she truly said, "If we all stop having clothes made, how will the little workgirl earn her living". . . The art of dressing is here practised at its highest. To say that the frocks here indicate the fashions we shall see on the boulevards, in the Bois, or even at the races, would be, I think, too daring. But where we shall see them will be in many of those beautiful, artistic homes in Paris, the doors of which are not easily opened to foreigners. . . The crowning note is simplicity of line allied to richness of colour and material. This season there is evidently a general leaning towards the Oriental, which expresses itself definitely in turbans and Indian cachemires. Every mannequin had her pretty head enveloped in a coloured silk handkerchief, twisted like a turban, and in a shade to go with her gown. One very pretty girl had on a pink mauve turban and a gown in Liberty and mousseline de soie. The lower half of the skirt was in old rose Liberty, and the upper half in mauve mousseline de soie, slightly gathered both at the high waist and the knees. The corsage. . . was pure Mme Récamier style. . .' *'The Queen', 1910*

¶ It is not surprising that Poiret designed clothes for the stage; what is less well known is that the stage designer Bakst made a counter-attack into the world of *la haute couture.* The *mot d'ordre* was *'modernisme oriental'.* A commentator of the period remarks that:

'The origin of all these refinements is certain. Persian images and Russian decors have made our eyes greedy for novelty, for tasty colours and original movements. Perhaps there is a danger that these *Lise-Léon Blum in 'Gazette du Bon Ton', 1913* modes might absorb our attention too long. But, while awaiting the inevitable reaction, Oriental Modernism finds its supreme expression in the present play at the Renaissance. M. Rousin, the designer of the decor for *Minaret* and M. Paul Poiret, the designer of the costumes, have vied with one another in imagination and daring. Perhaps the decors recall *Sumarun* and the Munich School. . . but if the costumes are inspired by Persian miniatures and Japanese prints, it is with an anticipation so violently modern that they certainly strike the eye more by excess of novelty than by archaism and exoticism.

'In Act 1, in the interior of a harem coloured white, indigo and acid green, surmounted by a frieze of palms, the women are clad in blue, green, black and gold. In Act III, against a black and white background the women pass in procession clad in white and black, but all different. Hooped tunics, around the body, reveal slashed pantaloons; three-tiered skirts, like lamp-shades placed one over the other spread out from long corslets gripping the body like a bandage. Snall caps of pearls enclose the head hiding the hair and the ears. Every kind of material is used, pearls, furs, gauzes and brocades and even those materials stiffened with gold and silver thread which lend M. Jean Worms the look of a lacquered statuette.

'To complete the illusion, Mme P., in the audience seems to be dressed as if for the stage with her heavy silver headdress hiding the hair, and in the centre of which are fixed unbelievable black plumes.'

¶ It would be impossible to describe with more penetration clothes on and off the stage at this period. Of the success of Bakst there could be no doubt.

Gabriel Mauray in 'Gazette du Bon Ton', 1913   'In drawing rooms and studios, in tea-shops and theatres, in the lounges of smart hotels and transatlantic liners, in the compartments of trains de luxe, everywhere, at this moment, nothing is spoken of but the dresses designed by Bakst and made by Mme Paquin and M. Joire.

'But they are not spoken of as one usually speaks of such things. . . they are spoken of as if they were alive. In fact, each has its own life, its own individuality. . . And then, they have such exquisite names, deliciously evocative, the names of goddesses and nymphs. I love them all. *Atalante* enchants me; I am ravished by *Alcyone*. . . I am mad about *Aglae*. That white tunic the bottom of which is embroidered with pink pearls, and with an opening in front, gathered half way down the

160

leg with a blue cameo. . . that bodice of blue and silver caught in at the waist by another smaller cameo, also blue. . . And *Niké* — how rightly named! A real *toilette de Victoire*. A robe of flesh-coloured satin with full sleeves and slits in the corsage, belted with emerald green silk underneath the luxurious cloak of the same, with its ample draperies and rich border of black and white — a cloak worthy of an Eastern empress. . .

"I say that all these are of a rare fantasy, daring and novelty and that M. Bakst is an artist of the most precious talent, who has ideas in plenty, an imagination perhaps too rich, an exquisite sense of colour. I share the general enthusiasm for his creations. But I find excessive his taste for geometrical arrangements and for violent colours.'

¶ It was through the House of Paquin that Bakst's ideas were realized:

The most prominent couturiers of the time were Cheruit, Doeuillet, Doucet, Paquin, Poiret, Redfern, Worth.

'Madame [Paquin] told us some very interesting facts about some of her models. It appears that the celebrated decorative artist, Bakst, who designs the costumes for the Russian dancers, and has to some extent revolutionized the whole field of stage decoration with his Oriental ideas, went to M. Joire, Madame Paquin's brother, who manages the firm with her, with 12 wonderful designs for dresses "qu'il avait rêvé!" He declared that his great desire was to have them realized in Mme Paquin's establishment. "Certainly," said M. Joire, and immediately placed the workrooms and workers at his disposal. Today among Paquin's own charming models these artistic but decidedly eccentric models are to be seen. [The Bakst model was] in soft white satin, with coat of black, a bonnet of cerise leather lined with white and the lace veil falling from within the bonnet. Eccentric, yes! but also quite a picture and extremely interesting as the carefully worked out ideal in dress of a well known artist.'

'Christian Science Monitor',
Mar. 28, 1913

¶ In an interview given to a correspondent of the *Pall Mall Gazette*, Bakst explained the matter himself:

'I was led to this subject from having to design the costumes for Debussy's new ballet, "Les Jeux", which, being the music of the future, tries to express the ideas of the future. "What is the characteristic of

'Illustrated London News',
Mar. 14, 1913

'Moscha'. Fashion drawing by Paquin

the age?" This I asked myself before sitting down to evolve my costume. I came to the conclusion that it was its sportiveness. . .And now the costume that I have imagined is based on woman's desire for freedom of movement.'

¶ Looking at the pictures in the *Illustrated London News* one would never have guessed it. In most of Bakst's designs the woman is fettered firmly round the knees!

The idea of the captive woman which the Unconscious of this period of female emancipation found so certainly attractive, expressed itself in two symbolic kinds of skirt: the harem skirt and the hobbleskirt.

'The harem skirt, an obvious derivation of the Oriental impulse, *'Taste and Fashion'*, was worn by a few bold women, but they were chased off the streets *1937* with almost as much obloquy as those *Merveilleuses* who dared to appear in the streets of Paris in 1795 with their breasts uncovered. The harem skirt for day wear was never anything more than an eccentricity; but its counterpart, which followed the same essential outline, the hobble skirt was worn by almost every woman. The narrow skirt of 1910 was an astonishing change from the flowing skirts which had prevailed for the last fifteen years. No longer was it necessary or even possible to lift the skirts when crossing the streets. The voluminous lace under-petticoat was abolished completely. The day of "frillies" was over, and an entirely new feminine aesthetic had been born.

'A fashion writer in 1910 remarks: "The hobble skirt is past — if it can indeed ever be said to have arrived so far as good fashion is concerned". But this is merely an expression of personal opinion, or perhaps hope, which is by no means borne out by the facts. The comic papers in 1911 are full of jokes about the excessively narrow skirts and the difficulty which women find in moving about in them.'

¶ It was all very peculiar:

'Never since Englishwomen took to outdoor activities had there *C. Willett* been a fashion so hampering and inconvenient as the Hobble skirt. *Cunnington.* One might see in the streets women trying in vain to mount the step *'English Women's* into an omnibus; a staircase called for gymnastics, and it was impos- *Clothing in the* sible to stoop without disaster. The tight skirt produced the "present *Present Century',* fashionable slouch", and sadly interferred with the Englishwoman's *1950* characteristic stride, so scorned by races less active. Indeed, it was even discovered that the Hobble skirt had a charm of its own, and we are told that "the tied-in effect at the feet has at least served a purpose in checking the ungracefully long stride, the outcome of the athletic sports nowadays indulged in by the fair sex. The short little tripping steps necessitated by present fashions possess a certain pleasing feminity". And we are assured that "the present fashions are almost wickedly clever".

¶ It was the Suffragettes themselves who provided the most astonishing spectacle of the divergence between the conscious and the unconscious in the minds of women:

C. Willett Cunnington. 'English Women's Clothing in the Present Century', 1952

'It is difficult to avoid using the popular name given to the epoch which might, more correctly, be called the "Tubular", with emphasis on vertical lines. It coincided with the Militant Suffragette movement whose activities in demanding greater emancipation seemed appropriately countered by the symbolism of the Hobble skirt; and the spectacle of fashionably dressed Militants, in the tightest of narrow skirts, demanding more freedom, supplied a beautiful example of the irresistible power of Fashion over Reason.

'That a restricting style of dress so obviously opposed to the march of events managed to keep Englishwomen in bondage for five years — in fact until six months after the opening of the first Great War — and that immediately the war was over the Hobble skirt was adopted once more, at least for a short time, is a very remarkable event in the history of Costume.'

¶ Yet these were the days of Mrs Pankhurst and 'Ann Veronica'.

C. Willett Cunnington. 'English Women's Clothing in the Present Century', 1952

'There is plenty of evidence that an "emancipatory urge", quite apart from any political movement, was affecting large numbers of Englishwomen. The economic pressure was telling, and the ranks of the Idle Rich were thinning. It was no longer possible for more than a few to sustain the extravagant cost of Edwardian fashions, and by 1908 the shadow of approaching war was inclining the mind to realism. The fairyland of frillies and chiffon and languorous charm was dissolving. A harsher, more masculine spirit began to reign. Moreover, in the middle of 1910 the eponymous figurehead of that epoch passed into history, and a younger sovereign seemed more appropriate to face the approaching storm.

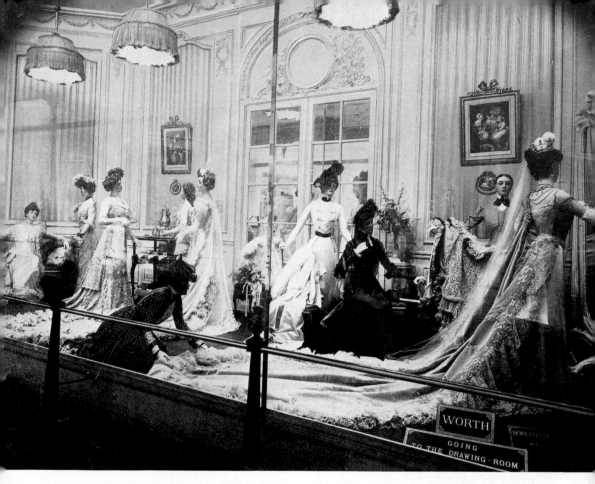

Above: Fashion display by Worth. Below: Hats of 1906 and 1907.

Above: the Committee of the Ladies' Kennel Association, 1908.

Below: 'Inexpensive Millinery' of 1911, and a yachting cap of the same year by Robert Heath.

'The new style of dress was no longer favouring the middle-aged; the straight up-and-down lines were those of youth, vigorous and markedly non-sensual in their absence of curves. All sorts of Classical effects were considered appropriate additions, but these, for the most part, were borrowed not from the Greeks direct, but via the Directoire and Empire modes, undergoing modifications in the process.'

¶ And the same authority concludes that —

'In trying to estimate the significance of the fashions of that eopch just before the war of 1914–18, we must recollect that a steadily increasing number of women were earning their living, and that the function of fashions was developing in a new direction. The belief that all the advantages, such as they are, of the modern democratic world have developed entirely since the first Great War flatters the post-war generation unduly. Already before that event fashions were aiming at giving the appearance of proficiency, and the non-domestic career was attracting a great many women who, nevertheless, preferred to be well dressed.'

C. Willett Cunnington. 'English Women's Clothing in the Present Century', 1952

¶ Certainly, if woman was still tied round the ankles she was no longer overwhelmed by the sheer weight of her clothes:

'Another noteworthy feature of the present century is the reduction in the amount of clothing worn, a process beginning about 1908 and reaching a climax of insufficiency twenty years later. At that date, at least in summer, the total weight of clothing often did not exceed one pound (a figure ascertained by actual weighing); and although there has been some slight increase since, there has been no return to anything approaching the burden of the Edwardian fashions.'

C. Willett Cunnington. 'English Women's Clothing in the Present Century', 1952

¶ Early in 1912 the extremely narrow skirts, plain to the ankles, showed signs of changing. A close-fitting, straight effect was still aimed at, but 'draperies' were coming in, especially in the evening, either in the form of an overdraping of some flimsy fabric over the main dress, or by a tunic, or by the catching up of some portion of the skirt here and there. It was this catching up of the skirt upon which fashion was to play its variations during the next three years. Lace tunics were very fashionable even with day dresses, and there was a passion for wearing rich materials over plainer ones. By 1913 or the beginning of 1914 the

165

tunic with a draped skirt had established itself to give a kind of lampshade effect.

But the most startling innovation in dress at the end of 1913 had nothing to do with skirts; it was a fundamental change in the form of

dresses at the neck. *Les décolletés du jour*, known in England as 'V-necks', created an immense amount of public excitement. High necks in the daytime, supported by little pieces of whalebone, had been considered essential for so long that it was thought a tremendous innovation when blouses became open at the throat. Old gentlemen whose mothers, in the middle of the preceding century, had thought nothing of baring their shoulders, now began a clamour against the immorality of the modern girl in exposing her neck. The fuss about the V-neck was a wonderful opportunity for contemporary moralists to make fools of themselves, and it was eagerly seized upon by the clergy of all denominations.

As a matter of fact the V-necks of 1914 were extremely modest. Although the collar disappeared altogether in some models, in others it merely retreated to the back to form the so-called Medici collar. In any case, the indignation of the unco' guid had, as usual, no effect whatever. Open necks became universal. A commentator of the period remarks with astonishment that 'even *serious* materials, as one may call blue serge, submit to this cut-open front rule'. The triumph of the exposed throat was complete, and the victory which had been gained by the women of 1914 was not likely to be allowed to slip by the emancipatory years of the War or the pleasure-loving decade which followed.

CHAPTER VIII

THE RUMBLINGS OF CHANGE

THE KING had not only accepted into his circle some of the most successful financiers of the day, but had even hobnobbed with tradesmen. The new 'Shopocracy' realized that titles, not only knighthoods and baronetcies but even peerages, were not beyond its reach. But the startling thing to old fashioned peers was not that shopkeepers became peers but that peers sometimes became shopkeepers. An encyclopaedia of the period thought it worth while to devote a whole article to this astonishing development.

'Every Woman's Encyclopaedia', 1910

'TITLES IN TRADE

'Those who are still young can remember the consternation caused by members of the aristocracy who took to trade as a means of money-making. To-day, when even sovereigns compete with their subjects and with the subjects of other sovereigns for the "nimble sixpence" which may be earned in trade, the feeling does not exist, or, at least, not to anything like the same extent. Few peers indeed would echo the sentiments expressed by the late Duke of Rutland, who, when a young man, wrote:

' "Let laws and learning, wealth and commerce die,

But leave us still our old nobility."

'The Marquis of Londonderry is a coal merchant. Indeed, he was the first peer to sell coals retail, for the great coal-owners, like the Earl of Derby, had, naturally, sold coals wholesale for a very long time.

'Another peer who deals in one of the chief commodities of life is Lord Rayleigh, whose dairies are justly celebrated for their milk and dairy produce. Lord Rayleigh has a great reputation as a scientist, and, in association with Sir William Ramsay, discovered one of the rare gases of the atmosphere, named argon.

168

'Lord Sudeley is the owner of a flourishing jam business, and makes a speciality of whole fruit jam.

'So many brewers have been made peers that it is one of the recognised jokes among a certain section of the Press to speak of the peerage as the "beerage." People may buy their "Bass" from Lord Burton, and their "Guinness" from Lord Iveagh, while the late Lady Meux owned or was largely interested in a well-known brewery.

'The Earl De La Warr, who has done so much to make Bexhill one of the most popular seaside resorts on the south coast, has had a good business experience, and is the proprietor of the Sackville Hotel at Bexhill.

'Another peer interested in hotels is the Earl of Leitrim, who was one of those peers who considered it his duty to go to the front during the South African War.

'There are many titles in connection with finance in the City, apart from those famous men who have made fortunes in trade and have had titles bestowed on them for one reason or another. Their name is legion, and, naturally, they have no place in this article.

'One of the first peers to go into business was Lord Archibald Campbell, one of the sons of the late Duke of Argyll, and brother and heir presumptive to the present Duke, who is husband of H.R.H. Princess Louise.

'Lord Archibald is a managing partner in the famous banking house of Messrs. Coutts and Co. Out of business, he is an author who has written several poems, and a painter whose home is decorated, to a great extent, by the work of his own brush.

'The Hon. Claude Hay, M.P., the son of the Earl of Kinnoull, is a partner in Messrs. Ransford and Co., stockbrokers, and so is Mr Charles Scudamore Stanhope, the brother of the Earl of Chesterfield, while two brothers of the Earl of Yarborough are also members of the House, as the Stock Exchange is always called.

'Another member is Lord Acheson, while Lord Lurgan's brother, Mr. Francis Cecil Brownlow, and Lord Dudley's brother, Mr. Ward, are partners in the firm of J. B. Millar and Co.

'Lord Charles Montague is head of the firm of Messrs. Montague, Oppenheim and Co.

'In connection with the Stock Exchange, it is interesting to recall the fact that the Duke de Vizeu, the eldest sone of Don Miguel of Braganza, who was reported to have come to an agreement with King Manuel of Portugal to support his Majesty in the event of his restora-

tion to the throne, worked as a clerk in the office of Messrs. Basil
Montgomery, Fitzgerald and Co., and is said to have been a very good
clerk indeed. He married Miss Anita Stewart, the daughter of the
Chicago millionaire, commonly known as "Silent Smith," because he
seldom spoke to anyone. The wedding took place at Dingwall, and was
the first Royal wedding celebrated in Scotland since Mary Stuart was
a bride.

'Lord Wolverton was engaged in the tin-plate business in New York
before he went into the family banking firm of Messrs. Glynn, Mills
and Co.

'The Earl of Ranfurly, who traces his ancestry back to William
Penn, the founder of Pennsylvania, and owns much property in the
irrigation colonies of Victoria, had at one time the largest fruit farm
in Mildura. He is a skilled gardener, and, besides supervising his men,
used to do a great deal of pruning and planting himself.

'The late Marquis of Bute became a wine merchant as the result of
an experiment which he was induced to make by his researches. He
was a great antiquarian, and he discovered that in pre-Reformation
days the Welsh monks used to make wine from grapes grown near
Cardiff. He, accordingly, had some vines planted about six miles from
that flourishing town, and the first vintage resulted in the production
of forty gallons of wine. Some years later the vintage produced a gross
sum of £3,000, which was more than the whole experiment had cost.
Some of the wine was of such excellent quality that it fetched £5. 15s.
a dozen.

'The first peer who actually opened a shop in London was the Earl
of Harrington. It was called the Elvaston Fruit Stores, after Elvaston
Castle, Derby, one of the seats of this peer. The stores were situated
near Charing Cross, where apples and other outdoor fruit, as well as
fruit grown under glass, and vegetables, in addition to flowers, could
be bought.

'As women in a less exalted social sphere are going into business and
competing with men, so titled women are starting businesses of various
kinds. Some of them are inspired with the purely utilitarian view of
making money for themselves, while others have for their primary object the benefiting of those who need financial assistance.

'Among the ladies in trade, priority of place belongs, naturally, to
the duchesses. The Duchess of Abercorn has a most successful
creamery at Barons Court, the Duke's seat in Ireland.

'The Countess of Essex, who is one of the peeresses America has

170

given us, for she was Miss Adela Beach Grant, of New York, had at one time the idea of running a laundry in association with Mrs. Hwfa Williams, who is equally well known in the most select circles of society. Eventually, however, it was found to be too great a trouble, and the idea was abandoned. Lady Wimborne, who at one time was so notable a hostess in London, had a shop in Bond Street, where Bibles and Church books were sold.

Lady Molesworth has established a jam factory at Walters Hall, near Minster-on-sea. At her old home large quantities of jam used to be made, and in one year, it is said, nearly a ton was manufactured. Berween three and four years ago it was decided to convert the old brewhouse adjoining the hall into a factory, and to go into the business on a larger scale. The building was accordingly given a new roof, and was fitted with a cooking plant capable of turning out half a ton of jam a day. All the goods made at Walters Hall are "Coronet Brand," and are guaranteed to be made of pure, unadulterated fruit and pure sugar, a highly desirable condition in these days when certain un-scrupulous manufacturers introduce other ingredients into their products. At first Lady Molesworth did not supply the trade, as her private connection was so large that it kept the factory as busy as she wanted it to be.

'Just as people who care about buying their dairy produce from a peer can do so, so ladies could until recently buy flowers from a woman of title, for Lady Angela Forbes had a flower shop in George Street, Portman Square, which she called "My Shop." She served in it her-self, and her portrait, standing at the door, was reproduced in many of the illustrated papers when she started business.

'Another titled woman connected with the flower industry is Lady Eileen Wyndham-Quin, daughter of Lord Dunraven, who runs a violet farm at Adare, her father's Irish seat.

'The products of the soil have a great deal of attraction also for the Hon. Frances Wolseley, the daughter of Field-Marshal Viscount Wolseley, the famous soldier. She has a school for woman gardeners at Glynde, Sussex. It is interesting to recall that she is the heir to her father's title under special remainder.

'Not only are certain titled men interested in hotels, but also titled women. Lady Burton has a fine hotel at Aviemore, which commands a lovely view of the Cairngorm Range, while the widowed Lady Augusta Orr-Ewing has another hotel, with good golf links attached, at Dunskey, near Stranraer, in Wigtownshire.

'One of the hardest worked members of the aristocracy is Lady Auckland, who, after having been reduced from — it is said — £20,000 a year to comparative poverty, opened a shop for artistic furniture and seventeenth century silver. Instead of leaving the practical work to subordinates, she used herself to be at the office by ten o'clock in the morning, while she personally attended to her clients.

'In the dressmaking world the name of Madame Lucile is one with which to conjure. It conceals the identity of Lady Duff Gordon, one of the survivors of the ill-fated Titanic, who, beginning in a small way, soon developed an enormous connection by reason of her enterprise, cleverness, and wonderful taste. It was she who introduced the idea of "emotional gowns," which were first worn on the stage by Mrs. Brown Potter, herself a society actress. From the stage, the idea was taken up in private, and for a time had a great vogue. Now, in addition to her other establishments, Lady Duff Gordon has comparatively recently opened an establishment in New York, where her authority is so great that one of the chief newspapers prints an article from her pen regularly every week.

'Another well-known dressmaker is Lady Affleck, who determined to go into business, and obtained an engagement at Selfridge's as a sort of critic. An account was opened for her, and she made purchases in the various departments. When these were delivered to her she wrote a report on them. This was so valuable that after a time she was offered a position as one of the chief saleswomen in the costume department, and those ladies who were waited on by Madame Julia will have the satisfaction of knowing that it was Lady Affleck who served them. In the neighbourhood of Edgware Road is a millinery shop which is managed by Lady Hope; while Lady Rachael Byng, a daughter of the Earl of Strafford, is the head of an artistic needlework shop.

'It may seem a curious thing for a woman connected with the aristocracy to keep a registry for servants, yet that is the occupation of Miss Edith Kerr, one of the daughters of the late Lord Frederick Kerr and a relation of Lord Lothian. Her establishment is in Lower Belgrave Street.

'Among the many activities of the Countess of Warwick was a shop for ladies' underclothing which existed for some years in Bond Street. There was no attempt to disguise the identity of the noble owner, for the name "Countess of Warwick" was inscribed in large letters under the window.

'In a similar way, the names of the Countess of Bessborough and the

172

The Countess of Warwick. Painting by Ellis Roberts.

Above: Slum children, 1910.

Below: East End interior, 1917.

Countess Duncannon were inscribed in letters of gold over the doorway of the shop which they had near Bond Street.

'Were one to go into more exalted circles it would be easy to lengthen this list, for even kings have not disdained to go into trade.

'The German Emperor, for instance, has a pottery business which is said to yield a turnover of about £20,000 a year, of which sum £10,000 goes into his Imperial Majesty's pocket as clear profit.

'The King of Wurtemburg owns two hotels which yield him a profit of £8,000 a year, while the King of Servia has a barber's shop and an apothecary's shop, and the Duke and Duchess Carl Theodore of Bavaria are the proprietors of a hotel at Tegernsee, not very far from Munich. The Duchess was the Infanta Marie Josepha of Portugal.'

¶ Still, it was a long call from 'titled women connected with the flower industry' and daughters of earls running 'artistic needlework shops' to the real workers whose position, in the decade before the First World War was anything but satisfactory. When we look back on the Edwardian epoch as a gay and carefree period we are, of course, thinking only of the privileged classes. Behind the bright Edwardian façade there was much poverty and misery, and the social conscience of the day was not sufficiently disturbed to do much about it.

'Something ought to be done by the authorities to wipe out the scandal of the homeless people who are forced to sleep out on these wintry nights. I walked home along the Embankment this morning at two o'clock with Bryan Carter, editor of the *Standard*. Every bench from Blackfriars to Westminster was filled with shivering people, all huddled up — men, women, and children. The Salvation Army people were out giving away hot broth, but even this was merely a temporary palliative against the bitter night. At Charing Cross we encountered a man with his wife and two tiny children. They had come to town from Reading to look for work. . . This unemployment question is really a great problem.'   *R.D.B's 'Diary', Dec. 24, 1901*

¶ By the strict letter of the Law people were not allowed to sleep out at all, at least at night. It was the duty of the police to 'move them on'. Jack London was moved to natural indignation by this absurdity:

'Among those who carry the banner,[1] Green Park has the reputation of opening its gates earlier than the other parks, and at quarter-past   *Jack London. 'The People of the Abyss', 1903*

[1] Slang phrase meaning "the homeless".

173

four in the morning, I, and many more, entered Green Park. It was raining again, but they were worn out with the night's walking, and they were down on the benches and asleep at once. Many of the men stretched out full length on the dripping wet grass, and, with the rain falling steadily upon them, were sleeping the sleep of exhaustion.

'And now I wish to criticise the powers that be. They *are* the powers, therefore they may decree whatever they please; so I make bold only to criticise the ridiculousness of their decrees. All night long they make the homeless ones walk up and down. They drive them out of doors and passages, and lock them out of the parks. The evident intention of all this is to deprive them of sleep. Well and good, the powers have the power to deprive them of sleep, or of anything else for that matter; but why under the sun do they open the gates of the parks at five o'clock in the morning and let the homeless ones go inside and sleep? If it is their intention to deprive them of sleep, why do they let them sleep after five in the morning? And if it is not their intention to deprive them of sleep, why don't they let them sleep earlier in the night?

'In this connection, I will say that I came by Green Park that same day, at one in the afternoon, and that I counted scores of the ragged wretches asleep in the grass. It was Sunday afternoon, the sun was fitfully appearing, and the well-dressed West Enders, with their wives and progeny, were out by thousands, taking the air. It was not a pleasant sight for them, those horrible, unkempt, sleeping vagabonds; while the vagabonds themselves, I know, would rather have done their sleeping the night before.

'And so, dear soft people, should you ever visit London Town, and see these men asleep on the benches and in the grass, please do not think they are lazy creatures, preferring sleep to work. Know that the powers that be have kept them walking all the night long, and that in the day they have nowhere else to sleep.'

¶ Even those who were employed seemed, sometimes, little better off:

Mrs C. S. Peel,
O.B.E.
'Life's Enchanted
Cup', 1933
'An ordinary pre-War wage for a working man was anything from 25s. to 30s. a week. How many of the ladies who offered to go and talk to the poor could have attempted to house, clothe and feed a family on such a sum? How many could have worked surrounded by a tribe of small children, been kept awake at night by a teething baby, and yet have remained cheerful and uncomplaining?'

174

¶ Thirty shillings a week was by way of being a good wage. The average was near 20s:

'How does a working man's wife bring up a family on 20s. a week? Assuming that there are four children, and that it costs 4s. a week to feed a child, there would be but 4s. left on which to feed both parents, and nothing at all for coal, gas, clothes, insurance, soap, or rent. Four shillings is the amount allowed the foster-mother for food in the case of a child boarded out by some Boards of Guardians; therefore it would seem to be a justifiable figure to reckon upon. But for a woman with 20s. a week to spend it is evidently ridiculously high. If the calculation were to be made upon half this sum, would it be possible? The food for the children in that case would amount to 8s. To allow the same amount to each parent as to each child would not be an extravagance, and we should on that basis arrive at the sum of 12s. a week for the food of six people. That would leave 8s. for all other expenses. But rent alone may come to 6s. or 7s., and how could the woman on 20s. a week manage with 1s., or perhaps 2s., for coal, gas, insurance, clothes, cleaning materials, and thrift?' *Mrs Pember Reeves. 'Round About A Pound A Week', 1913*

¶ But many, far too many, had even less:

'A woman, now in fairly comfortable circumstances, told one of my investigators something of the struggle which she had gone through during the years when her husband was earning only 17s. a week. To make both ends meet with that sum for a large family of children was no easy matter. Each week, she said, as soon as she received the 17s. she put aside the money required for rent, and then planned out exactly how she could spend the remainder to the best advantage. The family never had a joint of meat, but occasionally she managed to afford 6d. for a sheep's head or to buy 6d. worth of "meat pieces". At the birth of a child she employed a woman for a week to nurse her, to whom she gave 5s. and her board. As soon as she knew that a child was coming she began saving odd coppers until the 5s. was collected, and so she was always able to pay the woman before she left the house· During the time she was nursing her children she lived chiefly upon bread and tea. Who can wonder that some of her children died during their first year?' *B. Seebohm Rowntree. 'Poverty', 1901*

¶ Even the children in the workhouse were better off:

175

Mrs Pember Reeves.
'Round About A
Pound A Week',
1913
'In Schedule A in the First Report of the Departmental Committee, with respect to the Poor Law Orders, a diet for a child of over two and under eight years is given, of which one day in any workhouse might be as follows:

Breakfast. — Bread, 5 ounces; fresh milk, ½ pint.

Dinner. — Roast beef, 1½ ounces; potatoes or other vegetables, 4 ounces; fresh fruit-pudding, 6 ounces.

Supper. — Seed-cake, 4 ounces; cocoa (half milk), ½ pint.

'No mother on 20s. a week could secure such food for her children. It is not supposed that the Departmental Committee appointed by the President of the Local Government Board would prescribe an extravagant diet, and it seems terrible that the children of the hard-working honest poor should be fed on a diet which is about half that prescribed as the most economical and very least that a healthy workhouse child should have.'

¶ Infant mortality was appalling, not only in London but all over the country.

B. Seebohm
Rowntree.
'Poverty', 1901
'When we examine the mortality of children under twelve months of age, we find the same terrible waste of human life proceeding in the poorer areas. Particulars have been ascertained regarding infant mortality [in York]. The results are as follows:–

Area No. 1 (poorest), out of every 1000 children born	247	die
„ No. 2 (middle),	„	„	184	before
„ No. 3 (highest),	„	„	173	they are
Servant-keeping class,	„	„	94	twelve
Whole of York,	„	„	176	months
				old.

'We thus see that in the poorest area one child out of every four born dies before it is twelve months old. In one parish in this area one out of every three children born dies in its first year. Such facts as these bring out in strong relief the adverse conditions under which the poor are living.

'It is sometimes urged that although the individual suffering indicated by a high infant mortality is considerable, it is not without some counterbalancing advantages, as the sickly children are thus weeded out. Even if this Spartan view be accepted, it must be remembered that of those who survive, a large proportion do so only with seriously enfeebled constitutions.'

Above: A masked procession of clerks in 1913.

Below: Demonstration by unemployed men in Trafalgar Square, 1908.

¶ Other investigators told the same tale:

'Whatever the exact causes are which produce in each case the sickly children so common in these households, the all-embracing one is poverty. The proportion of the infantile death-rate of Hampstead to that of Hoxton — something like 18 to 140 — proves this to be a fact. The 42 families already investigated in this inquiry have had altogether 201 children, but 18 of these were either born dead or died within a few hours. Of the remaining 183 children of all ages, ranging from a week up to sixteen or seventeen years, 39 had died, or over one-fifth. Out of the 144 survivors 5 were actually deficient, while many were slow in intellect or unduly excitable. Those among them who were born during the investigation were, with one exception, normal, cosy, healthy babies, with good appetites, who slept and fed in the usual way. They did not, however, in spite of special efforts made on their behalf, fulfil their first promise. At one year of age their environment had put its mark upon them. Though superior to babies of their class, who had not had special nourishment and care, they were vastly inferior to children of a better class who, though no finer or healthier at birth, had enjoyed proper conditions, and could therefore develop on sound and hygienic lines.'

*Mrs Pember Reeves.
'Round About A
Pound A Week',
1913*

'It seems strange to-day, but that some children were hungry was accepted, as wet weather is accepted. I can remember my mother helping to serve soup, which could be bought by the needy for a penny a jug, and hearing her say: "Fill that jug to the top, and give the children extra bread, that family never has enough to eat." In most towns in the winter such soup was provided for the poor, the meat and bones would often be given by the butcher, the vegetables by the green-grocer, bread to eat with the soup by the baker, and the soup would be made and served by charitable ladies. Neither the tradesmen who provided the materials for the soup, nor those ladies who served it, appeared to think it wrong in a rich country that families could be in such want that they would queue with jugs for a pennyworth of soup. There was nothing wrong with the people of that date, they were just as kind-hearted and easily moved as we are to-day, it was that the way they thought was different; poverty was something that happened — just as some people were born cripples, you helped, but you did not expect to cure them — indeed there were many who supposed that it would be upsetting God's purpose if you did.'

*Noel Streatfeild in
'The Day Before
Yesterday', 1956*

¶ It was not only the children who suffered:

Jack London.
'The People of the Abyss', 1903

'The statistics of London tell a terrible tale. The population of London is one-seventh of the total population of the United Kingdom, and in London, year in and year out, one adult in every four dies on public charity, either in the workhouse, the hospital, or the asylum. When the fact that the well-to-do do not end thus is taken into consideration, it becomes manifest that it is the fate of at least one in every three adult workers to die on public charity. . .

'Year by year, and decade after decade, rural England pours in a flood of vigorous strong life, that not only does not renew itself, but perishes by the third generation. Competent authorities aver that the London workman whose parents and grandparents were born in London is so remarkable a specimen that he is rarely found.

'Mr. A. C. Pigou has said that the aged poor and the residuum which compose the "submerged tenth", constitute $7\frac{1}{2}$ per cent. of the population of London. Which is to say that last year, and yesterday, and to-day, at this very moment, 450,000 of these creatures are dying miserably at the bottom of the social pit called "London". As to how they die, I shall take an instance from the morning's paper.

' "SELF NEGLECT

' "Yesterday Dr. Wynn Westcott held an inquest at Shoreditch, respecting the death of Elizabeth Crews, aged 77 years, of 32 East Street, Holborn, who died on Wednesday last. Alice Mathieson stated that she was landlady of the house where deceased lived. Witness last saw her alive on the previous Monday. She lived quite alone. Mr. Francis Birch, relieving officer for the Holborn district, stated that deceased had occupied the room in question for 35 years. When witness was called, on the 1st, he found the old woman in a terrible state, and the ambulance and coachman had to be disinfected after the removal. Dr. Chase Fennell said death was due to blood-poisoning from bed-sores, due to self-neglect and filthy surroundings, and the jury returned a verdict to that effect."

'The most startling thing about this little incident of a woman's death is the smug complacency with which the officials looked upon it and rendered judgment. That an old woman of seventy-seven years of age should die of SELF-NEGLECT is the most optimistic way possible of looking at it. It was the old dead woman's fault that she died, and having located the responsibility, society goes contentedly on about its own affairs.'

178

¶ Before she became too old she had probably been employed in some 'sweated' industry. Jack London cites another heart-rending case:

'Conceive of an old woman, broken and dying, supporting herself and four children, and paying three shillings per week rent, by making match boxes at 2¼d. per gross. Twelve dozen boxes for 2¼d., and, in addition, finding her own paste and thread! She never knew a day off, either for sickness, rest, or recreation. Each day and every day, Sunday as well, she toiled fourteen hours. Her day's stint was seven gross, for which she received 1s. 3¾d. In the week of ninety-eight hours' work, she made 7066 match boxes, and earned 4s. 10¼d., less her paste and thread.' *Jack London. 'The People of the Abyss', 1903*

¶ Things were no better in the clothing industry:

'I talked with a woman who was representative of that type which has been jerked out of its little out-of-the-way streets and has started on the fatal fall to the bottom. Her husband was a fitter and a member of the Engineers' Union. That he was a poor engineer was evidenced by his inability to get regular employment. He did not have the energy and enterprise necessary to obtain or hold a steady position. *Jack London. 'The People of the Abyss', 1903*

'The pair had two daughters, and the four of them lived in a couple of holes, called "rooms" by courtesy, for which they paid seven shillings per week. They possessed no stove, managing their cooking on a single gas-ring in the fireplace. Not being persons of property, they were unable to obtain an unlimited supply of gas; but a clever machine had been installed for their benefit. By dropping a penny in the slot, the gas was forthcoming, and when a penny's worth had forthcome the supply was automatically shut off. "A penny gawn in no time", she explained, "an' the cookin' not arf done!"

'Incipient starvation had been their portion for years. Month in and month out, they had arisen from the table able and willing to eat more. And when once on the downward slope, chronic innutrition is an important factor in sapping vitality and hastening the decent.

'Yet this woman was a hard worker. From 4.30 in the morning till the last light at night, she said, she had toiled at making cloth dress-skirts, mark you, lined up with two flounces, for seven shillings a dozen! This is equal to $1.75 per dozen, or 14¾ cents per skirt.'

¶ Newspapers and magazines, some of which could not, by any

stretch of the imagination, be called revolutionary, or even left wing, began to ask themselves the question —

'HOW THE POOR EXIST

'Attention has before now been drawn in these columns to the fact that while philanthropic schemes are always on foot for the betterment of the working classes, the weak point of a very large number is that they do not touch the very poorest of the poor. There are few artisans or workmen of any calling who, if they are in regular employment and, above all things, steady in themselves, cannot find comfortable rooms with the latest conveniences, cannot live a little way out and avail themselves of cheap trains or tramcars, and cannot taste of at least some of the comforts of home life; but, after all is said and done, such men and women have a backbone of their own in that they are in work all the year round and can pay. In the opinion of many people, however, more might be done in the way of reclaiming, or attempting to reclaim, that extremely difficult class to cope with, the irregularly employed, the unskilled people, who have to trust to luck too often to earn a living wage, and who are apt to sink lower and lower in social degradation till they become a pest and a nuisance, so rendering the problem ten thousand times harder to solve. There is plenty of room for work in this direction, as is evidenced by a census recently taken by the medical officer of health to the London County Council, together with the authorities of Finsbury, Fulham, Greenwich, and Southwark, of the homeless poor of the metropolis, the object being to ascertain the number of persons sleeping out in London. It was found that 1869 men and 312 women had been found on this particular occasion (Feb. 17) in the streets or on staircases, 827 men and thirty-nine women and children reporting themselves at the Whitechapel depot, while at the Church Army tent in Clare-market 300 men were chopping wood. Turning to the common lodging houses and shelters, it was found that they contained 23,690 people, 21,254 being single men, 1688 single women, 357 married couples, and thirty-four children under ten years of age, 1600 men of this total having received their tickets from the Church Army. There was also vacant night accommodation in the casual wards for 337 men, 213 women, and 117 women and children, the number of homeless persons (2481) found being greater by 684 than the number on Jan. 29 of last year, when the census taken did not extend over such a wide area; but the fact that the Church Army gave away many tickets for beds, as also did the

180

Salvation Army, suggested to the medical officer a difference of 2348. More pathetic still than even these sordid statements is the fact that 988 persons were that night turned away from common lodging houses, 742 because they had no money, 211 because the houses were full, while twenty-one others were too dirty, eight drunk, five bad characters, and one created a disturbance. It may at once be admitted that in all probability a large percentage of these people were "worthless characters", on whom little sympathy need be wasted, but that does not blind one to the fact that on a particular night in London nearly 30,000 men, women, and children were either utterly destitute or nearly so. As has been said before in these columns, the idle, dissolute scamp should be taken severely in hand and made to work; but, at the same time, there are thousands drifting daily towards the same degraded existence, whom it is yet not too late to rescue, and more of London's charity might with advantage be devoted to this kind of work than is the case at the present moment.'

¶ Of course, there were tentative efforts to bring about some kind of improvement. An eminent woman reformer tells us something about—

'THE ST. PANCRAS MOTHERS' AND BABIES' WELCOME   *'The Queen', 1910*
By the Hon. Mrs. Bertrand Russell, B.A.

'One of the first beginnings in the fight against infantile mortality and the ignorance of untrained mothers was made more than two years ago in London by the starting of the popular School for Mothers, or Mothers' and Babies' Welcome, as it reads in the lettering around a high and conspicuous building in the poorest part of St. Pancras, at 37, Chalton-street, Euston-road. In the large window is an invitation to the "baby consultations" with a beautiful picture of a baby, and underneath Blake's lines:

> I happy am, Joy is my name;
> Sweet joy befall thee.

'Just by the door is an injunction not to bring in any "comforter", and within doors the walls are covered with charts and pictures illustrating food values or showing the bow-legged baby, and the baby half strangled by the coils of rubber tubing attached to his feeding bottle. The large, light room is divided by a screen, at one end rows of chairs and space for perambulators, at the other end a dining table, where the daily 1½d. dinners are served to nursing and expectant mothers. These dinners are only given on the order of the doctor when she finds that the pregnant mother is in need of wholesome food, or that the nursing mother's milk is not sufficiently nourishing for the baby, and in winter the average daily attendance is over twenty. Of this number over half pay for themselves or are paid for by societies or private persons, while a few, after careful investigation, are given the dinners free, because of unemployment or illness in their homes.

'When the dinner is cleared away the screen is pushed aside, and the room is turned into a large classroom, or, on weighing days, a waiting-room for mothers and babies and perambulators. On Tuesdays and Fridays, from three to five, the babies rule supreme — the baby who is being weighed by either Dr. Dora Bunting or Dr. Mabel Hardie in the small warm room upstairs, the baby who has just been weighed and is being dressed in the ante-room, and the rows of babies waiting up and down stairs for their turn to be weighed. Once a fortnight each baby is brought, and the mother pays 1d. for the earnest consultation with the doctor over baby's progress and her own health.'

¶ Something was being done to try to tackle the intractable problem of prostitution:

Mrs C. S. Peel,
O.B.E.
'Life's Enchanted
Cup', 1933

'In order to obtain local colour for my books I procured an introduction to a lady who was employed by a certain Association to work amongst the unfortunate girls of the West End streets. We made friends and she told me much about her experiences and took me out with her once or twice. That woman was a saint if ever there was one; a hard-working, tolerant, humorous saint. She told me that it was not unusual for a man who had become interested in a girl to apply to Sister, as she was known, in the hope that the girl might be removed from the life of the streets. In few cases, however, could any kind of work which would appeal to them be offered to such girls. "The life gets its claws into them," Sister explained, "and after a time they are useless for regular work."

'I pushed my investigations further, visiting Homes for what were called "fallen" girls. Almost all of these places were financed by religious bodies. There would be, perhaps, a Sister in charge of a receiving station, to which the police or any other interested person would send some stranded girl who had already got into trouble or was in danger of doing so. From this temporary shelter the girl would be passed on to a Home, in some of which a girl was taken before her baby was born, then sent to the Infirmary

182

for her confinement, and received again with the baby afterwards.

'In one Home which I visited, in a large bare room were rows of cots. Every baby appeared to be screaming as hard as it could scream. After a day's work the young mothers would return to put their babies to bed, and to wash their clothes. They had the charge of the infants at night, rose early to attend to them, and then went out to work again. Perhaps it was not wonderful that the life of the street, hard though it might be, appealed more to young girls than this fifteen-hour day of respectability.'

¶ One of the main troubles was housing:

'The vast majority was engaged in most productive "dirty" work and were badly housed, the houses we lived in from when I was born in 1884 to when I left home in 1905 were more or less typical working-class houses. The house in which I and four of my brothers and my sister Blodwen were born in had no back-door, no water or any conveniences. It was one of a dozen small houses in a row, at each end of which there was a dry closet for admission to which we more often than not had to queue-up. In the dozen houses of the row lived upwards of fifty people, men, women and children, and all they had for the use of their bowels were these two dry closets.' *Jack Jones in 'The Day Before Yesterday', 1956*

¶ Seebohm Rowntree bears this out with chapter and verse, here are some of the cases listed in his records:

'Widow. Two rooms. Son thirty-two, messenger. Parish relief. Very weakly. Sober and industrious. House clean and fairly comfortable. Son consumptive; in sick club. Been twenty-five years in house and cannot get water laid on, though they offered to pay more rent. This tenement shares one water-tap with fourteen other tenements, and one closet with fourteen others. Rent 3s. 9d. *B. Seebohm Rowntree. 'Poverty', 1901*

Old widow. One room. Parish relief. Has a lodger who is a charwoman. Has been in better circumstances, and has some comfortable furniture, but is not clean. Has been confined to her room for twelve months. Drink may be cause of poverty here. This tenement shares one water-tap with eleven others, and one closet with fourteen other tenements. Rent 1s. 4d.

N.B. Both are living in very old premises, which are now let out in single rooms. There is only one water-tap for the whole block. There are

183

no sinks, slops being emptied down the street grating, or down one
in the yard. There are two closets in the yard, but only one is fit to
use, and is shared by fifteen different families.'

Bricklayer's labourer (25). Married. Two rooms. Three children,
school age or under. The stench here is abominable. The grating of
the street drain is $1\frac{1}{2}$ yards from the house door, and is blocked up.
There are twenty-three houses in this yard, and only one water-tap
for the whole number. Four houses join at one closet. There is one
ashpit for this yard; it is full to the top, and slime running down the
walls. Rent 2s. 3d.'

¶ People not only lived, they worked in such places:

Jack London.
'The People of the
Abyss', 1903

'There were seven rooms in this abomination called a house. In six
of the rooms, twenty-odd people, of both sexes and all ages, cooked,
ate, slept, and worked. In size the rooms averaged eight feet by eight,
or possibly nine. The seventh room we entered. It was the den in which
five men "sweated." It was seven feet wide by eight long, and the
table at which the work was performed took up the major portion of
the space. On this table were five lasts, and there was barely room for
the men to stand to their work, for the rest of the space was heaped
with cardboard, leather, bundles of shoe uppers, and a miscellaneous
assortment of materials used in attaching the uppers of shoes to their
soles.'

¶ It is small wonder that the public conscience was beginning to stir:

B. Seebohm
Rowntree.
'Poverty', 1901

'That in this land of abounding wealth, during a time of perhaps
unexampled prosperity, probably more than one-fourth of the population are living in poverty, is a fact which may well cause great
searchings of heart. There is surely need for a greater concentration
of thought by the nation upon the well-being of its own people, for no
civilisation can be sound or stable which has at its base this mass of
stunted human life. The suffering may be all but voiceless, and we
may long remain ignorant of its extent and severity, but when once
we realise it we see that social questions of profound importance await
solution.'

¶ Small wonder, too, that some of the investigators lost their tempers,
and, like Jack London, began to harbour dangerous thoughts:

184

'Society must be reorganised, and a capable management put at the *Jack London. 'The People of the Abyss', 1903* head. That the present management is incapable, there can be no discussion. It has drained the United Kingdom of its life-blood. It has enfeebled the stay-at-home folk till they are unable longer to struggle in the van of the competing nations. It has built up a West End and an East End as large as the Kingdom is large, in which one end is riotous and rotten, the other end sickly and underfed.

'A vast empire is foundering on the hands of this incapable management. And by empire is meant the political machinery which holds together the English-speaking people of the world outside of the United States. Nor is this charged in a pessimistic spirit. Blood empire is greater than political empire, and the English of the New World and the Antipodes are strong and vigorous as ever. But the political empire under which they are nominally assembled is perishing. The political machine known as the British Empire is running down. In the hands of its management it is losing momentum every day.

'It is inevitable that this management, which has grossly and criminally mismanaged, shall be swept away. Not only has it been wasteful and inefficient, but it has misappropriated the funds. Every worn-out, pasty-faced pauper, every blind man, every prison babe, every man, woman, and child whose belly is gnawing, with hunger pangs, is hungry because the funds have been misappropriated by the management.'

¶ Greater writers than Jack London began to ask awkward questions. If the test of greatness in a writer is the influence he exerts on his generation, three men stand out before all others, for it was they who changed the whole social climate of their time. They were Bernard Shaw, H. G. Wells and (to a lesser degree) Arnold Bennett. These three were the enemies of complacency, the great iconoclasts, the harbingers of change.

Shaw was the most provocative. He seemed to be attacking the whole basis of society, as indeed he was. The little barbed darts of phrases which he flung about with so much nonchalance had a way of striking in the flesh and festering there. He turned everything upside down. 'Vice', he said, 'is the waste of life. Poverty, obedience and celibacy are the canonical vices.' Such a doctrine might have suited the Edwardian Upper Classes well enough. They were not given to the practice of these particular vices, however they might waste their lives. But Shaw reminded them that 'the more a man possesses over and above what he uses, the more careworn he becomes'. And if there were poor in the land it was largely the fault of the rich. 'Every new yard of West End creates a new acre of East End.' And again, 'the true diagnostic of modern gentility is parasitism'. An uncomfortable, not to say an alarming doctrine.

Shaw was known to be a member of the Fabian Society, the existence of which was just beginning to be realized by the vast majority of English people. It had, however, been founded as long ago as 1883 and Shaw had been a member almost from the beginning. By lectures and pamphlets (particularly in 'Fabian Tracts') the doctrines were spread abroad. The Fabians played a part in founding the Labour Party in 1900, and its success in the General Election of 1906 startled those who had been brought up to think that.

> . . .'every baby born alive
> Is either a little Liberal
> Or else a little Conservative.'

H. G. Wells was a member for a time, but he quarrelled with some of the leading Fabians and from 1906 was inclined to temper his admiration with a certain amount of ridicule. Readers of *Ann Veronica* will remember his rather cruel picture of the kind of woman who fluttered round such movements and delighted in anything that seemed to be 'advanced'.

H. G. Wells. 'There was a wild light in her eye, and her straight hair was out
'Ann Veronica', demonstrating and suffragetting upon some independent notions of
1909 its own. Her fingers were bursting through her gloves, as if to get at once in touch with Ann Veronica. . . Everything, Miss Miniver[1] said, was "working up", everything was "coming on" — the Higher Thought, the Simple Life, Socialism, Humanitarianism, it was all the same really. . . Hitherto in the world's history there had been precursors of this Progress at great intervals, voices that had spoken and seared, but now it was all coming on together in a rush. She mentioned, with familiar respect, Christ and Buddha and Shelley and Nietzsche and Plato. Pioneers all of them. Such names shone brightly in the darkness, with black spaces of unilluminated emptiness about them, as stars shine in the night; but now — now it was different; now it was dawn — the real dawn.

"The women are taking it up," said Miss Miniver; "the women and

---

[1] No relation of Mrs Miniver, who attained such well-deserved fame in the Second World War.

186

the common people, all pressing forward, all roused. . . You must let me take you to things — to meetings and things, to conferences and talks. . . I must take you everywhere. I must take you to the Suffrage people, and the Tolstoyans, and the Fabians."

"I have heard of the Fabians," said Ann Veronica.

"It's *the* Society!" said Miss Miniver. "It's the centre of the intellectuals. Some of the meetings are wonderful! Such earnest, beautiful women (Such deep-browed men!). . . And to think that there they are making history! There they are putting together the plans of a new world. Almost light-heartedly. There is Shaw and Webb, and Wilkins the author, and Toomer, and Dr. Tumpany — the most wonderful people! There you see them discussing, deciding, planning! Just think — *they are making a new world.*" '

¶ The picture is not without malice. But Wells was just as much an enemy of complacency as Shaw himself. He knew all about the 'Stately Homes of England' for he had been brought up in one — albeit on the wrong side of the green baize door.

'The unavoidable suggestion of that wide park and that fair, large *H. G. Wells.* house, dominating church, village and the countryside, was that they *'Tono-Bungay', 1909* represented the thing that mattered supremely in the world, and that all other things had significance only in relation to them. They represented the Gentry, the Quality, by and through and for whom the rest of the world, the farming folk and the labouring folk, the trades-people of Ashborough, and the upper servants, and the lower servants and the servants of the estate, breathed and lived and were permitted. . . The great house, the church, the village, and the labourers and the servants in their stations and degrees, seemed to me, I say, to be a closed and complete social system. About us were other villages and great estates, and from house to house, interlacing, correlated, the Gentry, the fine Olympians, came and went. The country towns seemed mere collections of shops, marketing places for the tenantry, centres for such education as they needed, as entirely dependent on the gentry as the village and scarcely less directly so. . . I though this was the order of the whole world. . . It seemed to be in the divine order. That all this fine appearance was already sapped, that there were forces at work that might presently carry all this elaborate social system. . . to Limbo, had scarcely dawned upon me. . . There are many people in England to-day upon whom it has not yet dawned.'

187

¶ Wells was one of the first to depict members of the lower middle classes (for his heroes are never proletarians; after his visit to Russia, Lenin described him as a 'typical *petit bourgeois*') not as figures of fun but in the round as human beings. He even went so far as to rejoice that he had not been at a public school:

H. G. Wells.
'Tono-Bungay', 1909
'The public schools that had come into existence in the brief glow of the Renascence had been taken possession of by the ruling class; the lower classes were not supposed to stand in need of schools, and our middle stratum got the schools it deserved, private schools which any unqualified pretender was free to establish. Mine was kept by a man who had the energy to get himself a College of Preceptors diploma, and considering how cheap his charges were, I will readily admit the place might have been worse. . . We had one inestimable privilege at that school, and that was spiritual neglect. We dealt with one another with the forcible simplicity of natural boys, we "cheeked", and "punched" and "clouted"; we thought ourselves Red Indians and cowboys and such-like honourable things, and not young English gentlemen; we never felt the strain of "Onward, Christian soldiers", nor were swayed by any premature piety in the cold oak pew, of our Sunday devotions. All that was good.'

¶ To be thankful for 'spiritual neglect' — here was indeed something new and startling. Wells detested — as well he might — the narrow Evangelicalism in which he had been brought up:

The hero of Tono-Bungay paints a savage picture of the uncle and aunt with whom he is boarded out. They run a bakery 'in a back street — a slum rather — just off that miserable narrow mean high-street that threads those exquisite beads, Rochester and Chatham':

H. G. Wells.
'Tono-Bungay', 1909
'One might have doubted if either of them felt discomfort in this dusty darkness of existence, if it were not that they did visibly seek consolation. They sought this and found it of a Sunday, not in strong drink and raving, but in imaginery draughts of blood. They met with twenty or thirty other darkened and unclean people, all dressed in dingy colours that would not show the dirt, in a little brick-built chapel equipped with a spavined roarer of a harmonium, and there solaced their minds on the thought that all that was fair and free in life, all that struggled, all that planned and made, all pride and beauty and honour, all fine and enjoyable things, were irrevocably damned to

everlasting torments. . . They were the self-appointed confidants of God's mockery of his own creation. So at any rate they stick in my mind. Vaguer, and yet hardly less agreeable than this cosmic jest. . . was their own predestination to Glory.

> "There is a Fountain, filled with Blood
> Drawn from Emmanuel's Veins,"

so they sang. I hear the drone and wheeze of that hymn now. I hated them with the bitter uncharitable condemnation of boyhood, and a twinge of that hate comes back to me.'

¶ His heroines too have 'lost their Faith':

' "old-fashioned people. . . knew right from wrong; they had a clearcut, religious faith, that seemed to explain everything and give a rule for everything. We haven't. I haven't, anyhow. And it's no good pretending there is one when there isn't. . . I suppose I believe in God. . . Never really thought about Him — people don't. . . I suppose my creed is, 'I believe rather indistinctly in God the Father Almighty, substratum of the evolutionary process, and in a vein of vague sentimentality that doesn't give a datum for anything at all, in Jesus Christ, His Son.' " '

*H. G. Wells.
'Ann Veronica',
1909*

¶ This quiet acceptance was, in its way, even more alarming than the truculent announcement of Bernard Shaw that 'every genuinely religious person is a heritic and therefore a revolutionist'. What was the world coming to? Even the most complacent were painfully aware of the rumblings of change:

'With so much Socialism about, one doesn't know what may happen; and now the King is dead I expect it will get worse; I always felt that he kept things together somehow," she said vaguely. "Oh dear," she said, "how things are breaking up. There's Romola gone to China, and Sylvia disappeared out of our lives, and Harry has become a bore, and people are quite disagreeable about Sir Adam now that he no longer has the King behind him, and now, of course, the Court will become as dull as ditch-water." '

*V. Sackville-West.
'The Edwardians',
1930*

¶ Perhaps we may be allowed to conclude this chapter with a comment of the indefatigable Blumenfeld:

'Came up in the same train as the Countess of Warwick who was travelling *third class!* The world is indeed changing.'

*R.D.B's 'Diary',
Mar. 29, 1912*

189

CHAPTER IX

VOTES FOR WOMEN

So FAR we have deliberately ignored 'the Woman Question' in order to give it a chapter to itself. Social workers had long been aware that, bad as were the conditions of the lower paid male workers, those under which women were expected to work were much worse. We shall not attempt any extended and comprehensive survey but will content ourselves with a sample of what life was like, in the early years of the century, in the millinery trade:

Mrs C. S. Peel, O.B.E. 'Life's Enchanted Cup', 1933

'The life of our work girls interested me. They began work at 8.30 and left off at 6 o'clock. In those days there was no fixed scale of wages. Head milliners in the great houses were well paid. We paid ours £4 a week, and our second hand 25/-. The rank and file earned from 8/- to 16/- a week, and the little apprentices who made the head linings, picked up the special long pins which strew the floors of all millinery workrooms, and learned what they could, received half-a-crown a week. Some of our girls travelled to London by workmen's trains and sat in waiting-rooms, reading their novelettes until the work-room was open. It was not surprising that by 11 o'clock they needed food. In many workrooms no morning break was permitted and the girls would produce food from their pockets and try to eat it unobserved, with the result that material might be spoiled.

'The girls were obliged to go out in the dinner hour in order that the rooms should be aired, in conformity with the orders of the Home Office. A printed list of Home Office Regulations hung in each room and women inspectors might demand entrance at any moment to see that they were not ignored.

'Accordingly, girls who could not afford to go to a restaurant ate their meal where they could. We finally decided that an apprentice

190

should make 11 o'clock tea and the girls should be allowed a ten minutes' break at 11 o'clock to go down to the kitchen and drink it. It took Miss Brown all her time to see that the break did not extend to fifteen or twenty minutes. We also arranged that our staff should have the use of the kitchen and a couple of gas rings, which enabled them to eat their midday meal in comfort.

'Our workers were generally very gay; they would sing at their work, and chatter like a cage full of birds. The word of the head milliner was law, and any conversation not approved by her was brought to an abrupt end.

'One might have thought that girls living under such conditions would have resented customers who bought hats costing as much as eight and ten guineas, for that was not an unusual price when fashionable women wore afternoon hats on which there might be half-a-dozen feathers or a lancer plume, that is, a feather as much, perhaps, as a yard in length, on to each frond of which another frond was knotted. On the contrary, the girls enjoyed making these expensive hats and went short of food so that they might copy for themselves these costly models.'

¶ The trouble was that even the advances made by Trades Unionism were not always helpful to women:

'In upholstery, which ought to be a woman's trade, the men's *'The Queen', 1910* trades unions step in, and forbid teaching the females any of the paying branches. There is no such thing as real apprenticeship in upholstery for a girl. If she joins a trade class, the teacher is not permitted to instruct her in the art of stuffing or covering. She is not even allowed to be taught how to model and cut the removable chintz over-covers of chairs and sofas. She is never allowed to try her hand at draping. Yet classes are formed, teachers are paid, and girls spend long hours for the acquirement of such simple processes as running up seams and sewing on a little bit of fringe. Of course, this restriction is always faithfully reflected in the rate of the girl's future wages. I obtained the figures of the weekly wage paid by a first-class firm of upholsterers to a man and a woman worker respectively, who chiefly modelled and made up removable chair and sofa coverings. The woman who had managed to instruct herself, and was a first-class worker, got 18s. 6d.; the man (not a whit better in the output or quality of the same work) got £2. 2s.

'This unjust discrepancy of wages, paid for the very same work, must and will be levelled away. Women, I believe, will never enjoy such pay as men have received in their palmy days, because a quite inflated value has been placed on the work of the skilled male owing to powerful trade unions, to organised strikes, and, above all, to the idea of sex dominance in a community directed solely by the males. However, women's enfranchisement must work wonders (if wisely used), fairly to adjust conditions in the labour market as between male and female workers.'

¶ Dire poverty was not confined entirely to the lower classes:

'The following account of what a lady of education and refinement, who had formerly been wealthy, spent on food, will serve to illustrate how many distressed gentlefolks live.

Quarter of a pound of tea at 1s. 4d.	4
Quarter of a pound of butter at 1s.	3
One pound of sugar	1¾
Bread	3½
Biscuits	4
Fish for three days	4½
Meat	5
Vegetables	3
Milk and Eggs	10½
Total	3s. 3¼d.

'Every Woman's Encyclopedia', 1911 'If we add to this, three or four shillings a week for rent, the lowest for which a room can be obtained in a respectable neighbourhood in London, and the cost of clothes, laundry, coal, light and a trifle for travelling and postage, it will be seen that even those who are so fortunate as to get 10s. a week granted have nothing left for little comforts or enjoyments and no provision for sickness.

'Some ladies who have applied to the Association [Distressed Gentlefolks' Aid Association'] have been found trying to live on 2s. 6d. a week, and in one instance two sisters, who had been accustomed to luxury, were discovered trying to live on 2s. 6d. a week between them. One can realise what a rise of even a halfpenny per pound on the necessaries of life means to people thus situated and the suffering which is entailed by the rise in prices during winter.'

Mr Asquith intercepted by two Suffragettes, Miss Jessie Kenney (left) and Miss Vera Wentworth, as he left Toynbee Hall, 1908. Drawing by S. Begg, from the 'Illustrated London News'.

Above: Mrs Pankhurst and Miss Pankhurst, 1908.

Below: Suffragettes advertising the Summer Festival, 1913.

¶ Nor was the growing discontent of woman merely a matter of poverty:

'The home is the enemy of woman. Purporting to be her protector it is her oppressor; it is her fortress, but she does not live in the state apartments, she lives in the dungeon. In modern life the home, however gaily-decked, is for her but a glorification of the basement where live the slaves of slaves. I do not think that there is a more powerful enemy of Feminism than the home, an atmosphere more deadly to all ideas of freedom and equality than the rarefied, holy air of the fireside.'

W. L. George. 'Woman and Tomorrow', 1913

¶ The daughters of the prosperous middle classes were beginning to rebel against the conventions that held them prisoner in their fathers' houses:

'The world she discovered. . . had no particular place for her at all, nothing for her to do, except a functionless existence varied by calls, tennis, selected novels, walks and dusting in her father's house. She thought study would be better. She was a clever girl, and she made a valiant fight for Somerville or Newnham, but her father had met and argued with a Somerville girl at a friend's dinner-table and he thought that sort of thing unsexed a woman.'

H. G. Wells. 'Ann Veronica', 1909

¶ Well's novel was certainly creating a stir. Even an ultra-respectable women's journal like *The Queen* felt constrained to notice it, if not altogether with approval:

'New books have been scarce during the holidays, but many of us have read the much-discussed *Ann Veronica,* and *The Agony Column,* by Mrs. Dawson Scott, has also attracted some attention. The former is, of course, a clever book, but one rather regrets that it should have been called "A Modern Love Story". Even now not many young unmarried women would care to imitate Ann Veronica in the way in which she set social laws at complete defiance. And we who know the world — and man's nature — are inclined to doubt if the future of Mr. and Mrs. Capes, when they were married and settled, would have been as peaceful and prosperous as the author seems to indicate. But the book has charming passages, among others, the description of scenery in the Tyrol, the Blau See, the mountains, and so on.'

'The Queen', 1910

¶ The same admirable magazine was itself much concerned with the situation in which too many young women found themselves:

'The Queen', 1910 'That the gravest problems of our day resolve themselves, after a very little thought, into mere questions of housekeeping, is a truth that is constantly shown in fresh aspects, and all the world was reminded of it once again by Canon Lyttleton's outspoken pronouncements concerning the great waste of life in middle-class England. In our girls of well-to-do parentage we have, probably, the best human material that the world, in its long centuries of striving, has ever produced. Improved hygiene, a season of peace, the advancement in scientific knowledge, the softening in domestic manners, the safety of locomotion, have all combined for their making. Well-grown, fresh complexioned, clear-eyed, wholesome in body and mind, they are fit mothers of an imperial race. They ought to be worth having, for they have been costly to rear. Yet now that they are reared they are not used. Such work as they do is a mere pastime, and serves chiefly to hurry the fleeting years along. And they marry too late or not at all. Their parents and teachers even fear to speak to them of marriage and motherhood, lest their minds be attuned to blessings for them unattainable, lest the upshot be only a deeper discontent with a home shaped for them when they were children, and with an enforced spinsterhood. The imperial race is recruited from the less healthy and (one may even dare to say) the less good; and while there is loud outcry for the endowment of poverty-stricken motherhood, and for the diminution of the infantine death-rate among the overworked and the underfed, it is reckoned as of no account that these girls of the comfortable middle classes are already endowed with all that is necessary for their best advantage, and are blessed with a splendid health that is the sole heritage any human being can be sure of handing on to posterity.'

¶ What was wrong with a world in which half the human race (unfortunately, in England, rather more than half) was precluded from 'living its own life' — as that dangerous Norwegian innovator, Ibsen, had expressed it, a generation before? Could it be, as many theologians have thought, that Woman was intrinsically inferior to Man? Not all theologians, happily, were so blind:

'Every Woman's Enclyclopedia', 1911 'Archdeacon Wilberforce has shown with great perspicacity what an amount of mischief has been done by the misinterpretation and

mistranslation of the story of woman's creation. The word "rib" should have been rendered "side," or "half." Woman was not taken out of man, an inferior vessel, but was the other created half of the human race with distinct functions. On this mistaken translation of a word a whole structure of fallacious theories and deductions, gaining strength through the ages, has been raised. But, as the archdeacon pointed out, "a new era has dawned and woman was beginning to take her proper place in the world; and when this was achieved it would be of the utmost value to mankind." '

¶ The struggles of the early Feminists were beginning to bear fruit:

'The change in education is in large part a cause of this, and pro- *Charlotte Perkins* gressively a consequence. Day by day the bars go down. More and *Gilman.* more the field lies open for the mind of woman to glean all it can, and *Economics', 1905* it has responded most eagerly. Not only our pupils, but our teachers, are mainly women. And the clearness and strength of the brain of the woman prove continually the injustice of the clamorous contempt long poured upon what was scornfully called "the female mind". There is no female mind. The brain is not an organ of sex. As well speak of a female liver.'

¶ Some brave men joined in the struggle, on the women's side:

'I do not believe that women are fit to have a vote. That is why I *W. L. George.* want them to have it. I am convinced that woman's political outlook *'Women and* is narrow, prejudiced, and mean, that her support will, at the inception, *Tomorrow', 1913* be readily accorded to any measure that is definitely sentimental or definitely brutal, to any law which restricts public expenditure and well-doing. If there be such a thing as progress woman will be the drag upon the wheel. It is fruitless to argue that this has not been the case in New Zealand, for we must deal with women in general and, as we are talking politics, it is certain that Englishwomen know far more of politics than do their sisters in Germany, France, and the United States. But they do not know much. They are governed exclusively by their passions and their interests. They coalesced to procure the repeal of the Contagious Diseases Act, the working of which they were not familiar with, because their feelings and not their minds were stirred.'

¶ Women (such was the hope) would be the equals of men if only they were properly treated:

195

'This question of character lies at the root of Feminism. We believe that if the majority of women are what they are, inaccurate, petty, calumnious, dishonourable, and vain, it is because everything that could be done to develop these traits in them has been done. The ages have given woman the status of the slave and developed in her the characteristics of the slave; we believe that by inverting conditions, causing her to develop in freedom, we can give her the characteristics of the free woman. We do not believe that women are inherently inaccurate, petty, calumnious, dishonourable, and vain, and we can prove our contention by pointing to those women who have been partially emancipated by the arts and the trades. In the midst of the great inferior majority a class of woman has grown up in the course of the last twenty or thirty years, which is serious (sometimes too serious), public-spirited, and honest. That is the arts and crafts worker, the school teacher, the female doctor, the government inspector; briefly it is the type which, by earning its own livelihood, has learned to hold up its head. If numbers of women have thus been freed from the vices of their sex, induced by the tyranny of the other sex, we feel justified in contending that there are among the women still enslaved an immense number of candidates for freedom.'

'The Queen', 1910   'There is perhaps no branch of life, whether national or social or family, in which modern evolution has wrought greater changes than in that relating to the question of authority.

'Until comparatively recent years the phraseology of the Catechism, which teaches that observance of the Fifth Commandment requires that we should "order ourselves lowly and reverently to all our betters", had a real and definite signification. It has been reserved for the twentieth century to inaugurate a system of lawlessness in every department of human relationship. By lawlessness we do not necessarily mean a state of violent revolutionary methods, but rather the spirit which suggests that if the existing conditions of affairs, or the existing statutes, prohibit a course of action which the individual conscientiously believes to be right, then it is legitimate to contravene the present custom or law, in order to show the necessity for its amendment or repeal.

'This policy is peculiarly in favour with that militant band of ladies who, possessing an almost unprecedented sense of originality and humour, have brought many members of the Government to the verge of neurotic hysteria by the unexpected methods which they have adopted in order to keep their cause before the public.'

196

Miss Ogston defending herself with a whip after heckling the Chancellor of the Exchequer at a Women's Liberal Federation meeting in the Albert Hall, 1908.
Drawing by S. Begg, from the 'Illustrated London News.'

Isabel Pankhurst arrested

¶ 'That militant band of ladies. . . possessing an almost unprecedented sense of originality and humour' were certainly beginning to make a considerable noise in the world:

'The Militant Suffrage Movement, which attained world-wide celebrity and became a tremendous legend, began in a simple and almost unpremeditated fashion in 1903.

Ray Strachey.
'The Cause', 1928

'In that year a few of those who had been working among the factory women of Manchester met together and decided to form a new suffrage society, the Women's Social and Political Union. The leader of this group, Mrs. Pankhurst, had already been in the Suffrage Movement for many years. When she was quite young she had married Dr. Pankhurst, the barrister who had taken part in the test-case of the Manchester women ratepayers in 1868, and she and her husband had both worked for the Manchester Women's Suffrage Committee and the Married Women's Property Committee. They had been active Liberals, but after Mr. Gladstone had "thrown the women overboard" in 1884, they had gone out of that Party, and Dr. Pankhurst had taken a notable part in the promotion of the Independent Labour Party in Manchester. He had died in 1898, and Mrs. Pankhurst had afterwards lost faith in the Labour Party, as she had in the Liberals. She felt that the Manchester Suffrage Society was old-fashioned and tiresome, and chafed against the restrictions which democratic organisation involved. She had once before formed a separate suffrage society at the time of the trouble over the text of the Suffrage Bill, and now she began again, hoping that by a new group something more vigorous than the quiet propaganda of the old committee could be achieved. In 1904 she went herself to London at the time of the expected debate on the committee stage of Mr. Begg's Bill, and she listened from behind the grille while Mr. Labouchere talked its slender chances away. Below in the outer lobby a few Co-operative women and other sympathisers waited, and when at last Mrs. Pankhurst brought the bad news down there was a great deal of indignation. They went out of the House together, a little group of disappointed women, and tried to hold an indignation meeting in the street outside. Mrs. Elmy began to speak, and a little crowd gathered, but they were at once moved on by the police, since meetings of all kinds are forbidden near the House while Parliament is sitting. The women walked away, as they were ordered, and being joined by Mr. Keir Hardie, the only Member of Parliament who seemed to share their indignation, they went just beyond the forbidden ground

197

and held their meeting. And then and there at that little unnoticed gathering the militant movement began. Patience and trust were abandoned, and indignation and bitterness took their place.

¶ Here is a picture painted by another of the pioneers:

Helen Atkinson in 'The Day Before Yesterday', 1956
'It was decided to attack London. Annie Kenney, the mill girl, was chosen for the work. With two pounds in her pocket, she set off "to rouse London". When Parliament was next assembled Mrs. Pankhurst, Mrs. How-Martyn, who later founded the suffragette's fellowship, Annie Kenney and a few other women went to the House of Commons to plead the cause. When they got there, to their dismay they learned that not the slightest consideration would be given to the women's claims. But the occasion must not be wasted, the Lobby was full of M.P.s, so first one woman and then another jumped on to a settee, and began to speak. The police immediately seized them and hustled them out. Next morning ten offenders were charged, Annie Kenney and nine more. Sylvia Pankhurst was not arrested at the time, but because of a protest she made in court, she was also included. All received prison sentences. These women were the first Suffragettes to be imprisoned in London.'

¶ Let us hear an account of the same matter from a lady who was not a militant:

Mrs C. S. Peel, O.B.E. 'Life's Enchanted Cup', 1933
'Throughout the twentieth century until the War the doings of the Suffragettes were one of the chief topics of conversation. Since 1906, when the Women's Social and Political Union, led by Mrs. Pankhurst, had made London its headquarters, the public had become more and more excited about votes for women. In that year Mr. Keir Hardy (sic) had secured a day for the introduction of a Women's Suffrage Resolution in the House of Commons, and the Prime Minister, Sir Henry Campbell-Bannerman, had been persuaded to receive a Deputation consisting of representatives of all the organisations supporting "The Cause", as it had come to be called. It was hoped that the resolution would be carried by a substantial majority, and that the Prime Minister would be so impressed that he would then make a favourable announcement to the deputation.

'A Mr. Cremer opened the debate, taking the jocular tone which so infuriated women, referring to them as persons, the majority of whom were not bread winners, who had not to bear the burden and did not understand the responsibilities of life. . . The women who were present began to fear that the resolution was to be talked out. "Divide, divide", they called from behind the grille, for then they were put inside a cage like animals at the Zoo, and "Votes for Women" banners were pushed through its bars.

'There was a mild fracas and some of the women were ejected. It was regrettable that the militants, who up till then had done nothing more violent than interrupt meetings, did not realise that it was unwise to allow themselves to be irritated by a person whose purpose it was to irritate.

'In spite of this fuss, the Prime Minister did receive the deputation, agreed that the women's case was conclusive and irrefutable, and proposed to do nothing about it. He advised them to go on pestering and to exercise the virtue of patience.

'The deputation of "persons who had not to bear the burden and did not understand the responsibilities of life" numbered over 300, and represented all the organised women suffragists — a large number: 50,000 textile workers, 22,000 Co-operative women, 52,000 members of British Temperance Associations and 1,150 graduates — and was introduced by Sir Charles McLaren and led by Miss Emily Davies, the originator of Girton College, who had been working for the better education and enfranchisement of women for fifty years.

'That was the beginning of the real militant campaign. Although I did not approve of lawless deeds, I am convinced that in the end it was the spectacular propaganda of the militant suffragettes, under the leadership of Mrs. Pankhurst and her daughters, which did even more than the quieter efforts of Mrs. Fawcett's followers, or the War work of women to procure for us the status of citizens. The surest way of furthering a cause is to make martyrs of its advocates and the Government made martyrs of women who, after all, were only desirous of being put in a position to serve their country better than before.'

¶ Blumenfeld, with his journalist's instinct, happened to be on the spot:

'Witnessed a strange scene in the House of Commons this afternoon. About four o'clock there was a rush of women into the outer lobby. They attempted to hold a meeting, and for more than a quarter of an hour there was a desperate fight between the police and the women,

*R.D.B's 'Diary',
Oct. 23, 1906*

199

who were led by little Mrs Pankhurst, Miss Annie Kenney, and Miss Billington. These are the same women who created a scene some months ago. Eventually they were cleared from the House of Commons, after reinforcements of police had been brought up. There was a good deal of rough treatment and considerable horse-play, but the frail women could not resist the stronger policemen. Nevertheless, a good many police were scratched and torn. Ten of the viragos were taken to the police station, and were charged with rioting in the House of Commons. I suppose to-day they will be taken to prison, where they will, of course, threaten to go on hunger strike.'

¶ A most ingenious device for drawing attention to 'the cause' was operated in the House of Commons itself:

Roger Fulford.
'Votes for Women',
1957
'On October 28th 1908. . . while Members of Parliament were discussing the Licensing Bill the proceedings were suddenly interrupted by cries of "Votes for Women" close behind the brass grille of the Ladies' Gallery. Attendants dashed forward, and found that three ladies, Miss Helen Fox, Miss Muriel Matters, and Miss Tillard, had securely chained themselves to the grille, and padlocked the chains with yale locks of formidable proportions. The officials of the House of Commons could do nothing except put their hands over the ladies' mouths, who were none the less occasionally able to emit little squeaks of "Votes for Women". Reinforcements were summoned, and it was decided that the only thing to do was to remove the grille with the ladies attached, in a manner somewhat recalling Samson, who when involved in a difficult situation with a lady, removed the doors of the city.'

Ray Strachey.
'The Cause', 1928
'For the first year after 1906 the militants followed the course they had already adopted; they opposed the Government at by-elections, heckled Cabinet Ministers at meetings, and went on undiscouraged deputations to the men who refused to see them, only to be arrested in the roadway for "obstruction". They grew to be very experienced in such matters, and learnt how to circumvent the police by stratagems and surprises. They arrived in all sorts of guises, and appeared in all sorts of places. Now one would appear as a messenger boy, now another as a waitress. Once a party chained themselves to the railings in Downing Street; another was found chained to a statue in the lobby of the House of Commons. They sprang out of organ lofts, they peered through roof windows, and leapt out of innocent-looking furniture

vans; they materialised on station platforms, they harangued the terrace of the House from the river, and wherever they were least expected there they were. Their so-called "raids" upon Parliament became a regular feature of their work. They were only technical raids, strictly orderly in procedure. A meeting in the neighbourhood would be the first step; at this meeting a deputation would be appointed, and eight, ten, fifty, or a hundred women would then file out, either in procession or in small groups, and proceed quietly towards Westminster. As they neared Palace Yard they would be met by cordons of police, sometimes as many as a thousand strong, on foot and on horseback. They would then be ordered to turn back, and would refuse. The crowds which had been following them would close in, and a sort of confused scuffle would follow in which the women were usually knocked about, sometimes pretty severely. They would do no violence themselves, but merely persist in their attempt to go on, and finally, after varying periods of time, they would be arrested. Conviction for "obstruction" usually followed, although the suffragettes argued that the obstruction had been used against them, and protested that they were being deprived of the ancient right of petition. They claimed, moreover, that the responsibility for the disturbances lay with the Government, and called Cabinet Ministers and even the Home Secretary himself as witnesses. The result was, however, always the same: imprisonment for varying terms in Holloway Gaol.

¶ Not all those who wanted votes for women were militants. Those who thought that the vote of the House of Commons could be swayed by a Petition set out hopefully to obtain signatures. The document was couched in the traditional form:

'To the Right Honourable the Commons of Great Britain and Ireland in Parliament Assembled, The Humble Petition of the undersigned Parliamentary electors of. . . . .   *'The Queen', 1910*

'Sheweth

'That we, the undersigned, urgently beg that your Honourable House will, without delay, pass into law a measure for the enfranchisement of women by granting to them the Parliamentary vote on the same terms as it is or may be granted to men.

'And your petitioners will ever pray, etc.'

Two ardent workers for the Cause set out to attack "the Suburbs", and one of them (it would be interesting to discover, from the files of the

201

Suffrage Movement, who "C. J." might be) has left an amusing account of how they fared:

'It was an unpropitious January day when, armed with the above confession of faith, we started on our campaign in search of voters' signatures. . . Ringing in our ears was the cheerful prophecy of an ostensible sympathiser, "There aren't half a dozen signatures in the place." We kept up our spirits, however, in the face of this auspicious send-off, and our confidence was justified by the result, for the signatures obtained ran into hundreds, and, indeed, represented a very respectable proportion of the electorate. . .

'Almost without exception, the villa owner had always been of opinion (or so he maintained) that "ladies paying rates and taxes ought to vote". In a great majority of cases he manfully bore witness to the faith that was in him by appending his signature to our petition. The working man was vaguer in his views, but, on the whole, scarcely less friendly. . . Among all classes the women were generally, we found, on our side; but to this rule there were exceptions. One lady, who believed that woman's mission was to "train her mankind at home", certainly laid herself open to the retort that her training of the only ostensible male under her influence — her husband — had not been a conspicuous success, for his reception of us was, *par extraordinaire*, exceedingly rude.

'Another, of very different breeding, made the casual remark that she rather fancied she had signed a petition *against* women's suffrage, but she thought there was a great deal to be said on both sides, and she offered no objection when her husband gave us his signature which he did with apparent readiness. Is not some compassion unnecessarily bestowed upon the women who are "praying not to have the burden of the suffrage thrust upon them". . . .

¶ The militants however did not feel that all this 'peaceful penetration' was getting them anywhere, and they gradually evolved a whole series of ingenious techniques for harassing the authorities.

'*Punch*', *Jan. 1908* *Punch* came out with a few helpful suggestions of
'*Bargains for Suffragettes*
'Chains! Chains! Chains! Very strong, with automatic police-proof padlocks and railing attachment complete. State waist measurement. X2337. Lassoes! A bargain! 1s 11¾d. The *Evening Noose* says "They are bound to catch on." X7432.

Policeman's Uniform. Second hand, good condition. Splendid disguise for enterprising lady wishing to enter No 10 Downing Street. Good accommodation for those willing to try it on. X1762.

Boxing. Lessons daily to Ladies and Suffragettes. Especially useful for by-elections. M.P. dummies kept for practice. X8109.

The Pankhurst Porcupine Waistbelt. Great novelty. Full of good points!! Arrest cure at last!!! Each belt is a bodyguard in itself!!!! X6370. Parrot. Grey African (knows Winston). Can *only* say "Votes for Women!" but says it all day long. Only 2s if taken away. Purchaser's risk. Or will exchange for fumed-oak bookcase. X6358.'

¶ The Suffragettes were soon made aware that many, even of their own sex, were opposed to their activities:

'An anti-suffrage society of ladies had been formed in 1908 under the presidency of Mrs. Humphry Ward, and in 1909 a "Men's League for Opposing Women's Suffrage" came into existence. These two bodies amalgamated in 1910, and soon began to afford great delight and comfort to their opponents by the ineptitude and futility of their ways. Every meeting they held was of course largely attended by the faithful, and it was an easy matter to make converts to the Suffrage Cause when the opposite case was plainly put. So invariably was this result secured that some of the younger and more light hearted of the suffragists made a practice of introducing prearranged "anti"speeches into their own campaigns, drawing lots for the privilege of stating the false case. The real "antis" soon saw that a purely negative gospel was not very successful, and they therefore tacked on to it a demand for the increased use by women of the local government privileges they already possessed. The "logic" of their case was that women could properly be entrusted with municipal affairs, while imperial matters were outside their "sphere"; but the two doctrines did not combine very happily together. They had some trouble with their own members, particularly with the imposing array of Peers who were their vice-presidents, since these gentlemen objected just as strongly to the presence of women on borough councils as anywhere else (outside the home); and the spectacle of their troubles was a constantly recurring delight to their opponents. Debates, which were sometimes arranged between the two camps, were an unfailing joy; but so heavily were the "antis" defeated whenever they ventured upon this method of warfare that it became very difficult indeed to persuade them to adopt it.'

Ray Strachey.
'The Cause', 1928

¶ There was, however, growing annoyance even among people of liberal views against such activities as assailing Mr Asquith with horsewhips:

*Ray Strachey.
'The Cause', 1928*
' "Madam," wrote Mr. Churchill, "My previous attitude towards this question had, like that of many other members of the Liberal Party, been one of growing sympathy; and on the only occasion on which I have had an opportunity of voting on it in the House of Commons I voted in favour of the motion. I cannot, however, conceal from you that I have lately been much discouraged by the action of certain advocates of the movement in persistently disturbing and attempting to break up both my own meetings and those of other Liberal candidates. I fully recognise that these persons are not representative of the serious supporters of the movement, and I can only urge those who do represent them to exert their utmost influence to repress the foolish and disorderly agitation which is in progress, and which, so long as it continues, must prevent me from taking any further steps in favour of the cause which you have at heart." '

¶ There was no doubt that nuisance-value of the Suffragettes' tactics kept 'the Cause' in the forefront of the news. The militants were not content to attack Cabinet Ministers with horsewhips. They broke the plate-glass windows of departmental stores with hammers concealed in what were then known as vanity bags; they even slashed the Rokeby Venus in the National Gallery, a gesture which contained perhaps more than a hint of unconscious resentment against the Odalesque ideal of womanhood there displayed. Certainly the Andalusian peasant girl whose fair skin was thus mutilated by the militants was at the opposite extreme from the position adopted by 'advanced women'. Fortunately the experts were able to repair the damage and one has now to look closely to see the scars.

It seemed that there was no limit to what the champions of Female Suffrage were prepared to do:

*Ray Strachey
'The Cause', 1928*
'In February, soon after the fiasco of the Reform Bill, at attempt was made to burn down Mr. Lloyd George's country house, and although it was not proved to have been the work of the suffragettes, Mrs. Pankhurst was arrested and charged with inciting to commit a felony. She was tried at the Old Bailey and conducted her own defence, and after a long and exceedingly interesting trial she was found guilty,

Mrs Pankhurst being carried away by Inspector Rolf after the Suffragette attack on Buckingham Palace, May 21st, 1914.

Above: Suffragettes at Victoria Station standing guard over the coffin of Miss Davison who threw herself under the horses at the Derby, 1913.

Below: Suffragette sandwichwomen, 1914.

and sentenced to three years penal servitude. Under the conditions which had hitherto prevailed, this sentence would have been of little importance; for by adopting the hunger-strike she would have been quickly released. But the Home Secretary had grown tired of seeing the sentences treated with contempt by these prisoners, and in his determination to crush down these troublesome women he did not scruple to introduce a new principle into English law. The same Government and the same Parliament which could not find time to attend to the widely demanded Suffrage Bill, succeeded in passing an Act controlling the treatment of suffragette prisoners, which came to be known as the Cat and Mouse Act. This Act, which was actually so framed as to apply only to one class of prisoner, made it possible for the Home Secretary to release a suffragette on a ticket-of-leave when her hunger-strike should have brought her in danger of death; she was then to be allowed to go out of prison to recover, and immediately she was strong enough she was to be re-arrested, without a fresh warrant, and go on with the serving of her sentence, the days of recovery not being counted towards its fulfilment.'

¶ A tragic note was struck in 1913, when the Cause claimed its first martyr:

'The next day was Derby Day, and in the midst of all the gaiety and excitement of the race-meeting one of the militant suffragettes, Emily Wilding Davidson, introduced a sudden and tragic note. To call attention to her cause, to testify to its seriousness and its urgency, this woman, who had told no one of her intention, threw herself under the feet of the racing horses and was killed. Her action startled and indeed roused the country. People who sincerely thought that militancy was madness, and who saw no relevancy and no purpose in her sacrifice, could not but be startled by the deed. All over the world people read of it, and all over the world it was known that there were women in England who courted death for the conviction that women should be free.'   *Ray Strachey. 'The Cause', 1928*

¶ The public might call such women as Emily Davidson fanatics, as indeed they were, but it was compelled to notice that the enthusiasm engendered by the campaign for votes for women was shared by a great many of those, such as nurses, who were contributing something valuable to the welfare of the community:

205

'Illustrated London News', June 25, 1910

'The Suffragettes made what was, perhaps, the most memorable demonstration of their career on Saturday last, when, 10,000 strong, they marched four deep from Victoria Embankment to the Albert Hall. At the head of the procession came "General" Mrs Drummond, riding astride and immediately preceding the chief banner-bearer and the drum-and-fife band of the Women's Social and Political Union, under their drum-major, Mrs Leigh. Those sections of the procession which created the greatest interest were the band already mentioned; the 617 bearers of silver broad-arrows, one for each conviction of a Suffragette; the ladies in cap and gown; the hospital nurses; and the car on which sat Miss Howey in prison dress. At the Albert Hall over £5,000 was collected for the cause.'

¶ Hopes ran high, but the struggle was not yet over. Indeed, victory might have been delayed for another generation, if the World War had not shown that women were capable of standing shoulder to shoulder with men in the struggle for freedom. But these developments must be left to another chapter:

CHAPTER X

THE END OF AN EPOCH

THOSE OF US who, for the greater part of our adult lives, have lived under the shadow of conflict, find it hard to realize that war, when it happened in 1914, came, to the vast majority, as a great surprise. It was so long since England had been involved in any combat near her own shores; there had been no warning beacons lighted for many centuries, no peel towers manned for a hundred years. Besides, war was out of date; it would never happen again.

English visitors to the Continent were sometimes surprised to find that foreigners were not so sure:

'In the spring of 1914 I spent a few weeks in Switzerland, to complete the cure of my damaged lung, and often played Bridge with a Belgian, a Frenchman and a German. As events fell out, it was long before persons of these nationalities were to meet again in amity. After the children had gone back to school, I went on with Winifred Herbert to Mentone and spent happy sunlit days writing, while she painted, in the garden of a charming little hotel in the hills above Mentone, where stocks and carnations and anemones bloomed. There were unusually few English people in Mentone that spring. Almost all the guests at our hotel were Germans. It seemed to me that they were not quite so pleasant as in other days.

'I asked the hotel proprietor the reason of his change of clientèle "I regret it, madam, for I prefer the English," said he, "but one must live". He paused, and then added, "Perhaps your countrymen will not be here next year." His manner was so peculiar that it impressed me. "But perhaps it will be the other way about and we shall be here and the Germans will not," I replied lightly.

'In Paris, where I stayed on my way home, there was no gold to be

Mrs C. S. Peel,
O.B.E.
'Life's Enchanted
Cup', 1933

had. Why? I met my Bridge-playing French friend and asked him. He shrugged his shoulders. "One never knows, and it is wise to be prepared," said he.'

¶ It had been a 'brilliant' season both in England and France. Perhaps we may borrow the pen of a French Social gossip to help us to picture the scene:

Comte de Fleury in 'Gazette du Bon Ton', 1914

'In the motocars, the coupés, one sees, enveloped in lace, tulle, light satins full of reflections, ladies of all ages, but chiefly in the summer of life, the full flowering of their youth, like roses garnishing the dinner table, and who have also their drops of water, the tears of their coronets and necklaces on the flesh of their shoulders and the curls of their hair.

'There are *messieurs* in the depths of all the carriages. The open overcoat shows the black satin revers, the immaculate shirtfront, the piqué waistcoat. Their pumps shine. . . It is dinnertime, dinnertime in Summer, the heat of the day over. The heavens turn green and the last rays of the sun lend an orange tint to the sky which hangs like a velarium over the Bois de Boulogne.'

¶ '*Ce qu'on aura bostonné, valsé ce printemps, c'est incroyable*' is our author's nostalgic comment. The phrase could hardly sound more remote if he had mentioned the minuet or the sarabande.

One might have expected that France, the elder citizens of which still remembered 1870, might have had some inkling of the new threat. But no:

Anthony Glyn. 'Elinor Glyn', 1955

'The onrush of the war took the French upper classes completely by surprise. Elinor [Glyn] had already arranged to return to England for the season, being dissatisfied with French society, and had fortunately made her travelling arrangements well in advance. On the Quatorze Juillet she took the girls to Versailles to see the fireworks, let off in front of a large crowd assembled round the Bassin de Neptune. The holiday spirit seemed undisturbed and there was no suggestion of calamity in the air.

'On July the 23rd they went to a château near Paris for the weekend and both they and their hostess were surprised and offended at the sudden departure of the Austrian Ambassador, who was one of the guests. It was Fielder, Elinor's chauffeur, who mentioned that he thought

Above: Taking the oath at the Recruiting Station at the White City, December, 1915.

Below: Recruits assembling at Southwark Town Hall in response to Lord Derby's campaign, December 1915.

Picture postcards of the war years, French and English.

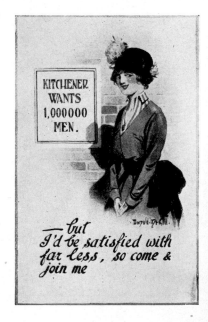

there might be going to be a war and everyone searched hurriedly in the newspapers to see what he could mean and with whom the war could be.

'The family reached England on July the 24th to find that English society was almost equally unaware of what was going on. . . Elinor. . . went, as usual, to Cowes. They found the place in commotion at a rumour that the regatta might be put off. Most people refused to take this seriously but Lord Ormonde, the Commodore of the Squadron, told Elinor that he thought there must be something in it, for Prince Henry of Prussia, who never failed to come, had cancelled his visit.'

¶ It was a glorious summer, one of the finest and warmest in living memory. The thunderbolt, when it fell, descended from a cloudless sky:

'Early on a lovely morning in June, 1914. I motored into Tisbury to get petrol or something. The newspapers had not arrived before I left. As the tank was being filled I idly noted a poster which said: "Murder of an Austrian Archduke."

Desmond Chapman-Huston. 'The Lamp of Memory', 1949

'There was an exquisite summer haze enveloping the soft, contented South Wiltshire landscape, and Austria and murdered Archdukes seemed foreign, foolish and far away. Here was England, happy rooted, secure, prosperous and, all things considered, one of the very few sensible countries in the world. Back home, I went for a ride on Win Green. The sea breezes from the English Channel delighted me and stimulated *Peking*, a white, almost full-blooded Arab with long mane and tail, to show what he could do in a gallop on the close Downland turf.

'That summer passed beautifully, as do all Wiltshire summers, good or bad. The Royal Wiltshire Yeomanry were camped near Pythouse in Jack Benett-Stanford's Park. We called on the Officers' Mess and, on the following Sunday, several young subalterns came to return the call and stayed to tea. They bore such well-known Wiltshire names as Herbert and Bouverie, Thynne and Awdry, Poore, Fitzmaurice, and many more, and their ancestors had been in, or closely associated with, the premier Territorial cavalry regiment since its foundation. Its badge is the Three Feathers because the Prince of Wales was always its Colonel-in-Chief, and it bore the proud motto *Primus in Armis*. I liked these agreeable young men as, a few days later, we sat watching their sports, admired their horsemanship, their

o

athletic prowess, their smart blue uniforms with white facings, silver chain shoulder-straps and Royal Red distinctions.

'Officers, non-commissioned officers and men were friends and neighbours and, so to speak, hereditary members of the Regiment. All the officers, and the majority of the men, brought and rode their own horses. Wiltshire is a county containing many one thousand acre farms with a splendid yeoman tradition, so the men were all comfortably off and good sportsmen.

'Little did I think that, because of the murder of the Austrian Archduke, I would soon have the honour of putting on their uniform.'

¶ There were some, however, who took the news from Sarajevo very seriously, among them the novelist who had become a specialist in prophesying the 'shape of things to come':

R.D.B's 'Diary',
June 28, 1914

'H. G. Wells came over to tea. While we were talking, news came that Austria's Crown Prince and his wife have been assassinated by a Servian. That will mean war. Wells says it will mean more than that. It will set the world alight. I don't see why the world should fight over the act of a lunatic.'

¶ The hard-headed business men were inclined to pooh-pooh the whole thing:

R.D.B's 'Diary',
July 29, 1914

'Mr Selfridge came down to see me at night to hear the latest news. He did not think the Germans would care to go to war. "They can't stand it financially," he said, "they wouldn't last till Christmas." '

¶ Germany invaded Belgium. The British Government's ultimatum expired at midnight on 3rd August. Next day we were at war.

Desmond Chapman-
Huston.
'The Lamp of
Memory', 1949

'On Monday, August the first, the party broke up, some to go to Cowes for Cowes Week, I to go to Fleet to my mother for a few days. By the time I arrived there I was so excited by the uncertainties of the international situation that I said if there was no definite news of peace on Tuesday morning I must go up to London and see what was happening. I left Fleet after luncheon; the train was crowded with Naval and Military Reservists recalled to their units by telegram. I thought them all very ancient!

'Waterloo Station was like Ascot Gold Cup day except that masses

210

of men were in khaki. Soldiers everywhere! As with difficulty I got through the platform exit into the seething mass of soldiers and civilians, Archie Rowan-Hamilton dashed up to me and said excitedly:

' "What are you going to join? Have you got into anything yet?"

' "No; I haven't even thought about it."

' "I don't know what I'm going to join, but I'm going to get into something immediately."

'Now Archie was the only son of Colonel Gavin Rowan-Hamilton, heir to Killyleagh, married and had a baby girl. They had a charming house on the Embankment near the Tate Gallery with purple stair carpet where I often spent very pleasant hours as both Archie and his young wife were keen on literature, music and art, and he was a fair performer on that difficult instrument, the flute. Married, settled, a father — Archie seemed to me too old for adventure!

'Like his father before him, Archie had gone to Woolwich and, thoroughly disliking it, had definitely decided against soldiering as a career. Nevertheless, when the Boer War broke out he volunteered, was in South Africa with his cousins, Archie Ava and Freddy Blackwood, got captured and was a prisoner of war for two years.

'By 1914 his life had purpose, shape, form, substance; was already firmly anchored in his home. All his chosen friends were musical and he belonged to a notable group that included Gustav Holst, Arnold and Clifford Bax, Cyril Scott and Norman O'Neill; he hoped to make a name as a composer. Yet here he was, prepared to give up everything, and set out on the great adventure to which he was so vocationally unsuited, yet for which he was so oddly prepared.

'A certain number of young men of the lower middle classes hung round in the autumn of 1914 until they could get commissions. Not so Archie: he at once joined a Territorial Battalion of the London Regiment as a private, was later on given a commission in the Second Battalion of the Irish Guards, where he had as brother officers Lord Kerry,[1] Captain Harold Alexander,[2] Siegfried Sassoon and young Kipling — Rudyard Kipling's only son.

'Archie went to France in August, 1915, and died of wounds in October.'

¶ The War had come but why should it make any difference? Thousands of tradesmen had cards printed and exhibited in their

[1] Afterwards 6th Marquess of Landsdowne, D.S.O. (1880-1936).
[2] Field-Marshall Viscount Alexander of Tunis.

shops: 'Business as Usual, during Alterations to the Map of Europe'. The professional soldiers were delighted, and if this sounds like a sneer, let us correct it by quoting the words of a man who was neither a lover of battles nor an uncritical admirer of the upper classes:

Charles F. G. Masterman. 'England After War', 1922 'Among those who had entered the Army itself, and had dawdled away their time pig-sticking in India or polo-playing in South Africa, the thing came with a great sense of relief. If they did not woo darkness as it were a bride, they at least realised that all their life had been moulded for this hour, and many went into battle singing, without a trace of fear. They fought; if they were wounded, they returned as speedily as possible to the front; they allowed no health certificates to interfere with their ardour. Some knew with certainty that they would be killed, but cared nothing so long as they were facing the enemy. In the retreat from Mons and the first battle of Ypres perished the flower of the British aristocracy; "playing the game" to the last, as they had been taught to play it all through their days of boyhood. They earned the extraordinary devotion of their men, and you may say with confidence nine-tenths of them thought of their men first. They did not form part of the armies that won the war. These were of a totally different character and temper; patriotic, stubborn, but not natural lovers of battle. Their tradition was only carried on by the chivalry of the air, where the boys from the public schools passed into the Air Service, in company indeed with boys of a very different class, with whom they would never have associated at home. In many aerodromes the average life of the individual was little more than a fortnight. In the useless slaughter of the Guards on the Somme, or of the Rifle Brigade in Hooge Wood, half the great families of England, heirs of large estates and wealth, perished without a cry. These boys, who had been brought up with a prospect before them of every good material thing that life can give, died without complaint, often through the bungling of Generals, in a foreign land. And the British aristocracy perished, as they perished in the Wars of the Roses, or in fighting for their King in the great Civil War, or as the Southern aristocracy in America, in courage and high effort, and an epic of heroic sacrifice, which will be remembered so long as England endures.'

¶ To many beside the soldiers war came as a relief. Perhaps it would solve among others, that intractable problem which for so long had bedevilled English political life: the Irish Problem? Things had

212

looked menacing enough on the other side of the Irish Sea for the last few years:

'In 1912 the Ulstermen in thousands had signed their Covenant, thereby pledging themselves to "use all means which may be necessary to defeat the present conspiracy to set up Home Rule in Ireland." From then on the Covenanter Volunteers had been drilling openly; in 1913 they began to arm. This aggressiveness, apt to characterize the Northern mind when conscious of right, was naturally not ignored in Dublin. As for England, she was impressed, if puzzled — for the Ulster attitude was, it appeared, as follows: She refused to be separated from England, with whom she felt as one. If Home Rule were endorsed (by England) she would at once fight. Fight whom? Why, England — though also, of course, the South. In the main, this peculiar expression of loyalty went down well — the incident known as "the Curragh mutiny" (General Gough's and his officers' refusal to march North for possible action against the Covenanters) showed how the wind blew.

*Elizageth Bowen.
'The Shelbourne',
1951*

'The South, therefore (in fact, as we know it, Ireland), began to raise its own Volunteers: these, formidable in numbers, resolution, and energy, represented the feeling throughout their country — they lacked only one thing, arms.'

¶ There were many who feared, not without reason, that we were on the brink of Civil War:

'Tension went on mounting: by July 1914 it was acute. Over the whole of Ireland that early summer hung a sinister, pre-thunderous hush. Compared to this, the alarms and panics of the earlier Home Rule crisis, back in the 1880's, might appear miniature and derisory: one can only say they had not been so at the time. Any conflict, on its course towards the solution, must give enlarging evidence of itself. Ireland in her 1914 extremity felt the eyes of the entire world to be turned upon her — therefore the Great War's outbreak, for quite another cause, was surprising; and, to be honest, something of a relief. As an interruption this came only just in time: so late as July 26 there had been the Howth arms-landing, with its ominous outcome. War altered the face of much, though not everything.

*Elizabeth Bowen.
'The Shelbourne',
1951*

'Such was the background against which Redmond's offer was made. Coming as and when it did, the offer was bold — and more, for it comprehended belief in the fundamental unity of all Irishmen.

Redmond's proposal was nothing less than that the Volunteers of the South and those of the North, forgetting their differences, should stand shoulder to shoulder in the undertaking to man and defend their country. From this might there not be born a whole better future? Sir Edward Carson, however, recoiled from the very thought; and Lord Kitchener, after a beetling glance at the South, made known his objection to arming "rebels". Further to aggravate sore feeling came Asquith's slowness in acting with regard to the Home Rule Bill — which, had the war not begun, must now have become law under the Parliament Act. "Redmond", explains Stephen Gwynn, "insisted that effect should be given to this consequence; but the Tory party denounced this as a breach of the political truce. Finally a compromise was arrived at. The Bill was to become law; but its operation was deferred till a year after the War. A pledge was also given that coercion should never be used against Ulster. . . . On this basis, the Home Rule Act received the Royal Assent on 18th September [1914]."

¶ John Redmond's great gesture came too late:

Elizabeth Bowen.
'The Shelbourne',
1951

'Two days after September 18, Redmond opened in Dublin what was to be a great recruiting campaign throughout the country: he called on the Volunteers to show their mettle by taking their place in the ranks of the Allied armies in Flanders. Thousands responded — going abroad to serve as Irishmen in the British Army, they wrote their own great, independent chapter of history. But another faction took up another stand: Sinn Fein began to assume control of the Volunteers who, turning away from Redmond, remained in Ireland. During 1915, with its tale of Allied reverses, the never-absent idea of seizing freedom by force loomed up again in immediate, tempting form. Sir Roger Casement negotiated for help from Germany. On that basis the 1916 Rising was planned — by a few leaders, in all but utter secrecy. The time set was Easter Day. Casement, having got wind of it, hurried to Ireland to say the thing was hopeless: Germany refused to promise support. Landing at Tralee, on Good Friday, he walked straight into a patrol and was arrested: on the same day the British Navy, acting on information, seized a cargo of arms coming in on a chartered ship.

'Officially realism prevailed: the rising was countermanded at the last moment. But two Volunteer sections ignored the order and, on their own, took action on Easter Monday. All through Easter Week while the fighting lasted the sun shone. The burning blue April weather, which hung over Dublin like a spell, gave even more unreality to the horror — what was happening was not easy to grasp.'

¶ For the moment however Ireland was forgotten. All eyes were concentrated on the heroism of Belgium and the fantastic prowess of 'General French's contemptible little army' in the retreat from Mons. The unfortunate phrase was invaluable to Allied propaganda, but perhaps at this distance of time it is permissible to point out that in all probability it was never uttered. 'Contemptibly little' was what the Germans meant; the German language having no means of distinguishing the adverb from the adjective. Be that as it may, Mons added yet another to the long list of heroic rearguard actions in the history of the British Army and as such it will always be remembered.

War is supposed to stimulate the production of poetry, and this was certainly true of the First World War, if not of the Second. The older and established poets rose to the occasion. Kipling, in a fine poem, recovered something of the apocalyptic fervour of *Recessional:*

Rudyard Kipling.

> For all we have and are,
> For all our children's fate,
> Stand up and meet the war,
> The Hun is at the gate!
> Our world has passed away
> In wantonness o'erthrown.
> There is nothing left to-day
> But steel and fire and stone. . .
>
> No easy hopes or lies
> Shall bring us to our goal,
> But iron sacrifice
> Of body, will and soul.
> There is but one task for all —
> For each one life to give,
> Who stands if freedom fall?
> Who dies if England live?

¶ Sir Henry Newbolt pictured England as a young knight keeping his vigil on the night before the battle:

Henry Newbolt.

England! where the sacred flame
   Burns before the inmost shrine,
Where the lips that love thy name
   Consecrate their hopes and thine,
Where the banners of thy dead
Weave their shadows overhead.
Watch beside thine arms to-night,
Pray that God defend the Right. . .

So shall thou when morning comes
   Rise to conquer or to fall,
Joyful hear the rolling drums,
   Joyful hear the trumpets call.
Then let Memory tell thy heart:
"England! what thou wert, thou art!"
Gird thee with thine ancient might
Forth! and God defend the Right!'

¶ One of the most popular of the early war poems was first published in *Punch* and was entitled:

In Flanders Fields

John McCrae

In Flanders fields the poppies blow
Between the crosses, row on row,
   That mark our place; and in the sky
   The larks, still bravely singing, fly
Scarce heard amid the guns below.

We are the Dead.   Short days ago
We lived, felt dawn, saw sunset glow,
   Loved and were loved, and now we lie
   In Flanders fields.

Take up our quarrel with the foe;
To you from failing hands we throw
   The torch; be yours to hold it high.
   If ye break faith with us who die
We shall not sleep, though poppies grow
   In Flanders fields.

¶ We should not forget that in those early days conscription had not yet been introduced. Those who joined up did so out of patriotism and idealism:

'Most of those volunteers of the prime were men of handsome and boundless illusions. Each of them quite seriously thought of himself as a molecule in the body of a nation that was really, and not just figuratively, "straining every nerve" to discharge an obligation of honour. Honestly, there was about them as little as there could humanly be of the coxcombry of self-devotion. They only felt that they had got themselves happily placed on a rope at which everyone else, in some way or other, was tugging his best as well as they. All the air was ringing with rousing assurances. France to be saved, Belgium righted, freedom and civilization re-won, a sour, soiled, crooked old world to be rid of bullies and crooks and reclaimed for straightness, decency, good-nature, the ways of common men dealing with common men. What a chance! The plain recruit who had not the gift of a style said to himself that for once he had got right in on the ground-floor of a topping good thing, and he blessed the luck that had made him neither too old nor too young. Rupert Brooke, meaning exactly the same thing, was writing: C. E. Montague. 'Disenchantment', republished 1940

> Now, God be thank'd who has match'd us with His hour,
> And caught our youth and waken'd us from sleeping,
> To turn, as swimmers into cleanness leaping,
> Glad from a world grown old and cold and weary. . .'

¶ Good poems were written by other young soldiers: 'Poets Militant', as the anthologies called them. Julian Grenfell sang of the ecstasy of battle and the fatalism of the soldier as one who had experienced both:

> And when the burning moment breaks, Julian Grenfell
>   And all things else are out of mind,
> And only Joy-of-Battle takes
>   Him by the throat, and makes him blind.
>
> Through joy and blindness he shall know,
>   Not caring much to know, that still
> Nor lead nor steel shall reach him, so
>   That it be not the Destined Will.

The thundering line of battle stands
    And in the air Death moans and sings;
But Day shall clasp him with strong hands,
    And Night shall fold him in soft wings.

¶ But soon a change was to come over the kind of poems which 'Poets Militant' felt impelled to write. It has been well summed up by one of the acutest social commentators of the period:

Charles F. G. Masterman. 'England After War', 1922 'The extraordinary fact remains, that in both the two great interpreting branches of literature, fiction and poetry, not only has the war given no real inspiration and the great victory passed unsung, but among the young men, bitterness and cynicism and contempt of human life and of the foolishness of men is far more noticeable than any of such new inspiration, as filled the world, despite the defeat of the better cause, a hundred years ago. I could name at least a dozen new novels and young novelists, men and women, who possess talent if not genius, and by every one of them is the same story told. There is, first, a picture of life before the war, greedy, sensual, money-loving, indifferent to any high or spiritual ideal. There is, second, the life during the war, in which the boys brought up amid such surroundings perish with valour and honour. And there is, third, when the story is continued, the life after the war, of a greedy, sensual, money-loving society: to which the vision of this enormous secular catastrophe has made no difference at all, except perhaps for a more determined resolve to grab the pleasures of an hour.

'The poets are still more remarkable. The first stage, vigorous, though limited, is represented by such an one as Rupert Brooke, writing with the same kind of *bravura* the things that schoolboys are taught to be, the right things to think of, when man begins to slay his fellow-man:

"Blow, bugles, blow! They brought us, for our dearth,
    Holiness lacked so long, and love, and Pain.
Honour has come back as a king to earth,
    And paid his subjects with a royal wage;
And Nobleness walks in our ways again;
    And we are come into our heritage."

'That stage soon passed and there came a long period in which all

218

the poetry of the war was that of loss and longing and regret. Tragic visions of the English countryside which they would never see again, tragic laments at the realisation that life would be cut off so young, with none of its possibilities realised, tragic acceptance, for the most part, of this necessary or unavoidable destruction of youth; as in Alan Seeger's poem before he died:

> "I have a rendezvous with Death
> At some disputed barricade,
> When Spring comes back with rustling shade
> And apple-blossoms fill the air —
> I have a rendezvous with Death
> When Spring brings back blue days and fair.
>
> "It may be he shall take my hand
> And lead me into his dark land
> And close my eyes and quench my breath —
> It may be I shall pass him still.
> I have a rendezvous with Death
> On some scarred slope of battered hill,
> When Spring comes round again this year
> And the first meadow-flowers appear.
>
> "God knows 'twere better to be deep
> Pillowed in silk and scented down,
> Where Love throbs out in blissful sleep
> Pulse nigh to pulse, and breath to breath,
> Where hushed awakenings are dear. . .
> But I've a rendezvous with Death
> At midnight in some flaming town,
> When Spring trips north again this year,
> And I to my pledged word am true,
> I shall not fail that rendezvous."

'And the third stage is one of complete disillusion and disgust; of hatred of the old men who have sent the young men to die; of hatred and contempt for the army command and staff; which has not even the sense to make itself intelligent enough to give a chance of living to the common soldier; of hatred and contempt of the politician and diplomat, whose actions have resulted in the young men of one nation slaughtering in all methods of torture and hideous mutilation the young men of another with whom they had no quarrel:

> "A thin line swinging forward to kill,
>   And a man driven mad by the din.
> Music-hall songs about 'Kaiser Bill'
>   And 'The march through the streets of Berlin.'
>
> Grey beards prattling round the fire
>   Of the good the war has done.
> Three men rotting upon the wire;
>   And each of them had a son.
>
> A soldier who once was fresh and clean
>   Lost to himself in whoring and drink,
> Blind to what will be and what has been
>   Only aware that he must not think.
>
> In the pulpit a parson preaching lies,
> Babbling of honour and sacrifice.
>
> .   .   .   .
>
> Fragments flutter in and out.
> Christ! what is it all about?"

'Such poets and novelists are facing reality, and perhaps it is better that reality should be faced than that we should live in a world of make-believe. But it is the record of men dying first in body and then in soul in a world where nothing worth preserving remains alive. It is an impreachment of man and of God. It carries with it nothing of the spirit of inspiration for some future generation, when

> "Earlier shall the roses blow,
>   In after years, those happier years.
>   And children weep, when we lie low,
>   Far fewer tears, far softer tears."

It is dust falling into dust, not in some high vision of heroic enterprise, but as a consequence of the infinite stupidity of mankind. You may

220

search in vain the whole of post-war literature of the young men and young women who should be inspiring such visions and dreams as poets like Shelley or reformers like Bentham and Hazlitt and Mill and the Utilitarians, still nursing the unconquerable hope even although the triumph of the old kings had appeared to make such hope a fantastic dream. To-day we are told that we have achieved a great victory for freedom; and all that we can find in literature is some boy, before he died, cursing those who have sent him to death, or some survivor exercising his mordant humour on the puppets and mannikins who rule mankind.'

¶ The public was, perhaps, first made conscious of the change in the writings of a young man called Siegfried Sassoon. If Rupert Brooke stands for the ecstasy with which young men entered the War, Siegfried Sassoon stands for their disillusionment. He has left us his own account of this development:

'While learning to be a second lieutenant I was unable to write anything at all, with the exception of a short poem called 'Absolution', manifestly influenced by Rupert Brooke's famous sonnet-sequence. The significance of my too nobly worded lines was that they expressed the typical self-glorifying feelings of a young man about to go to the Front for the first time. The poem subsequently found favour with middle-aged reviewers, but the more I saw of the war the less noble-minded I felt about it. This gradual process began, in the first months of 1916, with a few genuine trench poems, dictated by my resolve to record my surroundings, and usually based on the notes I was making whenever I could do so with detachment. These poems aimed at impersonal description of front-line conditions, and could at least claim to be the first things of their kind. The only one which antici-pated my later successes in condensed satire was 'Good Friday Morning', a jaunty scrap of doggerel versified from a rough note in my diary. Here I broke into realism by introducing my Muse to the word 'frowst'. Six years later, the reprinting of these lines in a New Zealand Socialist paper caused the editor to be prosecuted for blasphemous libel. After several days of law-court proceedings the editor was dis-charged — the jury adding a rider "that similar publications of such literature be discouraged". Nevertheless it summarized the feelings of thousands of other platoon commanders, and I consider it one of the most effective of my war productions.'

Siegfried Sassoon. 'Siegfried's Journey', 1945

221

¶ Soon it was no longer merely a question of introducing, in the name of realism, a few 'rude words'. Sassoon's disillusionment went deeper than that, and it is interesting to be told that it was H. G. Wells who first set him thinking along new lines:

Siegfried Sassoon. 'Siegfried's Journey', 1945 'On New Year's Eve I was alone in my hut reading *Mr. Britling Sees it Through*, which was more of a revelation to me than anything I had met with, and seemed to light up the whole background of the War. Someone was speaking his mind fearlessly; and since it happened to be the mind of H. G. Wells I devoured his pages in a rapt surrender of attention. Finally I came to a startling passage that checked my rapid reading. For several minutes I sat staring at the words. Then I copied them carefully into the small note-book in which I recorded my nocturnal ruminations. I was in the panoramic and retrospective state of mind induced by New Year's Eve, and this was what one of England's most powerful imaginations told me.

' "It is a war now like any other of the mobbing, many-aimed cataclysms that have shattered empires and devastated the world; it is a war without point, a war that has lost its soul; it has become mere incoherent fighting and destruction, a demonstration in vast and tragic forms of the stupidity and ineffectiveness of our species. . ." '

¶ In the absence of effective bombing quite a lot of people at home (including young officers on leave) were having a 'good time' and it was Sassoon's satirical attack on this in the poem 'Blighters' which gave so much offence:

Siegfried Sassoon. 'Siegfried's Journey', 1945 'My diary makes no mention of the next entertainment I went to in Liverpool. This was a Revue at the Hippodrome, to which I was conducted by one of my fellow officers who in peace-time had worked in the organization known as "Moss's Empires". It is probable that I spent quite an amusing evening, since my companion was a pleasant and intelligent person (less fortunate than myself, for he was killed at Bullecourt in April 1917). The Hippodrome show, however, provided me with a bit of material for satire. A couple of days before my departure from the Depot for final leave, I wrote the afterwards well-known lines called *Blighters*, in which I asserted that I'd like to see a tank come down the stalls at a music-hall performance where — in my opinion — the jingoism of the jokes and songs appeared to "mock the riddled corpses round Bapaume". Perhaps I was intolerant, but I found a good many people, — Thomas Hardy among them — who agreed with me. Anyhow it was my farewell to England, and as such it was the sort of thing I particularly wanted to say.'

¶ Older people, even those who were themselves serving, did not like this kind of thing at all. Desmond Chapman-Huston, who was certainly no dug-out, expresses this feeling in a passage written when the war was over.

'As I lay in bed in my quiet bedroom in South Street overlooking *Desmond Chapman-* the large garden at the back I read Rupert Brooke's recently published *Huston.* volume of *Poems.* *'The Lamp of Memory', 1949*

'It is now the debased fashion to jeer at Brooke's poetry and at all he stood for. I, like thousands of others, carried that volume throughout the war.

'If the wild, sweet music of youth that filled his verse was false, then we were false; if the patriotism he sang was pinchbeck, then we were pinchbeck; if the splendour he urged on youth was but a tawdry splendour then the thousands of untrained boys who shed their youth in France and Flanders in that grim autumn of 1914 and that soul-searching spring of 1915 died each one a tawdry death. If indeed God did not match each one of them and Britain with His hour then history has been wrongly written and they all survived to become crapulous, bloated Blimps, paper heroes, garrulous old chatterers who fought and won paper wars.

'There was no such thing as Mons or Passchendaele or the Menin Gate: as for the Cenotaph, and the Tomb of the Unknown Warrior in the Abbey they are merely falsehoods erected by a false people to false sons who all of them ran away in battle and falsely claimed a victory.

'Our Glorious Dead!

'According to the contemporary version, newly written and acclaimed, Glorious Liars one and all.'

¶ Most of the poets were young men of what would now be called the 'officer-class'. The ordinary soldiers contented themselves with a cruder kind of verse, in the form of music-hall songs. They kept their good humour. Even their disillusionment was expressed in humorous terms:

'There had been volunteers in the South African War; but in the *Christopher Pulling.* main up to 1914 the Army had been professional, and this was the *'They Were* first time that every family had personal links. They sang the songs *Singing', 1952* they remembered and liked, whether thay had anything to do with the War or not. The invasion of the music-halls by American ragtime songs had barely started. Men on leave in town and the war-time "flapper" liked bright, gay, and tuneful revues and musical comedies — "Tonight's the Night", "Chu Chin Chow", "The Maid of the Mountains", "The Bing Boys". Maudlin songs like *All Alone by the Telephone* and *Every Little While I Feel so Blue* got their hold on the memory; but the really popular ones of the period had the simple sentiment of *If You were the Only Girl in the World* and Alice Delysia's *If You Could Care for Me.*

'Pacifism had not yet come to be regarded as an interesting intellectual exercise, though America did produce a heart-throb, *I Didn't Raise my Boy to be a Soldier!*

'There was plenty of swing to the tune of *Over There*, George M. Cohan's song which the American contingent brought over in 1917:

' "Over there, over there;
  Send the word, send the word over there,
  That the Yanks are coming, the Yanks are coming,
  The drums rum-tumming everywhere;
  So prepare, say a pray'r,
  Send the word, send the word to beware;
  We'll be over, we're coming over,
  And we won't come back till it's over, over there."

' "There is the whole arrogance of the strength of the New World in its lines," Colonel Walter Elliot has written.

'The British Tommies, less grandiloquently, chanted *Take Me Back to Dear Old Blighty* and *I Want to Go Home*. They sang the old music-hall favourites like *Hello! Hello! Who's Your Lady Friend?* and *Who were You with Last Night?* and a few of the good old maudlin ones like *Never Mind* and *God Send You Back to Me*. They marched to Little Tich's song:

' "Hi! hi! Never say die!
  I'm one of the Deathless Army."

But they had their own versions of most of the songs written for and about them, and it was these, and the improvisations, that they mostly sang.

224

Photograph by F. J. Mortimer.

Directing the way at the Front. 'Yer knows the dead 'orse 'cross the road? Well, keep straight on till yer comes to a p'rambulator 'longside a Johnson 'ole.'

Sentry: ' 'Alt, who goes there?' He of the Bundle: 'You shut yer — mouth, or I'll come and knock yer — head off/' Sentry! 'Pass, friend.'

The Young and Talkative One: 'Who made that 'ole?' The Fed-up One: 'Mice.'

'There goes our blinkin' parapet again.'

'There was *Old Soldiers Never Die,* and there was

> ' "When this — war is over
> No more soldiering for me."

'There were simple ditties like

> ' "Left! Left! I had a good job when I left.
> Left! Left! I had a good home when I left.
> Left! Left! Oh, what a pity I left!
> Left! Left!"

'To the tune of *Three Cheers for the Red, White and Blue* they sang:

> ' "At the halt on the left, Form Platoon!
> At the halt on the left, Form Platoon!
> If the odd numbers don't mark time two paces,
> How the Hell can the rest form Platoon?"

'To the tune of *Auld Lang Syne* they sang *We're Here because We're Here;* and to a well-known hymn-tune they sang:

> ' "We are Fred Karno's Army, the ragtime infantry;
> We cannot fight, we cannot march — what earthly use are we?
> And when we get to Berlin the Kaiser he will say,
> 'Hoch! Hoch! Mein Gott! What a jolly rotten lot
> Are the ragtime infantry!"

'There was the famous *Madamoiselle from Armentières, Parlez Vous?*
There was

> ' "Oh! Oh! Oh! it's a lovely war!
> Who wouldn't be a soldier, eh?
> Oh! it's a shame to take the pay.
> As soon as *reveille* has gone, we feel just as heavy
> as lead,
> But we never get up till the sergeant brings our
> breakfast up to bed.

' "Oh! Oh! Oh! it's a lovely war!
What do we want with eggs and ham
When we've got plum-and-apple jam?
Form fours! Right turn!
How shall we spend the money we earn?
Oh! Oh! Oh! it's a lovely war!" '

¶ Even the ordinary soldiers began to ask themselves before long if the men at the top really knew what they were doing:

C. E. Montague. 'Disenchantment', republished 1940

'Long ago, perhaps, the commons of England may, on the whole, have accepted the view that while they were the fists of her army there was a strong brain somewhere behind, as good at its job as the fists were at theirs; that above them, using them for the best, mind was enthroned, mind the deviser, adapter, foreseer, the finder of every new means to new ends, mind which knew better than fists, and from which, in any time of trial, all good counsels and provident works were sure to proceed. If so, the faith of the general mass of the English common people in any such division of functions was now pretty near its last kick. The lions felt they had found out the asses. They would not try to throw off the lead of the asses just then; you cannot reorganize a fire-brigade in the midst of a fire. That had to wait. They worked grimly on at the job of the moment, resigned for the present to seeing all the things go ill which the great ones of their world ought to have caused to go well. For themselves, in each of their units, they saw what was coming. Some day soon they would be put into an attack and would come out with half their numbers or, perhaps, two-thirds, and nothing gained for England, perhaps because some old Regular in his youth had preferred playing polo to learning his job. The rest would be brought up to strength with half-trained drafts and then put in again, and the process would go on over and over again until our commanders learnt war, and then perhaps we might win, if any of us were left.'

¶ But was anything better to be expected?

C. E. Montague. 'Disenchantment', republished 1940

'Consider the course of the life of the British Regular officer as you had known him in youth — not to pick, the saving few, the unconquerably sound and keen, but the average, staple article made by a sleek, complacent, snobbish, safe, wealth-governed England after her

226

own image. Think of his school; of the mystic aureole of quasi-moral beauty attached by authority there to absorption in the easy thing — in play; the almost passionate adoration of all those energies and dexterities which, in this world of evolution towards the primacy of the acute, full brain, are of the least possible use as aids to survival in men and to victory in armies. Before he first left home for school he may have been a normal child who only craved to be given some bit, any odd bit, of "real work", as an experience more thrilling than games. Like most children, he may have had a zestful command of fresh, vivid, personal speech, his choice of words expressing simply and gaily the individual working of his mind and his joy in its work. Through easy contact with gardeners, gamekeepers, and village boys he often had established a quite natural, unconscious friendliness with people of different social grades. . . And then down came the shades of the prison house. . . You may leave school unable to tell what stars are about you at night or to ask your way to a journey's end in any country but your own. Between your helpless mind and most of your fellow-countrymen thick screens of divisions are drawn, so that when you are fifteen you do not know how to speak to them with a natural courtesy; you have a vague idea that they will steal your watch if you leave it about. Above all, you have learnt that it is still "bad form" to work; that the youth with brains and no money may well be despised by the youth with money and no brains; that the absorbed student or artist is ignoble or grotesque; that to be able to afford yourself "a good time" is a natural title to respect and regard; and that to give yourself any "good time" that you can is an act of spirit. So it went on at prep. school, public school, Sandhurst, Camberley. That was how Staff College French came to be what it was. And as it was what it was, you can guess what Staff College tactics and strategy were, and why all the little brown bundles lay where they did in the nettles and grass.'

¶ But — and it was a big but —

'While so many things were shaken one thing that held fast was the men's will to win. It may have changed from the first lyric-hearted enthusiasm. But it was a dour and inveterate will. At the worst most of the men fully meant to go down killing for all they were worth. And there was just a hope that in Germany, too, such default as they saw on our side was the rule; it was, perhaps, a disease of all armies and countries, not of ours alone; there might thus be a chance for us still.

C. E. Montague. 'Disenchantment', republished 1940

227

On that chance they still worked away with a sullen ardour that no
muddling or sloth in high places could wholly damp down. Many of
them were like children clinging with a cross crankiness to a hobby
of learning to read in a school where some of the teachers were good,
but some could not read themselves, and others could read but
preferred other occupations to teaching.'

¶ Doubts of another kind began to raise their ugly heads:

C. E. Montague.
'Disenchantment',
republished 1940 'One leaf that had gone pretty yellow by now was the hope of
perfect victory — swift, unsoured, unruinous, knightly: St.George's
over the dragon, David's over Goliath. Some people at home seem to
be still clinging hard to that first pretty vision of us as a gifted, lithe,
wise little Jack fighting down an unwieldy, dastardly giant. But troops
in the field become realists. Ours had seen their side visibly swelling
for more than two years, till Jack had become a heavier weight than
the giant and yet could not finish him off. We knew that our allies and
we outnumbered the Germans and theirs. We knew we were just as
well armed. We had seen Germans advancing under our fire and
made no mistake about what they were worth. Our first vision of
victory had gone the way of its frail sister dream of a perfect Allied
comradeship. French soldiers sneered at British now, and British at
French. Both had the same derisive note in the voice when they
named the "Brav' Belges". Canadians and Australians had almost
ceased to take the pains to break it to us gently that they were the
"storm troops", the men who had to be sent for to do the tough jobs;
that, out of all us sorry home troops, only the Guards Division, two
kilted divisions and three English ones could be said to know how to
fight. "The English let us down again"; "The Tommies gave us a bad
flank, as usual" — these were the stirring things you would hear if
you called upon an Australian division a few hours after a battle in
which the lion had fought by the side of her whelps.'

¶ So much for the fighting men. What of the women who were being
drawn into the conflict too?

Ray Strachey.
'The Cause', 1928 'The confusion of the first months of the war was tremendous. For
men the course of action was, on the whole, straightforward, but for
women it was perplexing in the extreme. The impulse of vehement
patriotism burned in their hearts, and the longing to be of service

228

'Tommy Atkins.' Photograph by F. J. Mortimer.

Women war workers, October 1916.

The first of the clippies, September 1917.

moved them; but there was little they could find to do. Even the women doctors, when Dr. Elsie Inglis approached the War Office with their offer of fully staffed medical units, were told, "To go home and keep quiet", and that the commanding officers "did not want to be troubled with hysterical women". It seemed almost as if the old anti-feminist argument was true, and that in a time of national crisis women were superfluous and irrelevant, passive creatures to be fought for, whose only personal function was to sit at home and weep.

'If this was what the civil and military authorities felt in the autumn of 1914, it was not what the women accepted. The Women's Movement had gone too far, and its ideals had penetrated too deeply for any such role to content them. They knew they were able and energetic; they knew that they had gifts to offer and help to give to their country; and rich and poor, young and old, spent their time in searching for useful work. It was not long before opportunities began to offer. The expansion of the nursing services, which had to keep pace with the expansion of the armies, absorbed thousands of eager women. The Voluntary Aid Detachments, which had been originated by Miss Haldane in 1909, expanded rapidly, and over eighteen thousand women enrolled in them and began their splendid supplementary aid to the Army Nursing Service. Hundreds of small private hospitals were prepared all over the country, and the Territorial Forces Nursing Service grew from under three to over eight thousand, and Queen Alexandra's Military and Naval Nursing Service from one to ten thousand. Depots for the preparation of surgical dressings, and comforts and appliances for the wounded sprang up in hundreds and were presently organised under the name of Hospital Supply Depots, which, in spite of official disapproval of this method, insisted on delivering their goods direct to the places where they were required. Motor ambulances, too, were endowed and staffed as fast as the works could produce them, and convalescent homes and care of the blind offered an opportunity to hundreds of women eager to "do their bit".'

¶ It soon became plain that women were needed not only for the subsidiary 'Services' but also in the factories if the flow of munitions was to be maintained. They were needed also for the mere business of administration:

'The great new munition centres which came into existence in 1915 and 1916 constituted an administrative problem of their own, but they *Ray Strachey.* *'The Cause', 1928*

229

were by no means the only directions in which women's labour was in demand. The Government itself called for thousands of them to staff the new mushroom Ministries in Whitehall. A hundred and sixty-two thousand women found employment in this way, being taken on at first without the least selection or care, and planted wholesale in the new temporary buildings. This army of clerks constituted a serious problem, all the more difficult to deal with because the Civil Service (like the Trade Unions) was very unwilling to trust any women with responsibility, or to allow them to rise to any of the better-paid posts.'

¶ The 'Whitehall Winnies' were regarded by the public as a rather poor joke. They were pictured as spending their whole time knitting or brewing cups of tea. They were none the less indispensable and it soon became obvious to far-sighted people that 'the women in the office' either as clerks or typists, had come to stay. For the first time women began to realize their power:

Ray Strachey
'The Cause', 1928

'Another change, even more vital to the Women's Movement than the approval of public opinion, was brought about by the war years, and that was the change in the outlook of women themselves. For the first time hundreds of thousands of them had experienced the joys of achievement; they had been of consequence and had done things they felt to be important; they had been encouraged to show enterprise and ambition, and they had been more or less adequately paid. The false and temporary prosperity of the war period had given women a taste of the power of money; the factory women had been better fed, in spite of the food shortage, than in the days when they did "women's work" in their homes. The married women had had the spending of the separation allowances, and their children were better dressed and in better health than had ever been the case before. They saw what the world was like for men; and neither Act of Parliament nor season of reaction, nor any other thing could thereafter take that knowledge from them.'

¶ There can be little doubt that for the greater part of the civilian population the war had improved their lot:

Charles F. G.
Masterman.
'England After
War', 1922

'The war was a "good time" for a great proportion of the working people, including, above all, the women and children. If the wage-earner was working in a home factory or workshop, he could often

230

earn prodigious wages — although at the expense of the wearing out of the human machine. The girls and the boys were all working also, the former in many cases receiving 20s. to 30s. a week instead of the 5s. or 6s. of pre-war days. In the average family the income soared far above the increase of prices, and none of the family need ever be unemployed. . .

'Women and children who were dependent on the soldiers received in separation allowances often much more than they had ever had paid to them to keep the home going, and without the cost of maintaining the bread-winner. The results became apparent as the years went by. I remember revisiting the region in South London where I once lived for nine years, which was then not far different from a concentrated slum. The place looked even forlorner than when I resided there, for repairs had ceased, and the Council had become indifferent to the sedulous cleansing of the streets, and torn paper and the debris of human existence occupied the narrow alleys between houses which looked as if at any moment they might collapse in ruins. The only distinction were the coloured cards put out in nearly every alternate house, showing that from each particular hovel some man had gone out to fight for his country; and it was to this "England" that he would return. But, on the other hand, the effect of the money that was pouring in was everywhere noticeable. The children were well fed, well dressed, well shod. The girls were adorned with cheap finery. The mothers were less careworn and could pay more attention to the children. And this same result was being obtained all over the country. "Families that were my despair before", said a medical officer of health, "are now clean and well cared for." That swamp of forlorn humanity round Dockland, Bermondsey, Wapping, South-West Ham, found itself for the first time well fed, and with good feeding came health and a new chance for the coming generations. Except for anxiety for those at the Front, many would have wished these conditions to continue for ever.

'It continued for nearly two years after the War. Its effects may continue for an indefinite time. For the first time for many decades the children of the poorest for seven years — say from three years old till ten — have had enough to eat. That should make a permanent difference to a whole generation. It is a pity that the length of the experiment could not have been continued longer and the world confronted with a new race who, from birth until the age (say) of fourteen, had never suffered from hunger. Perhaps had such a thing happened, the whole future of England would have been changed: and the permanently inefficient and the partially unemployable, and all that mass of low-grade life which is never quite healthy and consequently never quite happy, which now coagulates in certain congested areas in the great cities, would have been altogether broken up and have disappeared.'

¶ In spite of war conditions many people began to be better dressed than they had ever been before:

Mrs C. S. Peel, O.B.E. 'Life's Enchanted Cup', 1933   'When war was declared, waists were in the normal position, and boots had not been replaced by the smart shoes which are worn to-day. The silk stocking craze did not become general until 1917, when practically every woman was earning, and girls had an unusual amount of pocket money at their disposal. That was the time when, owing to the number of girls of good class who were working in the Ministries in the West End of London, and who lunched in Soho restaurants, that the smart Soho dress shop appeared.'

¶ Women were becoming 'emancipated', socially and alas! morally. It was at last inevitable that they should be emancipated politically:

Ray Strachey. 'The Cause', 1928   'The House of Lords had always been the stronghold of the league for opposing Women's Suffrage. Lord Curzon, who was still its president, was the leader of the House, and there were plenty of others whose opposition was known to be strong and influential — Lord Lansdowne, Lord Halsbury, and Lord Bryce, for example; the last of these all the more damaging because of the great share he had taken in advancing the education of women. It was true there were also strong friends — Lord Lytton, Lord Selborne, Lord Grey, Lord Courtney (the same who had reunited the divided factions of the suffragists in 1878), and many more; but the "antis" seemed to be the more numerous, and they had all that unknown crowd of silent Peers presumably on their side.

'As in the House of Commons, the second reading of the whole Bill passed off smoothly, and was carried without a division. There were some speeches on the Women's Suffrage issue, but it was evident that most of these were reserved for the three days' debate on Clause IV, and on 8th January 1918 the last fight began.

'Lord Curzon wound up the debate on the afternoon of the 10th of

January, and as he rose to speak there was a hush of excitement. One of the policemen at the door, friendly as the police always were to the women, went along the passage to the committee-room, where a number of them were gathered, and put his head round the door. "Lord Curzon is up, ladies," he announced, "but 'e won't do you no 'arm." And so it was. For the President of the Anti-Suffrage League was forced to strike his colours. He said, indeed, that the passage of the Bill would be the ruin of the country; women were politically worthless, and the whole ideal of the Women's Movement was disastrous and wrong; he felt bound to say these things, for he believed them. But when it came to action he could not give so certain a lead. The majority in the House of Commons had been too big, and if the Upper House rejected Women's Suffrage all that would happen would be that the Bill would return to them again with the clause re-inserted. "Are you prepared", he asked, "to embark upon a conflict with a majority of 350 in the House of Commons, of whom nearly 150 belong to the party to which most of your Lordships also belong. . .?" For his part, he said, he could not take upon himself the responsibility of "precipitating a conflict from which your Lordships would not emerge with credit", and he would abstain from voting, one way or the other, upon the clause. With that dramatic and wholly unexpected announcement the discussion ended, and the voting began; and the suffragists, as they waited for the figures, knew that their fight was won. One hundred and thirty-four Peers voted for the clause, 71 against it, and 13 abstained. The Representation of the People Bill was through both Houses; and on 6th February it received the Royal Assent and became the law of the land. The fifty years' struggle was over, and the sex barrier was broken down.'

¶ A comic comment on this is supplied by one of the most redoubtable of the old Militants:

'When the 1914 war broke out shortly afterwards, the King pardoned the Suffragettes who were in prison. Those who were "at large", of whom I am one, are not sure whether they are pardoned or not!'

Helen Atkinson in 'The Day Before Yesterday', 1956

¶ Few people had imagined when Kitchener signed men on 'for three years or the duration of the War' that the latter period would turn out to be the longer. But so it proved:

Mrs C. S. Peel,
O.B.E.
'Life's Enchanted
Cup', 1933
'As the dreary summer of 1918 drew to a close, one began to feel as if the War would go on for ever. The streets were dark, the clothing of the people was dark, for although few now wore mourning for their dead, gay colours were not seen, and the shops stocked little but black and grey material.

'Although the fear of starvation was over, food was still scarce and so dear that all but the very rich were obliged to put a strict limit to consumption. Inadequate nourishment and lack of warmth were weakening the stamina of the people. A specially severe type of influenza raged. Added to the long War Casualty lists were the names of those who had died of influenza or pneumonia, into which this type of influenza often developed.

'Then, when it seemed as if the misery of the world was too great to be endured longer, there came rumours of peace. Just as in August 1914 few of us could believe that a European war could happen, so now we could scarcely believe that peace could come. I was at the *Daily Mail* when the news came through on the telephone. We opened the window wide and could hear cheering and immediately somewhere near a wheezy old gramophone began to play "God Save the King". I longed to go into the street but could not, for whatever happens, newspapers must go to press. I was correcting proofs and my eyes kept filling with tears, tears for those to whom peace had come too late to save some one dearly loved. By the time my work was over, it was five o'clock and raining heavily, and there was no other way to get back to Alexander Square than by walking. Amongst all that I saw, one scene stands out. I went through the Temple which was deserted, and up one of those little streets which lead to Charing Cross, and there under an archway were two old women in jet-trimmed bonnets and capes, dancing stiffly to the strains of a barrel organ — an out-moded organ with one long wooden leg, played by an ancient, bearded man who might have been Father Time himself.

'That night in Trafalgar Square there was dancing and singing, flags were waved, confetti thrown. "Have we won the War?" roared the crowd. "Yes, we've won the War", came an answering roar. A song new to us was heard. "What shall we be when we aren't what we are?" chanted those soldier men. It foretold one of the grimmest tragedies of peace — unemployment.'

¶ But this was still in the future. There would be no doubt that *some* people in England were better off than they had ever been before.

234

'As the war progressed, business became more and more business; *Charles F. G.* the thoughts of romantic sacrifice were put aside. Each man did what *Masterman.* he saw his competitors doing, and tried to do it better, and stayed his *'England After* conscience by the belief that if he did it efficiently he was doing his *War', 1922* "bit" to win the war. And the result has been that while many historic families have been blotted out by death, and others by the loss of possessions due to high taxation or the fall of securities, the war profiteer is for the time triumphant. He purchases titles, he can obtain a safe seat in the House of Commons, he is dominant at the present time in that strange assembly. "I asked", said Mr. Keynes, "a Conservative friend, who had known previous Houses, what he thought of them". "They are a lot of hard-faced men", he said, "who look as if they had done very well out of the war." '

¶ Even the prosperous, however, did not find things *quite* the same:

'Surely there never was any time in the life of the world when it was *C. E. Montague.* so good, in the way of obvious material comfort, to be alive and *'Disenchantment',* fairly well-to-do as it was before the war. Think of the speed and *republished 1940* comfort and relative cheapness of the Orient Express; of the way you could wander, unruined, through long aesthetic holidays in Italy and semi-aesthetic, semi-athletic holidays in the Alps; of the week-end accessibility of London from Northern England; of the accessibility of public schools for the sons of the average parson or doctor; of the penny post, crown of our civilization — torn from us while the abhorred halfpenny post for circulars was yet left; of the Income Tax just large enough to give us a pleasant sense of grievance patriotically borne, but not to prostrate us, winter and summer, with two "elbow jolts" or "Mary Ann punches" like those of the perfected modern prize-fighter.

'Many sanguine well-to-do people dreamt, in the August of 1914, that the war, besides attaining its primary purpose of beating the enemy, would disarrange none of these blessings; that it would even have as a by-product a kind of "old-time Merrie England", with the working classes cured of the thirst for wages and deeply convinced that everyone who was not one of themselves was a natural ruler over them. For any little expense to which the war might put us the Germans would pay, and our troops would return home to dismiss all trade-union officials and to regard the upper and middle classes thenceforth as a race of heaven-sent colonels — men to be followed, feared, and loved. Ah, happy vision, beautiful dream! — like Thackeray's reverie about having a very old and rich aunt.'

¶ The 'twenties, for good or ill, did not turn out to be in the very least like that. Those who tried to put the clock back merely found that it no longer told the time. The Edwardian epoch, which continued in essentials until the First World War, was found, when hostilities had ceased, to have receded into the background of history. It was as remote as the *Ancien Régime* after the Napoleonic Wars. We have tried in our anthology, to present a fair picture. In many ways our own world is a better world, and yet it is hard to resist a certain nostalgia for a period when at least some people took it for granted that the world was a pleasant place to live in and saw no reason why the 'good time' should not go on for ever.

'*We are making a new World.*' *Painting by Paul Nash. London, Imperial War Museum.*

INDEX